"What does the biblical history in the C and societies of the twenty-first century? ㄴ. ..., ...g , a difference in the society in which you live, I implore you—learn the lessons God has for us as they are unpacked in *God and Political Justice*. These lessons teach us how we fail or flourish. Whether we fail or flourish is our choice, and consciously or unconsciously we choose. To choose well we need to know the amazing patterns the God who made us set for our flourishing. I especially liked the final chapters in which Landa Cope gives us concrete and realistic suggestions on how to contribute to the building of Christ's Kingdom in our world—irrespective of our individual place in society or its alignment with the values of the ultimate and final Kingdom."

Bob Moffitt
Author of *If Jesus Were Mayor*; President, Harvest Foundation

"Landa Cope takes the Scriptures seriously. She is a Genesis One Christian, starting her work where the Scriptures begin, 'In the beginning God,' and establishing a first-principles foundation for all that she speaks and writes. In her latest book, the panoramas she creates with words will sweep you into the alternative universe—the world of reality, not illusion, where God dwells and interacts in space and time with humankind. Read this book and stand ready to join the Wilberforce generation, a modern-day generation of Christians committed to creating godly culture and building nations for the glory of God."

Darrow L. Miller
Author of *Discipling Nations* and *Rethinking Social Justice*

"I have known Landa Cope for many years as a friend and coworker in many workshops and schools around the world. One of Landa's strengths is that she has a keen sense of current issues and how to frame them and in doing so help to make the body of Christ relevant for today in the midst of these complex human issues. To use this strength to help the body of Christ frame how we are to think about government is a real gift to the body of Christ. Most importantly for me is that in this strength she has a heart after God and starts any position she takes with a reference to a good God who has a desire to give us abundant life. This book will be one I carry with me and refer back to many times. Not so I can think right, but so I can live right. And most importantly to be able to represent God in a way that is true to his heart and glorifies him."

Matt Rawlins, PhD
Green Bench Consulting

"Landa Cope so clearly reveals for all who will read her great book that justice truly is at the very center and core of so much of what the world needs. God is a god of justice! His Law is good for the world. The practical challenges in chapter 26 are for every believer to pursue, while there is much for those specifically called to service in the many expressions of the executive, judicial, and legislative branches of government to meditate upon.

"In many ways *God and Political Justice* builds upon *The Old Testament Template* and provides a wonderful guide to help dig out the treasures of the whole Bible. I found myself thinking as I was reading that so many would get so much more out of their own study of the Bible if they would read this book like a foreword to the Bible itself. We can all gain a clearer perspective on what God has been trying to teach the world in human history and how we are to live as his followers in the twenty-first century."

Larry Baldock
Tauranga City Council 2001, 2010–2013; NZ Parliament 2002–2005

"If the Bible is the blueprint for God's design for justice on earth, then *God and Political Justice* is the manual on how to unpack it. The entire weave of God's justice plan is explained with such thorough and painstaking detail, from Genesis right up to Revelation. After reading this book, we have no excuse to claim that we don't understand God's views on this topic.

"In the twenty-first century, more than any other, rights-based governance is growing around the world. The biblical template on justice helps us grapple with this issue so that we can flesh out its biblical relevance in our current reality. For everyone who seeks to understand God's will in how the individual and the community can engage with contemporary political justice, I highly recommend Landa Cope's book. God's heart will be evident to you as you turn the pages. And that is the triumph of this book."

Sally Anne Param, PhD
Lecturer, Sociology and Social Psychology, University of Malaya

"To be exposed to Landa Cope's teaching is as exciting as discovering that the world is not flat—new dimensions, new understanding, new colors to biblical texts."

Francoise Andre
International Board, Food for the Hungry; Vice Chairman, Mercy Ships Int.

"This book has tremendous insights and a meticulous study from Genesis to Revelation in understanding God, the individual, and God revealed in the community. The principles of political justice and just governance are among the most difficult subjects to grapple with using our human finite understanding. Yet Landa Cope has taken the risk in describing methodically and convincingly what only very few can do, how to understand and deliver God's justice in an unjust world. This book is very relevant to our times and a must-read!"

Arnold J. Enns
President/CEO, COICOM (Latin American Confederation of Christian Communicators, Mass Media, Pastors and Leaders)

"The world would be a much better place if Christians would understand and live out the principles that Landa Cope is arguing for in this book. It has the potential to change communities and societies regardless of any particular cultural backgrounds. In every generation, the change comes from private initiatives, not from top-down, state-originated programs; if and when the people of God, 'the creative minority', 'the remnant', is able to create a critical mass, there and then the will of God is 'done [in our societies] as it is in heaven'. 'The call of God must be joined by the thinking of God to bear fruit', says Landa, and her book is able to help us grasp God's thinking in terms of good governance and political justice."

Marinela Blaj
Romanian Director, Schuman Centre for European Studies

"This is a breath-taking analysis of the principles of political justice and constitutional government from Genesis to Revelation. Landa Cope's grasp of the big picture of history and in-depth understanding of divine principles in Scripture is testimony to the years of research this book has taken. It is essential reading for anyone exploring a vocation in law or government."

Baroness Berridge of the Vale of Catmose
House of Lords, Westminster, London

"As the world cries for justice, Landa Cope unveils with clarity and passion God's heart in this matter. Landa never wavers in her intense commitment to understand and uncover the ways of God as he reveals his heart to mankind. Through her diligent and deliberate pursuit of God and his word, the story of his love and commitment to justice unfolds, guiding mankind from savagery to sonship. With intensity and precision, this book both breaks our hearts and thrills our souls. Most of all, it offers the hope of Jesus beyond the despair of sin."

Candace C. Sparks
Executive Director, The Crowell Trust

"Landa Cope is both a prophetess and an Esther for such a time as this. Of all the speakers and leaders I have known around the world over the last couple of decades, no one quite matches Landa for her passion to see nations discover the divine pattern of living. Some people think individual, others think local church, but Landa thinks nation. In fact, she thinks the world. But she sees the world through the lens of God's purposes for the multiple nations of the world."

Michael Cassidy
Founder, African Enterprise

"Many believe that the twentieth century was primarily about the restoration of the ministry of The Holy Spirit in the life of both the church and the individual lives of the believers. I and others are equally convinced that the primary issues of the twenty-first century for the church will be about the discipling of nations. The church is being both led by God and forced by social conditions to engage the nations on multiple levels. Landa Cope has written a book that ensures her role in the foundation-laying dimensions of this process. Her ability to focus on the central issue of justice, drawing wonderfully from the actions of God revealed in scripture, the Laws and the prophets from Old to New Testaments is highly impressive. This book will become a primer and a study guide on multiple levels in this response to obeying the Great Commission to disciple nations."

Dennis Peacocke
Founder and President, Gostrategic

"The originality of the book is the passionate case made for social justice, including and perhaps especially for the most marginalized people in our societies and our world. Perhaps it is an unhelpful stereotype, but conservative Christians are typically viewed as being more judgmental and less concerned about social justice—that the poor are poor because they are lazy, etc. Or that one should try to save their souls as the first priority and help them out a bit secondarily. I think this book could be a way to bring a wider range of Christians—and perhaps non-Christians—together to talk through issues of governance and social justice. A book that is so deeply grounded in Scripture, yet so passionate about social justice and the responsibility of all Christians to look for how God is calling them to respond, even in small ways, could be a text that brings people to a debate but a civil debate that might actually produce understanding and community action."

Dan Harris
Minister Counselor, U.S. Commercial Service (ret.)

"It was Landa Cope's life of integrity and clarity that pointed me on my own spiritual journey in the 1970s, having met her in a Muslim country. In her book, I am reminded once again of Landa's ability to articulate truth in a seemingly effortless way, calling us to true north. She gets to the heart of a matter faster than anyone I have ever known, identifying bottom lines and articulating the plumbline of God's character and ways. I found myself writing and underscoring feverishly as I read. How could you not want to follow this Savior?"

Janet Potter
Former Confidential Assistant to the Attorney General of the United States

LANDA COPE

God AND POLITICAL JUSTICE

A Study of Civil Governance from Genesis to Revelation

YWAM Publishing
Seattle, Washington

YWAM Publishing is the publishing ministry of Youth With A Mission (YWAM), an international missionary organization of Christians from many denominations dedicated to presenting Jesus Christ to this generation. To this end, YWAM has focused its efforts in three main areas: (1) training and equipping believers for their part in fulfilling the Great Commission (Matthew 28:19), (2) personal evangelism, and (3) mercy ministry (medical and relief work).

For a free catalog of books and materials, call (425) 771-1153 or (800) 922-2143. Visit us online at www.ywampublishing.com.

God and Political Justice: A Study of Civil Governance from Genesis to Revelation
Copyright © 2015 by Landa Lea Cope

Published by YWAM Publishing
a ministry of Youth With A Mission
P.O. Box 55787, Seattle, WA 98155-0787

Published in collaboration with The Template Institute
6 Jamaica Close, Capri Village, 7975, South Africa
www.templateinstitute.com

Library of Congress Cataloging-in-Publication Data
Cope, Landa L.
  God and political justice : a study of civil governance from Genesis to Revelation / Landa Cope.
     pages cm. — (The biblical template)
  ISBN 978-1-57658-834-5 (pbk.) — ISBN 978-1-57658-885-7 (e-book)
  1. Politics in the Bible. 2. Bible and politics. 3. Justice—Biblical teaching. 4. Christianity and politics—Biblical teaching. 5. Christianity and justice—Biblical teaching. I. Title.
  BS680.P45C67 2015
  261.7—dc23   2015002925

First printing 2015

Printed in the United States of America

To those who invested their love and passion for God and His Word into my life, with the prayer that the multiplication will continue to generations:

Joy Dawson

Campbell McAlpine
1918–2009

C. Gordon Olson
1907–1989

"Many people have compassion for the lost. I have compassion for God."
Wyn Fountain, 1918–2011

CONTENTS

PART III: POLITICAL LESSONS FROM JEWISH HISTORY

PART IV: JESUS AND POLITICAL JUSTICE

FOREWORD

It was 1999 when I took office as a Member of Parliament in the National Assembly. I was convinced that South Africa needed godly government and was committed to growing the numbers in Parliament—and in all spheres of public life—of "like-minded and like-hearted" people. I was also committed to holding the Executive accountable and to influencing legislation in line with my understanding of biblical standards.

More and more I found that the practical expression of my and my colleagues' application of our understanding of a biblical worldview did not resemble the God we intended to emulate and please—we came across as legalistic, judgmental, and irrelevant in today's world.

This observation became the motivation for my ongoing scrutiny of all things pertaining to our work as Christian politicians. It was at this point that I was introduced to Landa Cope and her work. Words cannot express how truly relieved I was that there was someone other than me tangling with these issues and coming to similar conclusions. I was elated and encouraged. The need to radically change our approach to our work was clear, and the increased clarity regarding what was and what was not our job as Christian politicians helped me move from closing people's ears with my words to being listened to and actually achieving results.

Possibly my favorite quote in this book falls under the heading "Our Call to Governance." Landa writes, "As God's people we are called into civil governance for the glory of God and the good of the people. Our goal is not to perfect the world or nation but to offer God's perspective, a better way, and allow society a choice." I say "possibly" only because I have found myself over the years sharing so many gems from an early reading of this work, concepts Landa has put so simply yet brilliantly

11

into words—concepts which I have wrestled with in practice and concluded similarly.

I am grateful to God beyond words for the gift of insight he has given Landa, and I know this kind of genius does not reveal itself without the proverbial "blood, sweat, and tears"! Thank you, Landa, for allowing God to use you as he has and for being prepared to do what it took to get here. You are a hero in my eyes—authentic and courageous!

Cheryllyn Dudley
Member of Parliament, South Africa
African Christian Democratic Party (ACDP)

PREFACE

Before I had ever written a word I was given two wonderful pieces of advice. Now that I am finishing my third book, I treasure those bits of wisdom like chunks of gold, ever getting more valuable. The first gem was "You know it is time to write a book when you have to." And the second was "You never finish a book, you abandon it." Those are true and faithful words.

For me a given book must have the sense of divine mandate on it. Not because I will not write anything else but because I cannot write anything otherwise. I do not have the focus, the brainpower, or the organizational skills to accomplish it.

I am severely dyslexic and probably ADD, and when my attention span is gone, no willpower on earth will bring it back.

When God puts a project on my heart, it comes with a divine imperative that will not let me lay it down. I get up each day that I am home, study the Word, and then sit in front of my computer. If there is nothing there, then I study the Word some more. Often there is nothing there. But often there is, and this revelational understanding so impacts me that I have to walk off the emotion of it on the beach with my dog. It leads to worship. It leads to prayer and intercession. Sometimes it leads to groaning with a labor that has no words. It is exhilarating and exhausting.

The labor pains of this book have taken five years of waiting and writing and a sixth of editing and polishing. As I look back, it seems impossible that I have stayed the course. But I had to!

Most of the book has been written three to five times. Each rewrite took me farther from my thoughts about God and political justice and closer to thinking that blew my thoughts away. I had to abandon the book finally because there was so much learning in the last writing that I could have written a completely different book at the finish of it. There is no end to the revelation and understanding God is able to give on any subject, let alone his understanding of civil governance. But finally God encouraged me this was enough for now.

This is not a definitive work on the Bible and political justice. The Bible is the only definitive work on the subject. This book is the best insight I have to offer after twenty years of study of the subject in Scripture. It is as uninformed as humanly possible by any other source than the Word of God from Genesis to Revelation. The book does not owe any debt to historical or current views on the subject. It is an attempt to let God speak for himself again from his source material, believing only a consistent and faithful return to his Word and the help of his Spirit will show any generation the way forward.

It is the best I have to offer you now but not nearly comprehensive of what God desires to give us in this age of change. Let's continue beyond these pages to the ever-growing revelation of the King of Kings and let our thinking be swallowed up by his.

Yours for His Highest,

Landa L. Cope
Cape Town, 2014

ACKNOWLEDGMENTS

Any work is finally an accomplishment achieved by a community of people, some who can be named and some for whom the contribution was untraceable by man but known to God. This book is no different, and here are some who played a role in helping me on the long journey:

From afar, Darrow Miller, Peter Tsukihara, and Matt Rawlins all conveyed key messages of encouragement at crucial points of drift. Each one was received as a lifeline with enormous gratitude.

Closer to home, a smaller group gathered here in Cape Town when I finished Part I and gave input on its strengths and weaknesses. They achieved the amazing combination of encouragement and questioning that led to my drawing the conclusion that I needed to rewrite it. Thank you, Patty, Wes, and Cherie!

Special thanks to Maureen Menard, who helped me wrestle with the New Testament and what changed in authority after Jesus came. These were vital discussions and helped point the direction for Part IV.

My Template Institute team of Erin Pennington and Leah Broomfield stuck with me from conception to birth with their unwavering confidence and encouragement that I would finish and that it was worth continuing. Invaluable!

Of course, Ryan Davis and the editorial team at YWAM Publishing helped make the text clear and make it flow, which is such a joy to any reader. They make me look so much better.

And finally, to my friends and donors, some of whom have prayed and given for more than thirty-five years, and who make this calling possible and journey with me no matter where the road goes—thank you, all.

INTRODUCTION

We want justice. We want peace. We want love. We want everything God offers. But do we want him?

This question presses us as we face a world void of solutions; a world crying out for an alternative to its failed convictions; a world crushed by poverty, unrest, overpopulation, natural disasters, and devastating diseases; a world longing to dream but with no vision; a world longing to change but seeing no options; a world pulsing with potential for a great age in the history of humanity but discerning no drumbeat to follow.

God is who we are looking for. He is the dream fulfilled, the one who offers us our destiny. But will we allow God to be himself? This is an odd question in a generation that insists so strongly for ourselves, Let us be us! Fair enough, God says. But you must let me be me.

In this book we pursue political justice, a desire of every heart, the cry of billions, and the demand of the peoples of many nations. We have only one concern—what does God say? We turn to only one book—God's book. In the Bible, God does not say what we want him to say. He does not tell us how to take control and make our nations good and just. He does not tell us how to legislate sin out of our towns and streets. He does not give us a strategy.

Instead, through Scripture, God tells us our story and his purpose, taking us on an unrelentingly tragic journey through the history of humanity. In Genesis we begin with an amazing vision of possibility for God's human creation. The cosmos is made for our inheritance. We are co-regents with God in dominion. Perfection, regal authority, and eternal comradeship with our Maker are ours. Our position is breathtaking.

From the third chapter of Genesis on, however, it is a very different story. We are in free fall from sin, and beginning with fratricide, we get all the way to human genocide by chapter 6. What is that all about? Nearly ten generations of human destruction end in a violent, global, catastrophic flood. Why even read this stuff? What is the point? Where is God in all this? Why not just skip ahead and get to justice in the New Testament? Because this is God's selected history, and he wants us to understand it. If we want his blessing, we will have to understand his thinking. Do you want him or your idea of him? You have to make a choice.

Finally hope reasserts itself as God calls a man to father a tribe, a new nation to reveal God. But from the first generation of Abraham, lying, cheating, and multiple difficult families take star roles in the story. Within four generations we are back to the near fratricide of Joseph and the genocide of the Shechemites. This is followed by more than four hundred years of slavery as God deals with Abraham's legacy.

Reprieve comes again in the form of the exodus from slavery and the law given to Moses to disciple the nearly free nation of Israel. God begins to speak for himself and gives clear, concise, and very specific instruction for how to achieve justice in a community. Five books, ten commandments, and one small nation should be doable. God is with Israel. They make a covenant with him. Finally we are moving forward.

God's chosen nation has some good years and some bad years, but it all hits the fan again. Only two thousand years pass from Joshua to the last kings of Israel and the total destruction of the promised nation! Sure, there are highs and lows between those markers. There is David. Yes, our best political leader, only a murderer and an adulterer. But he had a heart for God? Yes, he did. And there is Solomon. Yes, the pinnacle of national history. A man of great wisdom from God in governing but with so little wisdom in his personal life. He is the king of Israel's greatest age but also the father of the kings who will in one generation begin to tear it all apart and take the nation to total destruction. What does this all mean? While much of what God wants is achieved, even a certain amount of political justice, the story deteriorates into bloody chaos again.

Why read this stuff? Why dwell on this difficult story for hundreds of pages? We haven't even come to the prophets and a few hundred more pages of pain! Surely God wants us to put this awful history behind us and get to Jesus, peace, and joy. More than a thousand pages of torture for what, when we now have the good news of the New Testament? Is there a point?

God has a point! He is telling us who we are, what we were made to be, and what we have become. He is telling us what he has had to witness, weep over, and address in order to bring us back to our destiny. He is telling us about the unrelenting suffering of God and his human creation, of all creation, because of the misuse of our human authority. He is telling us the cost of ignorance, the cost of lostness, the cost of the dream behind giving humankind authority in the first place. He is telling us that everything has been tried in human history and failed. He is telling us that we want the wrong kind of king, that we are looking for the wrong kind of kingdom, and that every time he tries to steer humanity in the right direction, we refuse him!

When we reject the Old Testament pain, we are rejecting God's view of humanity and reality. We are saying that we don't want this God to be God. We don't want this to be the truth about who we are. We do not want this to be the story. We want Jesus! And Jesus does come.

When Jesus comes, his male peer group is slaughtered. When he comes, his own people work with a pagan empire to execute him. He is not the king his people want. "But he is resurrected. He ascends!" He does, and the Spirit comes, the power of God in human beings to carry out God's destiny. "Yes, this is the one. This is the king we asked for." The growth of the church explodes, and the good news sweeps the known world. "Yes, this is the wave we were waiting for." But then it begins: persecution from within, believers ganging up on believers, and from without, political domination and persecution from imperial governments with different agendas. The church struggles to be God's church, and we continue to argue about what kind of king Jesus actually is, all the way through the first three chapters of Revelation.

If God has not come to give us control, if he has not come to give us peace and comfort, if he has not come to stop sin and violence, then what is the point? Why are we still here on earth suffering?

That is a very important question, and you will have to walk through what God has walked through and see what he has seen before you understand what he understands about justice, on earth and in heaven.

PART I

IT ALL BEGINS IN GENESIS

CHAPTER 1

WHY DISCIPLE A NATION?

All over the world today Christians are discussing discipling nations. There are many terms used in the movement—transformation, spheres and domains of influence, the seven mountains, the vocational mission—but we are all talking about what Jesus meant when he left us with parting instructions to disciple all nations. We are trying to understand what that means and to apply ourselves in this age of the church to do it.

There can be only one legitimate reason for discipling nations, and that is to make Jesus known. The only way to know the Son of God in depth is by saturation in his revealed Word and radical application of it through daily obedience to the Holy Spirit. The only way to know Jesus as he relates to political justice and in his role as King of Kings is to exhaustively study the Scriptures he studied and the message he brought in fulfilling them.

In this book we are undertaking that study of God's Word from the perspective of political justice and just governance. The only way to restore political justice to God's design is by *so* hearing the heart of God and *so* seeing the perfection of his thoughts and ways in his Word that we *see* him and, therefore, *know* what we must do to help create more just nations and communities, to be a more just people.

THE KINGDOM OF GOD IS A SOCIAL CONTRACT

In Matthew 22:36–40 Jesus summarized the whole teaching of the law
in two sentences. When asked, "Teacher, which is the greatest commandment in the Law?" Jesus replied: "*Love the Lord your God with
all your heart and with all your soul and with all your mind.*' This is the
first and greatest commandment. And the second is like it: '*Love your
neighbor as yourself.*' All the Law and the Prophets hang on these two
commandments" (emphasis added).

The message of the kingdom of God, as summarized in the royal
law of Matthew 22, is a revelation of who God is, who you and I are,
and how we are to live together as a community. The last century of
Christianity has emphasized what God says about *me*, the individual,
what he requires of *me* and will do for *me*. With our emphasis on salvation, we stress personal blessing, personal sin, and personal holiness.
Understanding how God relates to *me* is not wrong, but it is incomplete,
out of perspective with the bigger picture of what God is showing us in
Scripture. We learn from the whole of the Bible to live out the nature and
character of God in community and nation. In other words, I reveal my
faith and my knowledge of God through how I treat you and how I consent to your treatment by others. My commitment to Jesus is also a commitment to my community. "In everything do to others as you would
have them do to you; for this is the Law and the Prophets" (Matt. 7:12).

THE KINGDOM OF GOD IS HEAVENLY AND EARTHLY

If we are to think like the God of the Bible, we must begin where he
begins—and God begins with the creation of the cosmos, the earth,
and everything in it. Just two chapters are dedicated to this space-time
creation event—not a great deal of explanation for such a monumental
happening. But these two chapters lay down the foundation stones of all
biblical thought. They lay down three themes fleshed out by the whole
of the Bible: Who is God? Who am I? How am I to live with you, my
neighbor? Without Genesis 1 and 2, our thinking about God and life
will drift toward either mysticism or rationalism.

Mysticism holds a magical view of reality and sees solutions in
terms of invisible powers in unseen places, while rationalism sees reality

as a purely material manifestation and solutions as solely pragmatic and man-made—things we can see, taste, smell, hear, touch, and measure. Without a clear understanding of Genesis 1 and 2, we begin to develop a duality between the seen and unseen world. We begin to define kingdom reality in terms of either miracles *or* science, heavenly *or* earthly, visible *or* invisible, secular *or* sacred, spiritual *or* unspiritual, losing the powerful message of Christ—Creator of *all*. Paul emphasizes this integrated reality of God's kingdom in Colossians 1:15–17: "The Son is the image of the invisible God, the firstborn over all creation. For in him all things were created: things in heaven and on earth, visible and invisible, whether thrones or powers or rulers or authorities; all things have been created through him and for him. He is before all things, and in him all things hold together."

In Genesis God declares that these two realities, seen and unseen, visible and invisible, are *both* created by him and are *both* under his authority. He places humanity in dominion over both realms on earth and tells us that our destiny as a human race is to multiply, fill the earth, and create communities, or cultures. Therefore, those who seek to think like God and find his solutions and direction must marry the realities of the seen and unseen, and the individual and community, as part of the one and only kingdom of God.

OUR STRUGGLE

As believers today, our struggle with a split concept of reality is often revealed in our dualism between the Old and New Testaments. Jesus acknowledges our tendency toward this in Matthew 5:17–19:

> Do not think that I have come to abolish the Law or the Prophets; I have not come to abolish them but to fulfill them. For truly I tell you, until heaven and earth disappear, not the smallest letter, not the least stroke of a pen, will by any means disappear from the Law until everything is accomplished. Therefore anyone who sets aside one of the least of these commands and teaches others accordingly will be called least in the kingdom of heaven, but whoever practices and teaches these commands will be called great in the kingdom of heaven.

In other words, greatness in the kingdom of God is being able to marry and live both Old *and* New Testament values. The Old Testament emphasizes nations and how we live together as a community here on earth, and the New Testament emphasizes the individual, salvation, and reaching the lost for a future in heaven. These must be married to see God and his kingdom clearly. The revelation is progressive, and we do not leave the beginning in the Old in order to achieve the end in the New. One builds on and fulfills the purpose of the other, revealing the full purposes of God. Political justice is about authority in heaven and on earth. And the pursuit of godly justice requires an understanding of the Old and the New.

GOD DELEGATES AUTHORITY AND POWER

The essence of government entails who has the authority to do what, when, and where, and where the power comes from to execute it.

Genesis 1 and 2 give us a summation of God's foundational values and where he places authority and responsibility. The delegation of and power to carry authority in the kingdom of God is the basis of every legal and justice issue and is therefore the values base for governance. In other words, this is the template of ideals we, as believers, are working toward for civil law in a fallen world. Our goal is to move toward God's values and rightful authority by restoring his thinking in and through our lives, our families, our vocations, and our communities.

In Scripture we find God's establishment of rights and responsibilities, authority and power. Every person has rights, and with those rights comes the weight of responsibility. However, no one has all rights and all responsibilities at all times, in all places, or over all things. The rights of men and women, animal rights, the earth's rights, rights of workers, rights of immigrants, nations' rights, border rights, community rights, individual rights, religious rights, parents' rights, children's rights, the right to speak, the right to communicate, the right to know, spousal rights, property rights, rights of ownership, sexual rights, the right to protest, the right of civil disobedience, the right of parental disobedience, the right to religious freedom, the right of religious disobedience, reproductive rights, prisoners' rights, the rights of the poor, the right to reputation, tribal rights, victims' rights, owners' rights, the right to work, the right to live, and more are all present and defended in Scripture. We can rightly say that Scripture validates, and in some cases historically creates, the concept of rights, privileges, and responsibilities.

CIVIL LAW

The burden of civil governance is to sustain and secure these God-given rights. It is very difficult and never perfected. But we are to work for the highest level of justice possible in the situation and then continue to work for a still higher level, while at the same time upholding the rights society has already established and securing the rights God gives but society still denies. Our focus, rather than on ourselves as Christians, should be on those whose rights are most abused: the widow, the orphan, the alien, and the poor.

OUR CALL TO GOVERNANCE

As God's people we are called into civil governance for the glory of God and the good of the people. Our goal is not to perfect the world or nation but to offer God's perspective, a better way, and allow society a choice. We are not the Jews in the promised land; we are God's people in Babylon, God's people surrounded by nations in darkness, offering salt and light.

We have influence, but we are not in control. We are not defending God's kingdom; his kingdom is already established. We are not here to "bring back the King"; the King is already coming. We are ambassadors of light, helping to dispel darkness. We are salt, preserving and changing the flavor of our communities' choices. We are salt that can bring healing. We offer an alternative to the lies of the lawless one. And we are preparing to deliver God's justice beyond the borders of this world and time.

As citizens, peacekeepers, and governors of a nation, our objective is to win our nations to the highest level of justice they will accept. Having been loved into the kingdom of God ourselves, we must not think that we will beat the lost into understanding God's values of political justice. We must win them over to God's thinking through our defense of his laws and values and by revealing his superior blessing in our lives.

To what end do we pursue this passion of the kingdom? That all may see the glory of the Lord, that some might be saved, and that all be blessed.

CHAPTER 2

THE ORIGINS OF POLITICAL JUSTICE

Genesis 1–2

On hearing of *the fall of man*, those who would truly know God should ask, "Fallen from what?" Nothing in the kingdom of God will make sense until we understand the purpose for which God created all things.

The tragedy of human history is not the fall, but what we lost through the fall. The unsurpassable joy of the kingdom is not conversion in and of itself but the progressive redemption of the stunning, perfect destiny God created for humanity and all of creation.

Genesis 1 and 2 tell us that God conceived of replicating and multiplying his perfect Self and the love and fellowship of the Trinity by creating human beings in his image. First he created space, then matter and time, then the perfect environment for every living thing—water for sea creatures, sky for winged creatures, and land for creatures that move along the ground. Finally, God created those for whom all of this was designed, the purpose of the cosmos and pride of creation. God made humankind, and he made them in his image. Then God declared all of this good!

God took earth in his own hands to form first-Adam's physical being. He breathed his own breath into lungs of clay, giving divine life to his created being. God took from the side of first-person Adam to form second-person Adam; from that single handful of soil and that one breath, God created a second person sharing the identical image of God with first-person Adam. And from them—Adam male and Adam female—human beings made in God's image would multiply and fill the earth.[1] God provided everything everyone would ever need: a perfect, sustainable biosphere where life, fellowship, devotion, love, work, creating, stewarding, and multiplying would never be diminished. And God declared all of it good!

God walked daily with us, his human race, in the garden. He gave us dominion over all the creatures of the sea, air, and land. Our mandate was to multiply, fill the earth, and cultivate it. The word translated "cultivate" in Genesis 2:15 (NASB) is rooted in the same word as *culture, cultus*. God was telling us to populate the earth and create cultures. Our destiny as human beings was to multiply, migrate, and create miniature kingdoms, tribes and nations, revealing the nature and attributes of God through our life together as neighbors, co-rulers of the earth, and co-heirs of the kingdom. To the human race, collectively, God gave authority and power on the earth. Governance was mandated from the very beginning of God's revelation of himself and his human heirs. By giving humanity freedom, limited sovereignty, and authority, God invited us to share in governance of the kingdom.

Culture and community were conceived in the triune nature of God. He gave the human race the potential to multiply his nature and character through individuals, families, tribes, and nations . . . forever. God's glory, revealed through us, was to fill the earth with diverse communities of human beings committed to loving each other as God loves us. And God declared this "very, very good." It was so good that God declared one in every seven days a day to sit back and appreciate the beauty and perfection of the productiveness of his—and our—creative work of building communities. God called this day the Sabbath.

THE PERFECT PURPOSE

There can be no biblical understanding of any domain or dominion on earth without first understanding God's design and purpose before sin and the fall. We were not made for sin. Sin happened, and we must deal with it. But we do not have governance, science, education, family, business, the arts, communication, and all of culture *because* we are fallen from God's ideal. We do not have nations and cultures *because*, after sin, there was no other way we could exist. All of these arenas of society exist because we are created in the image of God, and they *all* reveal him. We don't bring God into our family, community, or work. He was there all the time. Each is a means to know, see, and worship God. We rediscover God in our life and work. Creating families and communities that reflect God is our worship now and forever.

Civil governance and the political process are not an unfortunate result of the fall. They are God's revelation of himself as King, the one who has all authority and all power over all things, and yet who, without fear, delegates real authority and power to those he governs. In fact, giving authority and power away is part of how he governs. God conceived of autonomy, sovereignty, rights, and freedoms; he seeks to redeem them, not destroy them, in his kingdom.

BOUNDARIES AND LIMITS

Of course, God has created boundaries to all authority and power, to all autonomy and sovereignty and every freedom. God is not naive! Nor does he desire us to be. He sets boundaries on rights. In his Word he details the proper use of freedoms and transparently tells us the consequences of exceeding those limits. But—and this is a significant counterpoint—he leaves us free and able to test those boundaries to see if we choose to agree with him. What daring, what confidence, what love God must have to risk human failure rather than refuse us the opportunity to achieve our destiny. God will not cheapen the value of human life with the simple formula of control, not because he cannot, but because he will not!

CREATED TO GOVERN

In spite of the reality of sin, human beings are created by God to govern. Being made in the image of God means, in part, that human communities have to decide how and by whom we are governed. We, like God, need to delegate authority to someone, somehow, somewhere, or perish in anarchy. The only governance more deadly than *bad* governance is *no* governance. As peoples we have to devise some level of consensus because individuals do not have enough power to rule the many.

We are given, by God, the freedom to experiment, make choices, create, and even rebel. After the fall, alienated from "the God who knows," our experimentation on how to govern ourselves evolves in a vacuum of ignorance. Our experiments are not expressions of values in diversity, but become expressions of diversity in ignorance and control. All human cultures reflect and defend some level of truth because it is the only way to survive. But, tragically, all cultures also develop glaring holes of deception that devalue human life and dignity.

Our Distorted Concept of Governance

Inevitably, after sin, humans have to figure out where "the right to govern" comes from. All human models are top-down systems of the few over the many. "I have the right to rule because I have the most powerful army. I can make you obey." "I have the right to rule because I have the most money and can hire the most powerful army, and I can make you obey." "I have the right to rule because my father ruled you and he had the most money and the biggest army, and he gave them to me and I can make you obey." "I have the right to rule because god has the most power, and god told me I can make you obey." "I have the right to rule because I am god and I can make you obey." In later centuries, human models of governance developed a new twist: "I represent you, and therefore I have the power to make you obey." But in all human designs, the power is at the top, controlling the masses at the bottom.

God's Template for Governance

Millennia into human history, God speaks. Choosing Abraham, God decides he will reveal to one people in space and time his template for building a nation. They are not yet a people and will never become a perfect tribe or nation, but he will use this one nation to teach all nations his ways—through the Scriptures, through the Messiah, and finally, through the Spirit and the global body of Christ.

When, through Moses, God speaks for himself on civil governance, what he says shakes the foundations of humanity's concept of the right to govern. "I don't want to *make* you obey," he says. "I want you to choose it. I will not force you, but I will seek to convince you that my ways are perfect." In Deuteronomy God essentially tells the Jews his template for a nation. He gives them the authority to choose who will govern and over what they will be governed. He tells them whom he would choose and over what they should be governed, but he leaves the decision to them. Through Scripture, God then tells us the story of four thousand years of choices made by the Jewish people and says to us, "What do you think? Was I right? Were they blessed when they obeyed? Were they blessed when they disobeyed? Now, what do *you* want to do?"

CALLED TO GOVERN

For God's servants in all of history, the simplest task in governing is discovering what would be best for our communities. God's perspective is knowable. Our most difficult task as believers is being convinced of that knowability, living this conviction from generation to generation. Our second most difficult challenge is convincing enough people to have the will and power to bring change in our nation. Having been won by love into the kingdom of God, we will not gain political influence in the nations by force. In politics we will have to learn God's way of wooing and winning every bit as effectively as in evangelism.

When we are called to governance through political office, party politics, military service, law enforcement, judicial roles such as paralegal, judge, lawyer, or public defender, or any other vocation supporting the justice system of our nations, we are called to this arena to do what God would do and does. We are called to offer people the best choices, work to convince them of the value of these choices, and help them institutionalize these choices in justly enforced law. This is a God-sized task, and God gives accounts in Scripture of his ongoing struggles with Israel to help guide us.

CALLED AS CITIZENS

As citizens of a nation, all believers are called of God to personally support what God considers justice for the people. We are called to raise our voices, not on God's behalf (God is fine), but on behalf of what justice demands for the people from God's perspective. We, God's people, do not win or lose in the political process; our blessings are eternally assured. God does not win or lose; he is eternally blessed. But the people we seek to serve with justice and freedom will win or lose based on the decisions they make. Our grief, our angst, our suffering is for them, not ourselves. We have lost nothing; we agree with God and we have the blessing of our choices. When thwarted, we regroup. We recommit. We rededicate ourselves to the cause of the people and the highest levels of justice with which they will allow us to serve them. We do this because we love them as ourselves, and as God loves us. Like Jesus, we love the world and are willing to lay down our lives in the service of the human race whether we are accepted or rejected.

England's William Wilberforce has been in the public eye because of the film *Amazing Grace*, which gives an overview of his life. Wilberforce loved God and desired to serve him with all his heart. He wanted to be a preacher, but he knew that God had called him to Parliament. Wilberforce spent decades fighting legalized slavery. Was it worth an entire life? I am sure there were days Wilberforce felt it wasn't. But history, as well as the kingdom of God, records his contribution to the justice of God through the system of law in his time.

God wants to raise up a generation of Wilberforces ready to take on the legal issues of our day—issues such as modern slavery and human trafficking, masses of people who have no legal recourse or defense, global flaunting of use of violence, crippling poverty, insufferable treatment of prisoners, economies built on the backs of economic slaves, poor development of land and use of resources, and blatant tyranny and denial of human rights. From God's perspective, work is not a privilege; it is a right. Health is not a privilege; it is a right. Life is not a privilege; it is a right. And we can go on and on.

But—and this is another very significant counterpoint—before we are able to defend the justice that God desires to restore in our societies, we must see what God sees, feel what God feels, and value what God values. So we continue through Genesis and the line of history God has highlighted to sharpen our perspective.

CHAPTER 3

THE RED THREAD OF VIOLENCE BEGINS

Genesis 3–9

From the moment God's order is broken in Genesis 3, the fruit is violence. The human race enters a spiral of violence, setting humans against humans, humans against animals, and humans against the earth. Sin and its consequences produce fear of creation, sorrow in childbearing, and frustration in work. And, most devastating, sin produces in humans shame, a sense of rejection, and the loss of identity. Human creatures, separated from their Creator, begin to look to themselves for validation and to their work and the material world for the source of their value.

God's wonderful human creatures no longer know who they are, where they are from, or why they are here. They no longer recognize a source of meaning in God. Separated from their Creator, humans must fend for themselves to establish their value. The fruit of this loss of perspective is tragic: a race disastrously turns in on itself and the world that surrounds it. God tracks the tragedy's influence as an escalating history of bloodshed—the red thread of violence—through all of Scripture. The dreadful outcomes begin immediately.

SELECTED HISTORY

It is important to remember that God is not attempting to tell all of human history in Scripture. Myriads of things are going on simultaneously. God is intentionally selecting those parts of the story that will affect all of history and exemplify the universal human condition. He is writing the "urgently need to know" version of our origins. With this in mind, there is no doubt that, from God's perspective, the immediate devaluing of human life, which results in escalating violence, is the gravest consequence of sin. Throughout Scripture, God is trying to limit the damage of the fall and the loss of human value while bringing us back to our value in him. Anything that devalues human life, then, is counter to kingdom strategy.

THE TREE

You cannot produce a just society by seeking to eliminate human choices. First of all, it is impossible to administrate, and second, it is contrary to the very nature of the thing God is trying to save.

The Bible presupposes that the image of God in the human race includes freedom, choice, and limited autonomy. In order for choice to be real, there must be at least one way in which choice can be expressed. Nothing in the garden of Eden is denied Adam except the fruit of one tree, the tree of the knowledge of good and evil (Gen. 2:17). Whatever our interpretation of this passage, clearly the tree represents a choice and specifically the choice of whether to obey or disobey God's authority—to recognize or deny that our human authority has a source and limits. The possibility of choosing and the consequences of our choices are a fundamental theme in all of Scripture.

A RATHER LARGE GARDEN

In fairness to God we must put this one "tree" in perspective. The garden of Eden extended from the Euphrates River at its northeast border to the river Nile, or possibly the Wadi of Egypt in the southwest (Gen. 2:10–14). Either way it is a very big garden, encompassing much of what we now know as Iraq, Syria, Turkey, Jordan, Saudi Arabia, Qatar, UAE, Kuwait, Oman, Yemen, Israel, Gaza, and eastern Egypt.

In this massive garden, full of trees, there is one tree that God has forbidden to Adam! This tree is not a trick of God to stumble humans by constantly confronting them with forbidden fruit. It is very simply and minimally an opportunity to express the freedom of choice. Without it, human beings would have been incarcerated by God rather than being co-rulers and heirs of his kingdom.

Adam, male and female, chose to disobey God's one law. They ate from the only forbidden tree in the garden. The first sin, the first injustice, is committed. It is a crime against God's created order. We have a created order because that is how God has made the cosmos. We have crime because God has made humanity free and able to make choices. We have consequences because the cosmos, humanity, and our choices are all real.

Consequences are not arbitrary "smacks" of God. They are the outcome of the reality of the universe we live in and the reality of our choices. Sin is not sin because God just decided to forbid it. God forbids certain behavior, calling it sin, because it will destroy us. The consequences are not judgments of motive or value but the real outcomes of our real choices made in a real universe. God is trying to protect us.

Gravity is real. I jump, I fall, I am hurt. Similarly, breaking God's laws had and has a devastating impact on us and the world we live in. Whether we mean to break the law or not is a separate issue. God is real. I am real. The cosmos is real, and the consequences of my actions are real. Thinking about murder and committing murder are two very different issues. They are both sin because they destroy, but one has more grave and tangible consequences than the other. One destroys me, which is tragic, but the act destroys another and that in turn begins to destroy the community. One is a moral dilemma between God and me. The other is an issue of justice between the community and me. Regardless of my motive, the fact of death has consequences.

Just as our own choices have natural consequences, the choice of Adam, male and female, to disobey God in the garden had unavoidable consequences. The tree was there; therefore, temptation was there as well. Temptation is contained in the fact that we are capable of choice. Adam chooses to disobey. The reality of *knowing* good and evil enters the world. Sin and disobedience are no longer only a possibility; they and their consequences are here and wreaking their havoc. The crime of chapter 3 was not that evil was a possibility. The crime was doing evil.

And the consequences of that crime were not arbitrary acts of punishment. They were the built-in consequences of breaking God's created order. And the breaking of that order must have boundaries lest it escalate into total destruction.

At this point in human history, God is the judiciary. He is dealing with lawlessness in the human race directly. We can look at Genesis 5–9 as a template of values for the judicial process, and we will see these same values in the due process God reveals through Mosaic law. We will assume here that none of us is God and therefore our proceedings will need checks and balances against human error and corruption. God alone is able to administer *pure* justice.

The Hebrew definition of *justice* is the restoration of order, or "right order." With that in mind, the resetting of tension between equally important values always motivates God's actions. We will come back to this understanding of "right order" in future chapters.

TRIAL #1: HIGH TREASON

God vs. Adam

Our first offense takes place in Genesis 3 and is the first act of human lawlessness. Adam was not ignorant of the law. God had made this one regulation of the tree clear, along with the consequences of breaking it. But Adam broke the law. There is no malice here, except for the actions of the serpent. But the law has been broken. Right order has been broken.

God begins these proceedings by seeking out the accused. He takes *testimony* from Adam male and Adam female, and they both, more or less, plead guilty. I suppose we could say that the serpent's testimony is inadmissible, or useless, as he is known to be a professional liar. It is not that God needs testimony in order to know what the truth is. So why bother with it? Could it be that owning our actions is an essential part of the redemptive process? Could the declaration of the truth be part of what restores justice?

To the *natural consequences* of shame and guilt they already experience, God adds *correction* to the sentence. They must leave the garden. They and their progeny are banned. They will no longer live forever but will age and finally die. At this point in reading, it is difficult to see why

God decrees such a permanent and irrevocable sentence for Adam's sin. But we will not get to the end of Genesis before we see the horrendous impact of this first act of lawlessness on the development of all human society. The gravity of God's sentence reflects the grave consequences of our loss of God's perspective. God must act swiftly, or the human race will destroy itself. He will *limit the human potential for destruction* by limiting the length of our life.

God intervenes to help lessen the tragic impact of humanity's actions on humanity. He sacrifices part of his beloved animal creation on behalf of his beloved human creatures in order to help diminish their shame and guilt. This first bloodshed provides clothing for Adam, male and female, but also foreshadows both the consequences that will inevitably flow out of choosing to break the law and what will be necessary to finally resolve the guilt and shame and separation from God it has produced. Blood has been shed. Sacrifices must be made.

God finds his human creatures and the serpent guilty and sentences them to life in exile from the garden. For Adam male and Adam female this means their experience will now include multiplied labor, sorrow in multiplication, and ultimately a death sentence through a limited life span. Adam now names his helper Eve.

Elements of Trial #1

- **Freedom and choice:** These are built-in realities in the kingdom of God.
- **Law:** Human freedom is not without boundaries, and therefore God has established laws.
- **Responsibility:** We are responsible for the freedom we have been given and the boundaries God has created.
- **Consequences:** The boundaries God has created are fixed, and natural consequences will be experienced regardless of any external circumstances.
- **Trial:** Part of the redemptive process is reinforcement of God's laws.
- **Testimony:** Part of the redemptive process is allowing the accused to own responsibility for their actions.
- **Judgment and sentence:** Part of the redemptive process is closure, placing the injustice in the past and creating a clear

understanding of the altered boundaries of the garden for the future. Choices are real and irrevocable. We must understand the impact they will have.

- **Correction:** The corrections are based on the overall destructiveness of the crime to the community present and future.
- **Compassion:** Regardless of their actions, the guilty are human beings created in the image of God and their integrity is to be preserved.
- **Recognition:** There is to be recognition of the innate human value of the guilty regardless of their crimes.

As we continue through Scripture, we will find that these trial elements match the values found throughout the Old and the New Testament.

Trial #2: Fratricide

God vs. Cain

We have no idea how many children Adam and Eve had after leaving the garden and before the birth of Cain and Abel. We can assume many, since they lived a very long time. As we begin Genesis 4, Eve, renamed by her husband in the previous chapter, is giving birth to Cain. God selectively preserves the story of Cain and Abel because it is a key turning point in human history. Cain's murder of his brother reveals that in one generation the consequences of the loss of God and his perspective of reality lead to the progressive devaluing of human life, and now murder.

Cain premeditates and murders his brother! The story is a familiar one. Abel is a shepherd. Cain tills the soil. They understand that there is a God but no longer understand what this God wants. In order to get God's blessing, they each bring an offering of the fruit of their labor. God "prefers" Abel's blood offering because it accurately symbolizes the consequence of sin and the necessary path to redemption, the shedding of blood. God was not accepting Abel and rejecting Cain. He was correcting Cain's perception of what he wanted and was trying to teach him. Rather than accepting correction and learning, Cain becomes defensive and angry. He turns God's instruction into a false value judgment of himself and a personal identity crisis.

God appeals to Cain to stop reacting and to understand that he is accepted. It is his offering that is rejected. Cain's temptation to cling to his idea of what should be sacrificed will destroy his relationships with God and his brother. He can overcome his temptation by accepting God's instruction. But Cain does not accept God's perspective and chooses murder instead. Cain, full of shame and of anger toward God, comforts himself by killing his own brother. Fratricide is conceived.

The Trial

God takes evidence by questioning the witness. "Where is your brother?" Cain lies: "I don't know." Cain then asks God, "Am I my brother's keeper?" Cain questions whether he has any responsibility for another human, even his brother.

God brings forensic evidence in the form of blood found in the ground. The material world is *real*, and evidence can be found. Evidence can be real, guilt and innocence can be real, and a judicial finding can be true and just. Our distortion of reality and misrepresentation of facts, intentional or not, do not change reality. Abel is dead. Cain killed him. God evaluates the evidence for Cain's benefit and finds him guilty.

A sentence is pronounced. Having preferred himself over his brother, Cain receives a life sentence in exile. He loses his land, vocation, family, and community. Having preferred self over another's life, Cain loses his life as he knows it. Correction will protect the community while sustaining Cain's life. He may think his life is more important than anyone else's, but God does not. However, God does value Cain's life.

The Appeal

Cain appeals God's verdict, and *God is willing to hear him*. Cain says that the punishment is too severe. Not only is he losing his land and family; he is also losing the protection they provide him, and he will surely be murdered. What an interesting argument from a man who has just murdered his brother! However, Cain is arguing God's perspective: "human life has value," even his. God agrees with him. The sentence should model a different set of values than the crime.

Cain's crime is the devaluing of human life. God's desire is for Cain to value human life. If the crime is the devaluing of human life, how do we enforce the law and correct the criminal? In this case God marks

Cain so that his *life* is protected. Seven being the number representing perfection, Cain's life is worth seven times another man's (Gen. 4:15). *And* another man's life is worth seven times his. The meaning? Life is *perfectly* sacred.

Elements of Trial #2

- **Appeal process:** Even the guilty are to have a voice.
- **Modification of sentence:** Judicial review may be part of the redemptive process.
- **Forensic evidence:** The material world does not lie.
- **Protected rights of the convicted:** All human life is sacred.

TRIAL #3: ANARCHY

God vs. the Human Race

In just five short generations from Cain to his great-great-great-grandson Lamech, human violence escalates beyond imagination. Lamech boasts in Genesis 4:23–24 that he has killed a man for merely slapping him and that seventy-seven deaths would be required to avenge Lamech's life. God's act of leniency on Cain's behalf has not resulted in humility and increased understanding of the value of life. Instead it has been twisted to serve egocentric arrogance. Cain's relatives have turned God's leniency into an excuse for self-serving violence and murder. A single murder has grown into a culture of violence. How will God stop the violence and yet preserve his precious human creation?

Nine generations after Adam, here is God's evaluation of the human race: "Now the earth was corrupt in God's sight and was full of violence. God saw how corrupt the earth had become, for all the people on earth had corrupted their ways. So God said to Noah, 'I am going to put an end to all people, for the earth is filled with violence because of them. I am surely going to destroy both them and the earth'" (Gen. 6:11–13).

The culture of violence had become universal. God finds murder in the heart of every human being with the exception of Noah. Preservation of the human race will require correction of the entire community. The human race has so completely lost God's understanding of the value of life that they are going to self-destruct slowly and brutally. God is looking for a way to save humanity before the race is completely destroyed.

God decides that the only just way to apply mercy is to destroy the human race quickly and preserve the life of the most righteous man he can find to give humans a second chance at survival. This is not *fairness* to Noah and his children. They are not good by God's standard, as will soon be revealed, but they are the best God has to work with. This leniency God is showing is not on behalf of Noah and his family. It is for the survival of the human race.

God faces a dilemma. If he does nothing, the human race will self-destruct, taking the rest of creation with them. He must intervene. If he is to intervene, he must be true to himself and his character. If he were *only* just, he would wipe out the entire human race because of their addiction to blood. If he were *only* merciful, the violence would continue and increase exponentially as it had since Cain, and humankind would destroy itself. How will God stop the violent destruction of the human race in a way that does not destroy humankind itself? The objective is redemption, not annihilation. If God did not value us, his problem would be easily solved.

The dilemma is to hold two perfect attributes in tension: justice and mercy. Choosing one or the other misrepresents who God is and destroys God's order. Neither one by itself is justice. Justice in the kingdom of God is holding onto and reinforcing both, a very painful task because there are no simple answers.

The Trial

In the third earthly trial God finds the human race guilty of murder and genocide in thought, word, and deed. He pronounces the death penalty. However, he will spare one man (the most righteous he can find) and his family in order to spare the future of the human race. He will give humanity a second chance: justice in tension with mercy.

This sentence is devastating to God and everything he values in creation; it is only possible for him to execute this sentence because of his great love for humankind. He knows this is the only way to save the human race from themselves. However, he promises *he will never do it again*. Listen to his heart: "Never again will I curse the ground because of humans, even though every inclination of the human heart is evil from childhood. And never again will I destroy all living creatures, as I have done. 'As long as the earth endures, seedtime and harvest, cold and heat, summer and winter, day and night will never cease'" (Gen. 8:21–22).

The Death Sentence

Death is the consequence of sin from Adam on. Violence and bloodthirstiness spread like wildfire throughout the human race. God's attention is not only on the individuals like Cain who commit murder but also on the communities that breed violence and murder. God's focus is not on abstract solutions but on deterrents to violence. The judicial solution must actually decrease violence. If it does not, it is not redemptive and we must find another.

If we are to think like God, we must recognize that we are dealing not only with violent individuals but with violence as the culture of humankind. If we seek only to rehabilitate individuals, we will allow for the continual perpetuation and escalation of human violence. We must seek solutions that also provoke change and rehabilitate the communities where violence breeds. Again, we must maintain a kingdom tension between the responsibility of the individual and the responsibility of the community.

While God makes it clear that he will never use global destruction as a deterrent to violence again, he also puts into place two additional corrections in humanity's sentence. For the second time he severely decreases the human life span, and for the second time, in the flood, he sacrifices his beloved animal kingdom. He then gives us meat to eat. It does not stretch the imagination to think that there was widespread cannibalism. But God does not give us the blood:

> Then God blessed Noah and his sons, saying to them, "Be fruitful and increase in number and fill the earth. The fear and dread of you will fall on all the beasts of the earth, and on all the birds in the sky, on every creature that moves along the ground, and on all the fish in the sea; they are given into your hands. Everything that lives and moves about will be food for you. Just as I gave you the green plants, I now give you everything.
>
> "But you must not eat meat that has its lifeblood still in it. And for your lifeblood I will surely demand an accounting. I will demand an accounting from every animal. And from each

human being, too, I will demand an accounting for the life of another human being.

"Whoever sheds human blood, by humans shall their blood be shed; for in the image of God has God made mankind. As for you, be fruitful and increase in number; multiply on the earth and increase upon it." (Gen. 9:1–7)

God's objective is clear. He is trying to stop the violence and brand the sacred value of human life into our thinking.

A Taste for Blood

God created us frugivores, eating the seeds of plants and trees. But we have literally acquired a taste or need for blood. First we read: "God said, 'I give you every seed-bearing plant on the face of the whole earth and every tree that has fruit with seed in it. They will be yours for food. And to all the beasts of the earth and all the birds in the sky and all the creatures that move along the ground—everything that has the breath of life in it—I give every green plant for food.' And it was so" (Gen. 1:29–30). Now we humans and many animals have become carnivores, as we saw in Genesis 9 above.

The consequences of sin continue as God sacrifices more of his animal kingdom to deal with our blood lust. What an incredible commitment to human freedom and redemption.

Elements of Trial #3

- **Community guilt:** Not only are individuals responsible but communities are responsible for creating the environment that breeds crime.
- **Permanent consequences:** Severe limit to human life span.
- **Outcome:** A drastic, unrepeatable, one-time attempt at starting over. God begins again with Noah and his family.

CHAPTER 4

THE RED THREAD OF VIOLENCE CONTINUES

Genesis 10–37

In Genesis 10 God turns his attention for a moment from humanity's decline into violence to celebrate with us his unfolding dream of the proliferation of people, tribes, and nations and their migration throughout the earth. God points out that each tribe has their own lands, borders, languages, families, and mighty leaders—elements of cultural life that are celebrated, defined, and protected throughout Scripture. God loves diversity. Nation creation and nation building are dynamic parts of the kingdom. Migration and immigration, rather than being a problem, are a natural part of God's ongoing plan. Culture, in all of its elements, reveals God. He loves the developmental process.

If we do not take a moment to stop at chapter 10 and remember God's ultimate plan for nations, entering into joy with him as it unfolds in spite of sin, we will become weary and disillusioned with the history Genesis reveals to us. But if we see what God sees, we will want to persevere. We must remember that all of these nations, languages, and peoples will be gathered before God in Revelation (Rev. 7:9). All their kings and leaders will be bringing gifts into the City of God (Rev. 21:24). No matter how despairing the journey, God's desire is to make peace with his human race. And he will succeed.

But, for now, the violence continues.

TRIAL #4: IMPERIALISM

God vs. Babylon

By the time we reach Genesis 11, the human race has conceived of a new kind of violence—political tyranny—and we return to the "red thread of violence."

> They said to each other, "Come, let's make bricks and bake them thoroughly." They used brick instead of stone, and tar for mortar. Then they said, "Come, let us build ourselves a city, with a tower that reaches to the heavens, so that we may make a name for ourselves; otherwise we will be scattered over the face of the whole earth."
>
> But the LORD came down to see the city and the tower the people were building. The LORD said, "If as one people speaking the same language they have begun to do this, then nothing they plan to do will be impossible for them. Come, let us go down and confuse their language so they will not understand each other." (Gen. 11:3–7)

Some say that chapter 11 is the origin of languages. I see no compelling reason in Scripture to draw this conclusion. Language development is a natural by-product of time and distance. Nothing in creation indicates that God prefers uniformity. Why assume uniformity of language? Overwhelmingly, creation demonstrates that God loves diversity. Furthermore, diversity of language is part of what we see redeemed in the coming kingdom: "There before me was a great multitude that no one could count, from every nation, tribe, people and language, standing before the throne and before the Lamb" (Rev. 7:9).

This does, however, seem to be the beginning of our not being able to *understand* each other's languages and the start of our great confusion in communicating with each other. Could this have been God's way of safeguarding diversity in the development of cultures and nations?

Where would we get the idea that God would want one uniform language? Certainly it does not come from Genesis or creation.

God does not desire one land, one government, one economy, one culture, and one language ruling the earth and all of humankind. The imperial dreams, birthed here in Babel, will spread throughout every region of the globe as man seeks to dominate his fellow man from Babel to Assyria, China, Greece, Persia, India, Macedonia, and Rome. From the Huns, Vandals, and Goths to the Franks, Vikings, Mongols, Aztecs, Ottomans, Africans, British, Russians, Japanese, and more, each conqueror has been convinced that theirs was the one government, one economy, one language, and one culture that should dominate the cultures surrounding them.

The human race has now invented two political poles: pre-flood anarchy and post-flood tyranny. Both lead to unbelievable violence. God's design for humankind is self-governance and freedom, but without God, humanity's authority is abused. How can God's human creation be saved from their own violent nature while keeping their freedom and the image of God intact? While the human race begins to debate political freedom versus control, God is trying to solve a completely different dilemma. How does he keep the rights of the individual and the rights of the community intact while holding in check the violence and tyranny?

Elements of Trial #4

Freedom and choice have led human society to a dangerous turning point. The abuses in the scheme in Babylon must be so great that there is no alternative but to bring correction again through permanent consequence. God has the testimony of Babylon's own words and knows their community's sin will destroy human destiny. Remember, God has promised that he will never destroy all of humankind again as he did in the flood. Justice demands that he act. Compassion demands that the correction be swift and universal. The boundaries of God's law are being crossed, and recognition of the innate value of human life demands intervention.

God sovereignly applies a corrective change in order to make the most excessive abuses of power impossible from here on. He weakens universal tyranny with confusion in communication. Considering the centuries of violence brought about in the name of empire *with* our limited language ability, who could disagree with God's decision?

A NATION FOR ALL NATIONS: ABRAHAM

In Genesis 12 God initiates the next part of his plan for redeeming and ultimately reconciling the human race to himself. He calls a man from Ur to leave his land, family, religion, tribe, and culture in order to reveal God's design for building a family and nation in his image. Ultimately, through this new nation, God will bring the One who can reconcile all people to their Creator and make atonement for all the blood and violence. God had let the human race go their own way (Acts 14:16), learning as they went the destructiveness of their own hearts. Now God will reveal to everyone his template of values for nation building. God calls Abraham to pioneer this new tribe.

WHAT "NATIONS"?

It is important here to consider that God's definition of *tribe* and *nation* is dynamic. It is more than the definition commonly used in anthropology and missions of a "monoethnic, monolinguistic, monoreligious grouping." While relevant to an in-depth study of culture or strategic missions planning, this definition of *nation* is too narrow when applied to "discipling nations." It denies the forward movement and change that is automatically required by the migration and immigration that is part of God's overall plan. Nothing sets Abraham apart from the people he leaves except that God has called him to migrate (Gen. 12:1–2). But he is the beginning of a new nation.

Nations existed in the Old Testament that did not exist when Jesus sent out his followers to disciple nations in the New Testament, and today there are nations that did not exist when Jesus spoke those words. The birth and death of nations is a dynamic process that continues throughout human history. We are called to bless and disciple whatever nations there are in our time, including new nations as they come into existence.

DIFFICULT BEGINNINGS

Returning to Genesis, we walk through twenty-two chapters of the story of Abraham and his offspring, much of which is dominated by lying to foreign kings, fighting over land, sowing seeds of family infighting and future tribal conflicts between Ishmael and Isaac, the betrayal of Esau by Isaac, more tribal conflict, more lying to foreign kings, the tyranny of Laban, and Jacob's return to Canaan.

Our only solace in the pain of all this unrighteousness is knowing that Israel does not yet have the law of God to guide them. They love God, for the most part anyway, but there is very little difference between their understanding of the value of human life and of how to live and the thinking of the nations that surround them. They have the call of God to build a new nation, but they do not have God's revelation of how to do it. They are "chosen," but they are neither wise nor good. And this is perhaps part of God's point in detailing their history. The call of God must be joined by the thinking of God to bear fruit.

TRIAL #5: GENOCIDE

God vs. Israel

In Genesis 34 we come to the tragic tale of Jacob's daughter Dinah and the prince of the Shechemites: "Now Dinah, the daughter Leah had borne to Jacob, went out to visit the women of the land. When Shechem son of Hamor the Hivite, the ruler of that area, saw her, he took her and raped her. His heart was drawn to Dinah daughter of Jacob; he loved the young woman and spoke tenderly to her. And Shechem said to his father Hamor, 'Get me this girl as my wife'" (Gen. 34:1–4).

The sexual encounter in verse 2 is most often rendered as the rape of Dinah. But some Hebrew scholars believe a more accurate interpretation would be "sex outside of marriage."[1] Regardless, it is clear that Shechem loves Dinah, and they want to do the honorable thing and marry. Jacob's sons, however, turn this into an opportunity for what can only be described as genocide. Treacherously they agree to the marriage on the condition that all the males of the Shechemite tribe be circumcised. They then turn the physical weakness of the Shechemites into an opportunity to destroy the entire tribe and take all their possessions.

Three days later, while all of them were still in pain, two of Jacob's sons, Simeon and Levi, Dinah's brothers, took their swords and attacked the unsuspecting city, killing every male. They put Hamor and his son Shechem to the sword and took Dinah from Shechem's house and left. The sons of Jacob came upon the dead bodies and looted the city where their sister had been defiled. They seized their flocks and herds and donkeys and everything else of theirs in the city and out in the fields. They carried off all their wealth and all their women and children, taking as plunder everything in the houses. (Gen. 34:25–29)

How Could They?

In order to put this horrendous event in perspective, we must remember that circumcision is the one and only sacrament God has given the tribe of Abraham at this point. It is the one sacred thing God has given them to mark them as his holy, set-apart-to-God people, and Jacob's sons have used it to weaken, deceive, and slaughter their enemy. Can we even begin to imagine the pain of God's heart as, again, his act of mercy is twisted into a tool for violence against the object of his compassion: the human race? And, this time, by his *chosen* people!

There was no godly virtue in what the sons of Jacob did. There was no kingdom justice. Jacob knows the fledgling tribe is in trouble because of his sons' violent greed: "Then Jacob said to Simeon and Levi, 'You have brought trouble on me by making me obnoxious to the Canaanites and Perizzites, the people living in this land. We are few in number, and if they join forces against me and attack me, I and my household will be destroyed'" (Gen. 34:30).

An Inheritance of Violence

Abraham has lied to Pharaoh and King Abimelek about Sarah for financial profit. Isaac has lied to the same king about Rebekah for his own well-being. Jacob has lied to his father and stolen Esau's inheritance and blessing. He has manipulated his uncle. Now Jacob's sons have lied to the Shechemites over their sister Dinah, and they have turned their sister's honor into an excuse for genocide and the plundering of a whole tribe. Violence is escalating again, this time through God's own chosen people. God holds trial number five.

God finds the tribe of Jacob guilty of genocide and prepares to bring sentence, beginning with the need to flee again to Bethel, where Jacob offers a sacrifice. While they are there, God speaks to Jacob. But Jacob's sons—having already committed mass murder—nearly return to fratricide, jealous of their father's favored son, Joseph. They are going to kill their brother but decide instead to sell him to passing Midianite slave traders. Joseph goes to Egypt, and God prepares for the correction of Israel's culture of violence. God's objective is still to stem human violence, somehow restoring the human community's understanding of the value of human life without destroying us altogether.

The 430-Year Life Sentence

God has already promised he will not wipe out the whole human race again. He has given his precious animal kingdom to satisfy our bloodthirstiness. And still violence has continued to escalate. It has evolved into political tyranny, and now, tribal genocide. The violence must be stopped. God prepares the tribe of Abraham for two things: first, the breaking of their arrogance and willfulness as a community through 430 years in captivity—300 years of that as slaves—and second, the coming of the law of God through Moses. Israel's experience of losing all their rights to Egypt will become a constant reminder from God in the Mosaic law of why they are to treat others differently in the land God is going to give them.

Elements of Trial #5

God deals with community guilt and brings cultural correction through generational incarceration, limiting freedoms with the purpose of redemption. The goal is to redeem people while not destroying them or allowing them to destroy themselves. This is God's dilemma and ours.

We are fairly familiar with the rest of the story God selects for us in Genesis. Joseph is amazingly exalted in Egypt and is used to spare the destruction of his tribe. But after his death, the next pharaoh enslaves the tribe of Abraham. The people begin to cry out to God to deliver them from their terrible labor, and God begins to raise up a deliverer in Moses.

At this point you must be tired of the violence. Well, so is God.

It will take eleven generations in Egypt to prepare Israel to receive the law in the wilderness. This revelation of the great heart of God, made known in the Pentateuch, will begin to move the human race slowly toward greater political freedom and justice. More than any other single document in the history of humanity, the law of Moses will lead to the concept that the people being governed have the right and the responsibility to choose how, in what aspects, and by whom they will be governed. It will lead to the greatest understanding yet of the sacredness of life and the rights and responsibilities of every individual, family, tribe, and nation. And it will bring the highest quality of life that has existed thus far among the nations. It will not stop the violence, but it will make the world progressively less tolerant of it, and it will turn the attention of every just government of the world to stopping the violence inside and outside its borders. It will conceive the idea that all human beings, even enemy soldiers, prisoners, women, children, and foreigners, have rights. It will establish that the best way to achieve these goals is through self-governance.

But first we must look at the foundations Genesis has laid for our thinking.

CHAPTER 5

THE BUILDING BLOCKS OF THE KINGDOM

Three Beings and Four Institutions of Authority

Before we leave Genesis and move on through the other four books of Moses, we must take time to look at the tacit principles and values that God weaves into the first book of the Law. These truths found in Genesis run through all of Scripture and become increasingly defined as God's revelation unfolds. We have the benefit of hindsight. We can look at the revelation in Christ and the reality of the book of Revelation and then return to Genesis and see that the threads of these ideas were sown from the very beginning of God's creation. None of the threads God is telling us about is more important than what he is revealing about authority and power in his kingdom.

A KINGDOM IS MORE THAN A KING

A kingdom is the system by which a king delegates authority and power, the infrastructure through which a monarch creates liberty, jurisdictions, limits, and boundaries. The key to understanding any culture or nation lies in understanding where authority and power reside within the community. This knowledge will not only help get things done within the country; it will reveal the culture's foundational values. The essence of governance is defining and maintaining these designations, their authority, and their limits.

In Genesis 1 and 2, God establishes two institutions of authority—the individual and the family—that by default will grow into two additional institutions and evolve as peoples and cultures multiply. The overall institutional design of the kingdom of God includes four separate and limited sovereignties: the individual, family, government, and church. Each of these has a designated purpose in the kingdom of God and has defined boundaries of jurisdiction. The four immutable vessels of authority are as important in the kingdom as the objectives God has created them to accomplish.

In addition to these four institutions, Scripture reveals three types of beings in the kingdom of God that share in some level of delegated authority and power: God himself, human beings, and angels. We cannot discuss institutional authority and power on earth without addressing the reality of both the seen and unseen world, and the beings that influence them.

These issues of authority and power are part of what Paul refers to several times in his letters as the great mysteries of God kept secret but now revealed. Understanding what God has said in the Old Testament is essential to understanding what Christ has accomplished on the cross, what it means to have the kingdom within us, and what it means to disciple the nations.

Do I have authority? Who gave me that authority? Over whom do I have that authority? Who has the authority to stop me? What responsibility comes with that authority? Do I have the power to execute that authority? If not, where do I get the necessary power? These questions are fundamental to all explorations of law and governance and to understanding the kingdom of God.

POWER AND AUTHORITY

What is the difference between power and authority? This is an essential question for anyone interested in justice and kingdom building. Imagine the world's greatest body builder and weight lifter—the world's biggest, strongest man. Imagine this mammoth man holding a newborn. The question "Can he crush this infant's head?" is a question of power. Of course he can. He has enormous strength, and the baby's head is soft. The question "May he (does he have permission to) crush the baby's head?" is a question of authority, a completely different matter. In order to answer that question, you would have to address the issue of where that authority would come from.

Definitions of the word *power* emphasize capacity: Is one able? The presence or absence of the power to act does not automatically correlate with the authority to act or vice versa. Power is ability one either has or does not have.

Definitions of the word *authority*, on the other hand, emphasize the concept that it is "given." Authority is given to me. It is the right to use power. It is possible to have legitimate authority to act without the power to do so. Equally, it is possible to have the power to do something but not have the legitimate authority to do it.

Part of the meaning of the Hebrew word for *justice* is "right order." It can be thought of as "the antonym of 'chaos.'"[1] Justice is restoring God's right order on earth. It is giving the "right" individuals and the "right" institutions the "right" authority ordained by God, along with the power to execute it. Part of building the kingdom of God on earth, then, is seeking to give and to use legitimate authority and power.

In order to answer any question of authority, we would have to say where authority for this or that comes from. For instance, who has the authority to decide if the baby held by the big man lives or dies? The answer to these questions—from where and to whom does authority come, and what is the purpose of that authority—is the essence of law and, perhaps, the essence of a kingdom.

THREE BEINGS

Scripture, both Old and New Testaments, reveals a kingdom where God has shared his power and authority with his creatures and creation. He has given away limited power and authority with boundaries, responsibilities, and requirements attached to it, but it is genuine power and authority, nonetheless. And God will not take back what he has given, for to do so would destroy what he has created. He seeks to redeem rather than destroy what he has made. In the hierarchy of the Bible, three beings have authority and power: God, human beings, and angels.

God

It is clear in Genesis 1 and 2 that God is the author of all that is—the seen and the unseen world. He is the Creator behind all that is created. He is the Power behind all power and the Authority behind all authority. God is capable of doing anything he likes; he has all power. Equally, God has all authority; being God, he has the right to do what he likes. Most Christians, if not most religious people, will agree with these two statements at some level.

Once we move beyond these basic truths, opinions about how God works diverge. Has God delegated any of his power or authority? If he has, to whom and for what purpose has he delegated it? How much power and authority has he delegated? And would he ever revoke that power and authority? The answers to these questions, found in Scripture, give us God's definition of "proper order," and when applied, they tell us what God means by *justice*.

If we seek to institute justice, it must be a biblical definition of justice that we seek to institute. It must be a biblical set of rights our systems seek to secure and deny as well as a biblical set of boundaries imposed on those rights. In other words, just governance in the kingdom of God is, by design, a system of competing interests and rights held in tension by law. Justice is measured by whether the right people are making the right decisions appropriate to their God-given authority. Justice and morality in the kingdom of God are determined not only by what we choose but equally by who chooses.

When Saul, king of Israel, seeks to murder David, David has no moral or legal responsibility to allow Saul to kill him. He runs! He has the right as an individual to safeguard his life and no obligation to surrender to the authority of the king when the king is acting contrary to the law of Israel. There are borders set on the authority of the political leader, and there are rights secured for the individual, family, and tribe. In other words, there are limits to the king's authority.

God delegated authority to human beings in different capacities. But he did not delegate all authority, to anyone, for all things.

Human Beings

In Genesis 1 and 2, God gives direct-line authority to Adam, male and female:

> Then God said, "Let us make mankind in our image, in our likeness, so that they may rule over the fish in the sea and the birds in the sky, over the livestock and all the wild animals, and over all the creatures that move along the ground."
>
> So God created mankind in his own image, in the image of God he created them; male and female he created them.
>
> God blessed them and said to them, "Be fruitful and increase in number; fill the earth and subdue it. Rule over the fish in the sea and the birds in the sky and over every living creature that moves on the ground." (Gen. 1:26–28)

God decrees his human creatures to be second in authority over his creation. Adam, male and female, and their progeny are made in the image of God, and God gives them authority to rule the earth and the creatures that live there. We humans are co-regents of our planet and co-heirs of the kingdom with God. The enormity of this position will not become apparent until Jesus comes with the revelation of redemption. The New Testament writers will refer to our position as co-regents and co-heirs as part of the secrets and mysteries kept hidden from us from the beginning of time and now revealed to us by the Spirit.

It is exceedingly important here to note that there is no authority given in Genesis 1 and 2 over each other, human being over human being. We will return to this subject as we develop the authority of civil governance and discuss institutions.

If we are created free to make a choice, then there must be a choice to make. In other words, authority without power is unusable. God is not playing with language. God is establishing authority in his kingdom. As we discussed in chapter 3, God created a choice:

> Now the LORD God had planted a garden in the east, in Eden; and there he put the man he had formed. The LORD God made all kinds of trees grow out of the ground—trees that were pleasing to the eye and good for food. In the middle of the garden

were the tree of life and the tree of the knowledge of good and evil. . . . The LORD God took the man and put him in the Garden of Eden to work it and take care of it. And the LORD God commanded the man, "You are free to eat from any tree in the garden; but you must not eat from the tree of the knowledge of good and evil, for when you eat from it you will certainly die." (Gen. 2:8–9, 15–17)

The smallest building block of the kingdom of God, then, is the individual. We are sovereign over ourselves as God is sovereign over all else. We are created in the image of God and therefore have freedom and authority from God to make choices. We have the *right* to sin but we *ought not* to sin. We should not disobey God. However, we can and may. While we *can* sin, God will not bless it.

Angels

Adam male and Adam female are not alone with God in the garden. There are other beings in paradise. Angels, God's emissaries in both the seen and unseen dimensions of his kingdom, are third in God's hierarchy. They do not appear in Genesis 1 or 2, but the story that evolves starting in chapter 3 is that angels have a history with God before we were created. There are more than 290 references in Scripture in which angels are sent to accomplish various tasks on God's behalf and are delegated the authority from God to accomplish what he has sent them to do.

Our first contact with these beings is with a demon, an angel that has "fallen." The serpent in Genesis 3 is a disguised fallen angel. All of Scripture clarifies that both before and after Adam's rebellion against God, there were and are angelic beings, created by God for the service of the kingdom.

Angels' job descriptions vary. They are sent to assist in earthly wars between humans, influencing both seen and unseen powers in these battles. They are sent to dispatch wisdom and answers to prayer. They can be detained. They can scare animals. Sometimes they can be seen and sometimes not. They can change appearance and appear and disappear. They have capacities, or powers, we do not have. But they do not have sovereign authority. The picture God gives us in Scripture is one where angels "wait" on the Lord's command to act. When given a specific assignment, they are also given the authority by God to carry it out. But they have no authority to self-initiate. They are not co-heirs or co-regents of the kingdom of God as human beings are. They are, rather, highly valued servants.

Therefore, when angels usurp authority for themselves and engage in self-rule, they "fall." Fall from what? They fall from God's servant roster. They are no longer sent by God to do anything and therefore have no authority, or permission, from God to act on his behalf.

The angels who have rebelled and rejected the God who created them have lost their position in God's kingdom. They exist, and they maintain a certain amount of power (capacity), but they have lost their authority, as God no longer sends them to do his bidding: "the angels . . . did not keep their positions of authority but abandoned their proper dwelling" (Jude 1:6).

Satan, chief fallen angel, first shows up in Genesis 3 in the guise of a snake. He is there to tempt Adam, female and male, to doubt God's trustworthiness and their own capacity to understand his words.

Satan does not actively show up again until the book of Job, more than five hundred pages later. In the books of the Law, it is clear that when Israel sacrifices their own children in worship, they are worshiping demons (Deut. 32:17). Demons feature some in the Psalms but do not become a major subject until the New Testament. Throughout the Gospels and apostolic letters, demonic activity is common, and demons are prevalent in the Revelation of John.

In the parable of the weeds, Jesus reveals that while it is the Son of Man who sows the good wheat seed, or the people of the kingdom, the devil is the enemy who sows the bad weed seed, or the people of the evil one (Matt. 13:24–30, 36–43). In Matthew 25:41, Jesus says that "the eternal fire" was "prepared for the devil and his angels." In Mark 3:15 Jesus states that demons have no authority over us, and Luke 10 clarifies that they must submit to the name of Jesus. Paul makes it clear in Romans 8:38 that demons do not have the authority or power to separate you and me from the love of God. And John makes it clear in Revelation that Satan and his fallen legions of angels are defeated in the end.

For our purposes here then, fallen angels have retained some of their power (capacity) but none of their God-given authority (permission).

Where then do demons get their influence and apparent authority today? From the only other source of authority in the kingdom of God apart from God himself—human beings. For Satan to have any authority, the human being must literally give Satan authority over himself or herself and collectively over the culture.

Why is this relevant to a discussion of governance and political justice? It is very simple. Justice is, in part, assigning guilt and innocence, while creating a system of proper order. Proper order in the kingdom of God is to place responsibility on either God or human beings, since these are the only two beings who have sovereign authority. Angels are glorious servants to God and humankind. Demons are defeated schemers who have already been tried, convicted, and sentenced and are waiting for their incarceration. In the kingdom of God, the defense "the devil made me do it" is never valid, even when he was involved.

God and his autonomous humans have authority and responsibility in creation. When we consider the state of the world, Satan and his fallen band are minor players. We humans, on the other hand, are the key to blessing and cursing.

INSTITUTIONS

In addition to *beings* with authority and power, God created *institutions* as an extension of our individual, delegated authority and power. Beginning with family, God created institutions to help mediate the impact of individual choices on the human community. As a Person, God created the individual. As a Father, God created family. As a King, God created governance. And as Priest, God created religion.

There is no known human culture, primitive or modern, that lacks any of these institutions. These institutions are essential to the human design and experience. Without them, we would self-destruct. As imperfect as each may be in any given society, these flawed institutions are still better than none at all. The only thing worse than bad governance is no governance. When anarchy reigns, there are *no* borders on abuse. The only thing worse than bad parents are no parents at all. When we try to raise children in institutional care or foster systems, the abuse multiplies, although even those systems are better than no system. And, though we rightly blame much of human violence on religious beliefs, the only societies that are more violent are those that claim there is no god.

All societies have institutions because that is the way God created human culture to function. The question is whether these institutions will be, more or less, built on God's template of authority and purpose. Because God has given humans authority and power and therefore choice, individuals and groups will attempt to abuse that same power and authority. It falls to every culture and society to decide what boundaries it will place on the abuse of society by the individual and on the abuse of the individual by society. This challenge is not a problem that we can solve but a dilemma of competing values we seek to keep in tension through "proper order," or justice.

God is clear in Scripture about the types of authority and the boundaries on authority he desires in his kingdom. It is our challenge as citizens and as political servants to work toward these same definitions and limits in our own society. We do not seek to create perfection on earth. That is not possible. But we do seek the best justice possible for everyone possible and work toward a healthy tension between the rights and responsibilities of all individuals as well as the groups and institutions they create. We seek to bless our nations.

Four Institutional Authorities

Genesis 1 and 2 give us God's first two institutions. In effect Scripture indicates that all authority on earth emanates from the delegated authority God has given to individual men and women. In other words, the smallest unit of authority and power on earth is you. All of human culture builds on that foundation. Our view of the individual will be the foundation of the rest of our cultural values. And our view of the individual will build on our view of God.

The Sovereign Individual

As individuals, we are created in the image of God, free and sovereign over ourselves. In other words, we are not controlled but rather empowered to make choices. We do not make choices over all things, but within the limits of our power, we choose how we will respond and use the circumstances that are beyond our control. A French politician who was freed after six years as a guerilla jungle hostage said she had lost control of everything except control of the kind of person she was going to be.

God does not deny the facts of nature and nurture, but he adds and emphasizes the reality of a third fact: choice. Because all individuals are created free, the border of one person's sovereignty must end where another person's begins. Anarchy is the tyranny of the individual overriding the freedom of everyone else. Tyranny, on the other hand, is a relatively small group taking away the rights of everyone else. Each society sets limits on personal freedom, drawing boundaries on the abuse of the few by the many and on the rights of the few over the many. Without those limits, the community would self-destruct. The question is, will those limits be kingdom limits?

As we saw earlier, Genesis details the descent of our fallen human race into total anarchy and violence. From the second-generation fratricide of Abel, the escalation of violence is swift. Just eight generations later, God has to destroy human life before humans totally destroy themselves. God spares Noah and his sons in a desperate attempt to give humans a chance to rehabilitate. Then, from the time of Noah to the creation of Babylon in Genesis 11, the human reaction to anarchy inspires the idea of total control and the tyranny of the few over the many. Babylon conceives the idea that no one has rights but the few, and the first imperial dream grows from there, multiplying around the world with continuing violence. God works throughout human history, with the pendulum swinging from anarchy to tyranny and then back again. How can God keep the individual both safe and free? Exactly!

The Sovereign Family

While delineating the creation of the entire universe in just two short chapters, Genesis 1 and 2, God takes the time to oversee the creation of and to establish boundaries on the second human institution: marriage and family.

Volumes can and must be written about the implications of this passage for all of our cultures. But for the purposes of this book, we will focus on the question of authority. God delegates to first-person Adam the naming of the animal kingdom. In this process, Adam recognizes his "only-ness." The solution God and Adam come to is the creation of "otherness," or a differentiation of self. From first-person Adam's self comes another—second-person Adam, or Adam female. "Adam two" is literally taken from "Adam one." The one has become two, and the two will multiply. They now may join together again as one, if they so choose, creating an institution called marriage.

Who joins them? Who officiates this first marriage? There is no civil ceremony since there is no "state." It is not a religious ceremony since there is no priest. God does not indicate that he officiates, even though he is there. Neither family to grant permission nor community to be witness are present. So where does the authority for these two people to marry come from? It comes from the two of them. As individuals, as co-regents with God, they choose each other. They choose to limit their God-given sovereignty over their individual lives by giving themselves to each other.

Together with the children they may have, these two individuals—one male and one female, agreeing to join in a lifetime exclusive relationship, freely "giving" themselves to each other—form God's definition of *family*. The partners are co-equals as individuals, co-rulers in dominion of the earth, but they now sovereignly agree, mutually and exclusively, to belong to each other. God is their witness.

Now God makes an incredible declaration. He says, "That is why a man leaves his father and mother and is united to his wife, and they become one flesh" (Gen. 2:24). Even though it has no practical relevance to this first union (there are no parents), God purposefully creates a boundary on the definition of family—its authority and responsibility. The authority and responsibility for a family lies with the man, his wife, and their children. This new family is not an extension of their parents' authority. The new family is a new sovereign entity within itself, with rights and responsibilities. God seeks to strengthen the rights of spouses while diminishing the rights of the extended family. And this is before the fall.

The authority of parents over children and husbands over wives is the authority of "love" defined by God as sacrificial care of another. And so where there is tyranny in the family—couples trying to destroy each other or their children—we have to create legal boundaries to minimize the abuse of the individual within the family, and of that family within the society.

The Sovereignty of Government

Our next kingdom institution, government, evolves as the human race multiplies and fills the earth. Individual freedoms and the authority of the family have to be held in tension with the rights of other individuals and families—in other words, the community. Families, as a basis for social development, dominate earliest human history. But multiplication necessitates the evolution of tribes, or communities of families, and beyond that the evolution of nations, or communities of tribes.

With the loss of God's perspective in the fall, human understanding of both family and governance takes a top-down authoritarian form, losing God's emphasis on the importance of the authority of the individual as the basic building block of society. All forms of government prior to the writing of the Mosaic law are conceived with power and authority at the top.

When God speaks for himself into human history, he declares the authority and power of governance to be "in the people" being governed—in the solid foundation, the building blocks of society. As God reveals his values and ways through the law, he once again emphasizes the importance of both the individual *and* the family and community.

Formed first in Deuteronomy 1, government as an institution is given responsibility for negotiating conflicting freedoms and rights within the community. Responsibility means that in a just system—a system with proper order—the community defines and defends rights and sets limits. Because the people being governed are created free, God gives the people the right to choose how, by whom, and over what they will be governed as individuals, families, and groups. God reveals his definition of just authority and limits in the law, but we do not have to follow God or obey these limits. God has given us choice, and we may decide for ourselves as nations what we will call justice and must live with the consequences of those choices. If we want God's promised blessings, however, we must apply his definitions and limits. This dynamic relationship between God's law, our choices as nations, and God's blessing is illustrated throughout the history of Israel. God details what he said, what they did, and what resulted, all the way through the Old Testament.

The Sovereignty of Religion

As they do families and governments, human cultures all develop institutions committed to the worship of a god or gods. In spite of our separation from God through sin, we retain our awareness that there is something greater than ourselves influencing our lives and planet. And we seek divine blessing.

When God forms the priesthood in the law of Moses, he declares his right through this institution to speak for himself. Unlike civil law, the authority of the priesthood and the message the priests deliver come directly from God himself. The institution of the priesthood has the right and responsibility to represent God, but it does not have the authority to impose belief on anyone. Because we have the right as individuals to believe what we like, societies will have many religions. Like individuals, religions have the right to exist. However, they do not have the right to violate the freedoms of other individuals, families, religions, or nations.

Now we are at the heart of kingdom authority and the crossroads of civil law and political justice: the tension God has created in delegating authority to individuals, families, nations, and religions.

A System of Checks and Balances to Authority and Power

The Scriptures give us a system of competing authorities and powers, all created by God. Sin corrupts, but does not destroy, God's design. In discipling nations, working to teach the nations God's ways, we need God's thinking on not only the content of law but also the system of law he will bless. We must leave God's delegated sovereignties in place. Our starting point is the individual, created in the image of God with the authority to make choices. Building from the individual, we must seek through civil law to secure certain rights, including rights pertaining to personal conduct, thought, speech, family, faith, and political conviction and, of course, limits to those rights.

We do not seek to perfect our nations through political control. We, as God's ambassadors, seek to bless our nations through securing a just system of proper order.

Rights

We now have the biblical basis for the discussion of what we today call *rights*. Because individual lives are sacred and are the foundational building block of God's creation, individuals, no matter who they are, have rights. Because family is the most concerned, connected unit of any community and is ordained by God to hold the most influential role in raising children, families have rights. Because humans are social beings who need the extended family to thrive and prosper, communities have rights. And because God guaranteed us the right to choose, religious freedom is mandated, and therefore, religious institutions have rights. The authority behind each institution is God-given authority. And because these institutions together hold a competitive tension of rights, created by God, the question is not only "What would be right to do?" but also "Who in this case has the God-given authority to decide what is done, and how will we secure their right to decide?"

The challenge of civil governance, then, is to ensure the rights of the right people to make the decisions God has ordained are theirs, whether we agree with them or not, and to enforce proper limits on the scope of their decisions. If we have no borders on the freedom of the individual, we will dissolve into anarchy, the most violent of all systems. If we have no borders on the rights of governments, we will end up with tyranny, the second most violent of all systems. And if we have no borders on the rights of the many, we will end up with demagoguery, where a leader uses the tyranny of the masses over the few. Instead, we seek proper borders for each institution, reflecting kingdom justice.

CHAPTER 6

THE ESSENTIALS OF BIBLICAL THOUGHT

Five Foundational Assumptions

Before we move on with God's progressive revelation of his struggle for justice, we must look at five assumptions that all of Scripture corroborates. These five assumptions, along with the three beings and four institutions of authority, form the nonnegotiable threads in the biblical weave of God's thinking. Four of these assumptions are clearly stated in Genesis 1–3 and the fifth is hinted at:

- God is, and is who he says he is.
- God is the Creator of the material universe, seen and unseen, and his creation is good.
- Human individuals, male and female, are created in the image of God and are central to his purpose for all creation.
- Everything that God has created is damaged by the fall of man and sin.
- Everything that is damaged is redeemable through the blood of Christ.

It is impossible to overestimate the power of assumptions in our lives and cultures. We use them every day regardless of our religion, philosophy, or worldview. Assumptions lay the foundation of every culture and, therefore, our cultural definition of reality. Our "beliefs in action" will always be congruent with our tacit, unstated assumptions, sometimes even while contradicting our outspoken "beliefs in words." We may say we trust God while at the same time being riddled with fear and anxiety. We "love people" but "hate that group." We want freedom of choice but don't want to be responsible for the choices we make. Assumptions are always at work at the foundations of our thinking even when we are not aware of them.

FEET AND FLOORS

If you happen to be stuck in an international airport overnight, you will observe assumptions at work in what people do to get a night's sleep. In Asian cultures it is culturally assumed that floors are clean and feet are dirty. You take your dirty street shoes off at the door and put clean indoor slippers on your dirty feet when you enter a house. Home entryways in this part of the world are full of shoes for outside wear and slippers for inside wear. In Western cultures on the other hand, we generally assume floors are dirty and feet are clean. Therefore we are less prone to go barefoot, generally do not take our shoes off every time we enter a home, and have sanitary laws requiring us to wear shoes in restaurants and certain buildings.

When these two cultures come together for an unplanned night in an airport, the Asian travelers are stretched out on the floor for a fairly comfortable, at least horizontal, night's sleep. Floors are clean! But the Westerners are twisted and tangled into the airport lounge chairs, painfully assuring an uncomfortable night and a visit to the chiropractor. For them, the floors are dirty! We are observing two completely different maps of reality, two different worldviews, at work.

Who is right? Who is wrong? From God's perspective, floors and feet are both more or less clean and dirty. We could test the cleanliness and come up with a germ and bacteria scale to assess which floors and feet are dirtiest. But meanwhile, the Asians sleep on while the Westerners twist and turn all night in armchairs, each group locked into their cultural assumptions. This example is more entertaining than it is consequential. However, what happens when the assumptions we make are more significant?

Major cultural divides exist around questions of the existence and nature of God, the value of the individual and the group, gender, marriage, time, the material world and how it functions, land, the right to ownership, safety, and authority, including who has authority and who does not. The list is long, and the assumptions are extremely different, often painfully conflicting, and for the most part, silent.

GRID WORK OF REALITY

Our assumptions lay the grid for reality as we understand and practice it. We fit the information we receive through experience, family, culture, and education onto that grid. We measure the unseen world by that grid and act accordingly. We weave sophisticated tapestries of reality and truth that profoundly impact the way we see the world and how it works as well as what we perceive the problems and answers to be. Unchallenged, we rarely, if ever, question these tacit assumptions; in fact, we rarely even see them at work.

Our assumptions have profound implications. We all work with assumptions every day. We accept them as reality. We work to design solutions around these beliefs. We work to enact them as laws. But are they true? Are we building on assumptions that may not be true to reality?

How could any one of us evaluate the assumptions of a culture or the beliefs of an age? Our data and experience are limited. Not one of us was present at the origins of the universe. Not one of us has, nor can, travel to the extremities of the cosmos and document exactly how it works. We cannot know everything, but we all can and do know something. We are working with the information we have and with the assumptions our experiences and cultures have given us. We are all culturally blind.[1]

If our assumptions are true, our view of reality may be true. If our assumptions are false, our view of reality will be distorted, and our solutions, while well intended, may be skewed, producing outcomes we had not intended, or worse yet, creating even larger problems. Nowhere is this more true than in law and governance. If we are blind to *where* authority ought to be and to *what* authority ought to be given, and if we are blind to the values and rights that should be upheld by that authority, we are in serious drift from God's definition of justice.

But what if we are not left to our own understanding? What if there is an objective, infinite source with first-hand information and experience? Then there is the possibility that we can see clearly.

GOD'S FIVE FOUNDATIONAL ASSUMPTIONS

God gives us five revealed truths in Scripture on which to build our understanding of reality. These truths must be revealed by God because they are beyond our human ability to experience or know. All biblical thought and teaching is anchored in these five assumptions. As believers, we hold them to be true because God is real and he knows. He reveals these truths to us in the cosmos, in Scripture, and through his Son. When we hold these five biblical assumptions in place, we cannot drift far from a biblical view of reality, or justice.

Assumption #1: God is, and is who he says he is! The Bible is not an apologetic for the existence of God. It is inspired by God and assumes his reality. It is written for those who believe. The cosmos is God's apologetic for his existence, and nothing we discover in the material world can deny God, because it all reveals him. Galileo said that God wrote two Bibles, the cosmos and the Scriptures. In the Old Testament, *Elohim*, "Creator God," is one of the most often-repeated names of God, and in the New Testament, Paul declares all people responsible "since what may be known about God is plain to them, because God has made it plain to them. For since the creation of the world God's invisible qualities—his eternal power and divine nature—have been clearly seen, being understood from what has been made, so that people are without excuse" (Rom. 1:19–20).

Scripture opens with the assumption that "God is" and works from there to reveal his character, thoughts, purposes, and ways. God does not seek to prove that "he is" in the Bible. He seeks to reveal *who* he is and *how* he works. He reveals his unchangeable truths and shows how they work out in history, first through individuals, families, tribes, and nations, then finally through Christ's incarnation, death, and resurrection, and the body of Christ.

Any thinking that does not presuppose the reality of God is not biblical. He is real, and he is the basis of all that is true. Whether people know that or not is another matter. As believers, we must know this is true and build our life and our thinking on that reality. The key to thinking biblically is to build our reality on God's assumptions, and we begin with "God is" and "he is who he says he is." Thinking the way God thinks requires that we give up any cultural assumptions that deny this.

This foundational biblical truth—that God is and is who he says he is—is the basis for character and the value of one's word, and that is the basis of all truth in testimony, vows, contracts, commitments, promises, and covenants.

Assumption #2: God is the Creator of the material universe, seen and unseen, and his creation is good. God reveals to us in Genesis 1 and 2 that the cosmos, everything that is, has its origins in him. He is the First Cause, prime reality. He is revealed through his creation, including the material world. We are not to worship nature, but nature will lead us to worship. Creation has an objective reality apart from God. It exists and it operates by laws, and those laws are discoverable by people. The origin and sustainability of those laws are in God.

A philosophical brainteaser asks the question, "If a tree falls in the forest and no person hears it, does it make a noise?" The biblical answer is "Yes!" because the cosmos does not need human experience to make it real. It has a reality all its own and functions with or without humanity's presence through laws created by God. Humans are also real and add to, but do not subtract from, the objective reality of the created order.

The miracles of today are the science of tomorrow, because God is working within the universe he created, and we can discover how it works. God has a higher level of understanding of the laws of nature than we do, so the miracles will continue. He longs for us to discover the laws of nature and use them to benefit humankind and the creation he has given us. Understanding the material world *is* part of knowing God.

This second foundational biblical truth—that God is the Creator of the universe and his creation is good—is the basis of evidence.

Assumption #3: Human individuals, male and female, are created in the image of God and are central to his purpose for all creation. On the fifth day God created the sea creatures and creatures of the sky, and on the sixth day he created the land creatures, including the first human being. God made all the earth's creatures, but the human creature was and is unique. In Genesis 1:26, God creates the human species in his own likeness and gives the human race authority over all other creatures. We, not the lion, are the kings of the jungle. In verses 27 and 28, God clarifies his plan and purpose for his human creation. Like all the animals he has made, we are to multiply, migrate, and fill the earth with life. But unlike any of the rest of creation, we are given authority and responsibility over the earth and the material world. We are told to use our authority to *subdue* the earth and create things that are good. Like God, we create, work, plan, and move forward. Our work? We are stewards of God's material creation. The Creator of the universe delegates development and stewardship of the cosmos to us, the human community.

This third foundational biblical truth—that we humans are created in the image of God for a purpose and given work to do—is the basis of personal responsibility.

As we noted in the last chapter, it is important to observe that authority is given to the human race, male and female, over creation, but no authority is given to humans, male or female, over each other (Gen. 1:28). This will be significant when we begin to discuss boundaries for institutions and the jurisdiction of all authority.

Assumption #4: Everything God has created is damaged by the fall of man and sin. Authority presupposes the ability to choose and act independently. This means that authority can be used or abused. Some types of authority can be rescinded, but in that case authority is something "you have," not something "you are." God has not just given us authority to *have*. He has created us in such a way that authority is part of our identity. To take that authority away, God would have to destroy the very object of his creation, his image in us, reducing us to animals. The risk inherent in giving authority is real, and God takes that risk. In Genesis 3, we see just how serious that danger was and is.

In chapter 3 humans are new to the job of dominion. The only thing they have created so far is language, words to describe God's material world and each other. There is no sin in the garden. But there are choices. Of all the trees he created, God has told them there is one they may not eat from, the tree of the "knowledge of good and evil."

In Hebrew, the word for *knowledge* incorporates the concepts of both information and experience. (We recognize that in biblical language, to *know* your wife meant to have sex with her—not just to recognize her in a crowd, recall her name, and remember who her father is.) So the Hebrew understanding of what God was saying about the tree of the knowledge of good and evil was this: If you eat of this tree, you will not only have information about the possibility of temptation; you will become intimate with evil because you will have done evil. In other words, you will have introduced evil as a reality into your experience and into creation. If you do not act on the temptation, you will only know, or be intimate with and experientially understand, the fact that evil could exist. However, it does not exist because you have not created it, and therefore, you have no direct knowledge of evil itself. Your knowledge and experience are, at this point, only of the good.

But Adam ate the fruit of the tree of the knowledge of good and evil, and sin became a reality in creation. Because of the authority of the human race over creation, the introduction of evil has had devastating, escalating consequences. The fact cannot be erased. Everything is affected by it. We now live in a world polluted by sin.

This fourth foundational biblical truth—that everything God made has been damaged by evil—is the basis for crime, correction, and punishment.

Assumption #5: Everything that is damaged is redeemable through the blood of Christ! The fifth assumption that all of Scripture corroborates becomes progressively clearer as God develops his plan throughout the Old Testament and into the New.

Speaking of Jesus, Paul writes: "For God was pleased to have all his fullness dwell in him, and through him to reconcile to himself all things, whether things on earth or things in heaven, by making peace through his blood, shed on the cross" (Col. 1:19–20).

The fifth revelation from God, which will complete the kingdom assumptions on which we build our thinking, is that everything is redeemable through Christ.

In Genesis 3, sin enters the world. Adam, male and female, create access by acting on the potential for disobedience. Of all the trees in the garden, they eat from the one God has forbidden. I once heard the introduction of evil into creation compared to the release of poisonous gas into the pure air of an enclosed space. You cannot see it, smell it, or detect it in any way, but it is there nonetheless and it will have its progressive corrosive effect—on everything. Throughout the rest of the Old Testament, we will witness God helping his human creation understand what they have lost and preparing them to receive his ulti-mate solution, Jesus. We will see the corrosion of sin lead to insecurity, fratricide, genocide, and violence threatening global destruction. Even with the values and ways of God right in front of them through the law of Moses, Israel will continue the spiral toward destruction. God must help us. We cannot help ourselves. From the third chapter of Genesis on, we are not just *doing* wrong things, we have *become* wrong. We, as a human race and the earth we inhabit, are damaged. We now *know* evil.

God sends the perfect antidote, his Son, the Messiah promised for more than two thousand years. The great mystery of God is fulfilled in Jesus. Creation is real. The power of the human race is real. Choices are real, and the destructiveness of those choices is real. The earth is contaminated. We cannot change that! But God has a saving antidote. You do not have to take it, but if you choose to, the powerful, destruc-tive reality of sin's effect in and through you can be neutralized and you can then become a vessel of antidote. We become the salt and light in a fallen world, working to demonstrate the power and wisdom of God in all of life. We are restored to our lost authority and destiny.

God's way of restoring us is to first grant us a righteousness we can-not earn. This righteousness restores our ability to consult directly with God. Then, through the work of the Holy Spirit, God begins to reveal and remove the false thinking that sin and separation from God have created and to renew our minds with his perspective; we begin to think rightly, in God's way, about the cosmos, the earth, and everything in it, including the human race. We become emissaries of light and hope; we become purifying, healing, and sustaining salt in our fallen world, 24/7. Building on our original mandate from Genesis 1, the cultural mandate to fill, subdue, and cultivate the earth, we undertake to fulfill the Great Commandment to love God with our whole being and others as our-selves, and the Great Commission to disciple all nations. In all this we reveal the glory of the kingdom of God.

This fifth foundational biblical truth—that everything is redeem-able through Christ—is the basis of restitution and rehabilitation.

All biblical thought builds on these five revealed assumptions. If even one of these five precious truths is forgotten or ignored in our view of reality, our understanding of God's message and God's nature and character will be skewed.

Justice will not be kingdom justice unless it is built on God's thinking.

PART II

MOSES AND THE PRESCRIPTIVE LAW

CHAPTER 7

WE ALL WANT JUSTICE

As we prepare to look at the prescriptive laws of Moses in Part II, it is important that we first take time to consider two foundational concepts. The first is the importance of the meaning of our words and where we get those definitions, an idea we will explore in this chapter. The second concept, which we will take up in chapter 8, is the differentiation between moral and civil law.

WHAT ARE WE MISSING?

There is something in the New Testament that no longer seems to draw our attention. This was brought to my awareness in my own study and reading and began to bother me. Starting in the second chapter of Acts, the writer struggles to describe a response from people, using words and phrases like "bewilderment," "utterly amazed," and "amazed and perplexed." And those superlatives are in one single paragraph.

> All of them were filled with the Holy Spirit and began to speak in other tongues as the Spirit enabled them.
>
> Now there were staying in Jerusalem God-fearing Jews from every nation under heaven. When they heard this sound, a crowd came together in *bewilderment*, because each one

heard their own language being spoken. *Utterly amazed*, they asked: "Aren't all these who are speaking Galileans? Then how is it that each of us hears them in our native language? Parthians, Medes and Elamites; residents of Mesopotamia, Judea and Cappadocia, Pontus and Asia, Phrygia and Pamphylia, Egypt and the parts of Libya near Cyrene; visitors from Rome (both Jews and converts to Judaism); Cretans and Arabs—we hear them declaring the wonders of God in our own tongues!" *Amazed and perplexed*, they asked one another, "What does this mean?"

Some, however, made fun of them and said, "They have had too much wine." (Acts 2:4–13)

What does this mean, indeed?

All the people present that day in Jerusalem lived in or were visiting a very cosmopolitan city. This is not the first time they had heard foreign languages. There would have been different tongues around them all the time. This is certainly not the first time they had heard drunks in the street. So what is it that draws their attention and causes them to be "amazed"? This type of language of amazement continues throughout the New Testament as the message spreads from Jerusalem to the surrounding Gentile cultures.

In Pisidian Antioch nearly the whole city turned out to hear Paul (Acts 13:44), and in Lystra the crowds thought that Paul and Barnabas were gods and wanted to worship them (Acts 14:11–13). In Thessalonica, the people accepted Paul's words as the words of God, not as human words (1 Thess. 2:13).

To the believers in Rome, Paul declares the message he is preaching to be a mystery for all nations, hidden from the beginning of time (Rom. 16:25). To the Colossians, Paul says that this mystery hidden for ages and generations is now revealed in Christ, in whom are "all the treasures of wisdom and knowledge" (Col. 1:26; 2:2–3).To the Ephesians, Paul says he is an administrator of this great mystery and asks that they pray he will fearlessly make this mystery known (Eph. 3:2–3; 6:19–20). And Peter tells us that even the angels want to look into these things, but apparently cannot (1 Pet. 1:12).

WHAT HAVE WE LOST?

What is it that we do not seem to experience any longer in the preaching and the hearing of the gospel? What have we grown so accustomed to that we no longer notice it? Or is there something we have lost the ability to see in our modern understanding of the message of Christ? When left with questions like these, I assume that if the Bible labors a point, it is because that point will always need to be grasped in order for us to understand God and his message correctly. Something is going on here in Acts and throughout the rest of the New Testament church experience that relates to how these people perceived their god or gods. There was something about *this God* being proclaimed in all their languages that they could not fathom.

If we look at the gods in the age of the Old Testament, we see that they are perceived as deities of the land the people inhabit. They are the gods of the mountains or the plains, gods of the sea or the sky, gods of the moon or the sun. They are the gods of a *people*, a *land*: the Philistines, the Cretans, the Greeks, or the Medes. All these nations were perfectly willing to accept the credibility of another "god of Abraham" and later a "god of the Jews." People of different cultures spoke freely of the power of another nation's god or gods. They even devised military strategies based on the attributes of the enemy's god. This was the thinking of the Jewish people as well. It was not only "our god is the true god"; it was "our god is *our* god." These deities defined nationhood and who the people were. And the people were jealous for them.

THIS IS OUR WAY

We can imagine how human beings came to these views. These wonderful creatures created in the image of God but separated from the God of that image must try to understand "god" on their own terms. They have no doubt that there are powers greater than themselves. The world they inhabit is full of danger and empty of understanding. Why does the volcano erupt, or a storm destroy the fishing fleet? Who or what kills the corpse lying in the wilderness? Why is one farm prosperous while another fails; why does one baby live and one die? Where do dead people go, and where do babies come from? Do the babies carry the spirit of the dead person? Do I need a boat to travel to the next life? What do I need to take with me? Is every day a new day or the same day all over again? What will keep us safe—from weather, from monsters, from disease, from enemies, from each other? These are the questions of survival.

If we are living in mountains, we begin to find keys to surviving in those mountains. These discoveries are so important to life that they begin to take on meaning beyond information, becoming doctrines of faith. Imagine a fishing village struggling with low catches. In dire conditions, one fisherman pours his unfinished morning drink out on the beach as he gets into his boat. That day he catches more fish than the village has seen all season. Everyone wants to know, "What did you do? Where did you fish? What did you use for bait?" The bewildered fisherman does not know . . . the day seemed common. He did what he always did. Except? And then he remembers. He poured his morning drink out on the beach! That's it! That's what the god of the sea requires . . . a drink offering, a libation for the god of the sea to bless them. In order for the tribe to survive and eat, they must offer the sea a gift. And so it begins.

One step at a time, a people, a tribe, a nation lays down a system of ideas that experience, history, and the ancestors have taught is "the way" to be safe, to prosper, to be blessed. These ideas become beliefs, and these beliefs become the tacit basis for culture and religious faith. These ideas describe reality, or how things work. They keep the tribe safe, and generation after generation they become deeply woven in the group consciousness. Intricate systems of living become known as the Jewish way, the American way, the African way, the Latin way, the Asian way. They define who we are as a people and how the world works. We feel these beliefs very strongly. We would go so far as to say, "God gave us this way." (And even though we may not know it, God did give us some of our many beliefs. And the fact that God did speak to our forefathers has made us, in part, a great nation.)

Then imagine all these peoples joining up in Jerusalem, living in and visiting this cosmopolitan city. Some Galileans come along and say there is only one way. And they say it in the language that was designed to communicate "our way." The audience is amazed, bewildered, and perplexed.

The question for us is, If this is such an important biblical message, where have these incredibly strong feelings and reactions gone?

TODAY

"Well," we might say, "we live in a much more enlightened age now. We are no longer so controlled by those superstitions and taboos, at least not in most cultures." And in some areas of life, that is perhaps true. But is it possible that in other areas of life, thought, and belief we still, even as Christians, hold onto unbiblical cultural securities and comforts? Is it possible that we lay the message of Jesus over the top of these tacit, fundamental definitions of reality? Could it be that the gospel we preach today does not even begin to touch our cultural realities? Could this be why the global church of Jesus has such patchy blessing and why our lifestyle cannot be distinguished from those who live around us, except on Sunday?

Consider this!

WE ALL WANT JUSTICE

If we ask anyone in any country from any religion, with only the grossest of exceptions, to answer the following questions, we would get the same answer:

- Do you want political justice? Yes!
- Would you like to be a slave? No!
- Do you want people to be poor? No!
- Would you work for me for nothing? No!
- Should people be loved? Yes!
- Do you think we should kill people? No!
- Is it a good thing to steal things from others? No!
- Is telling the truth better than lying? Yes!
- Do you think people should have sex with other people's wives/husbands? No!
- Is it a good thing to disrespect your parents? No!
- Should a person be convicted of a crime they did not commit? No!

- Is abortion, drug use, lying, cheating, or stealing a good thing? No!
- Do you love your family? Yes!
- I don't have a car. Can I take yours? No!

We all want the same things, don't we? I have been to more than half the countries of the world, and I have yet to encounter a culture or a people crying out for more corruption, more poverty, less development, and no justice.

So, what is the problem? Why do we not have world peace, global quality of life, healthy and whole families, and crime rates of zero? Is it possible that when we use the words *justice, poverty, corruption, development, crime, peace, sex, property, freedom, kill, work, steal, disrespect, own,* and so on, we are not talking about the same thing? Are our definitions vastly different? Yes, sometimes they are! We seek the same values in name, but they are not the same values in meaning. When we watch the news and see the protesters' placard that says "We Want Justice," we would be wise to stop and consider their definition of *justice* before we agree or disagree.

Is it possible that this disconnect is just as prevalent among believers as it is among those of different faiths? If we are to "disciple all nations" in "kingdom justice," we must make sure our definitions are the same as God's. Otherwise, we may once again see "the King coming in all his glory" and be aware of only "a man on a mule." In other words, we may see Jesus bringing justice and not recognize it, because his work does not fit "our" definition of justice. Or, perhaps worse, we will preach a justice that is not God's at all, but a Jewish, American, Latin, Arab, African, or Asian version of justice.

What can deliver any of us from our cultural blindness?

THERE IS ONLY ONE SOURCE

There is only one place to go in order to understand the specific definitions God gave to these terms. We must go to the law of Moses and the rest of the Old Testament. In Scripture, God has given us a set of values by which to measure and correct our own personal and cultural definitions of reality. Jesus had mastered these by the time he was thirteen.

God lays out his biblical revelation of himself on a timeline, beginning with creation, the human community's descent into global violence, the flood, humanity's descent into violence again, and finally God's strategy of using one nation, starting with Abraham, to reveal his heart and purpose for all nations. Through Abraham and his descendants, God brings the law, his thinking on all of life, and his Son, his solution for the redemption of all creation. God continues to tell us two millennia of Jewish history, which are anything but good. The law will bless those who live by it, setting them free from tyranny, but only the Messiah will bring release from our slavery to sin and unveil the mystery kept secret for ages.

JESUS LOVED THE LAW

All of Scripture, old and new, refers back to and builds on the Pentateuch, what Jesus called "the Law." In Matthew 5 Jesus makes it clear that the entire Old Testament is the foundation for his message and his actions:

> Do not think that I have come to abolish the Law or the Prophets; I have not come to abolish them but to fulfill them. For truly I tell you, until heaven and earth disappear, not the smallest letter, not the least stroke of a pen, will by any means disappear from the Law until everything is accomplished. Therefore anyone who sets aside one of the least of these commands and teaches others accordingly will be called least in the kingdom of heaven, but whoever practices and teaches these commands will be called great in the kingdom of heaven. For I tell you that unless your righteousness surpasses that of the Pharisees and the teachers of the law, you will certainly not enter the kingdom of heaven. (Matt. 5:17–20)

If our thinking does not build on the values and definitions of the Old Testament, then we cannot understand where Jesus is taking us with his message. He is not giving us a sympathetic, spineless, feel-good broth. Jesus actually raises the requirements of Jewish law to a righteousness beyond what Moses could have comprehended. We do not reinterpret the Old Testament with the New, nor the New with the Old, but rather see them as a four-thousand-year line of thought that God is building. Together they are a continuum of ideas that begins in Genesis and builds toward Christ's ultimate return. They show us how we should live in the meantime.

It is impossible to define *justice* or *mercy* or *political justice* without God's definitions in the Old Testament. These concepts do not mean whatever we want them to mean simply because our understanding fits our gifts, personality, culture, or times. They mean something quite specific to God, and only he has the right to define them for us. If we seek to be God's ambassadors, then we must represent his policies, not the current policies of the world or even the thinking and policies of Christians in our age.

At this point you may feel like skipping ahead to the revelation of the "great mystery." But before you can understand the great mystery, you must labor with God through several hundred years and pages of painful Jewish history, even after the Pentateuch. Then, and only then, will you understand what Christ has done and what our message is today.

CHAPTER 8

THE TEMPLATE OF LAWS

Nowhere does the Mosaic law weave the values of the kingdom more delicately and beautifully than where it addresses public justice. Its weaving is so intricate that it is difficult to know which value thread to begin with in unraveling it. There are innumerable ways to look at and analyze what God is giving us in these scriptures on justice. For our purposes in this volume on government and civil law, we will use a matrix of three categories of crime—loss of life, bodily harm, and loss of property—and four categories of consequence—death penalty, life sentence, restorative correction, and punitive correction. Using these categories, we can examine all that the law stipulates as crime: the breaking of civil laws that have specific instructions for correction, remuneration, or punishment.

As we go, it will be helpful to picture the study of Scripture as mentally unweaving the threads of an ornate tapestry in order to understand the parts that make up the whole. The threads do not stand by themselves; only together do they produce the picture. But the threads are the foundational parts of the whole, laying out the grid work that makes the tapestry possible. As with the reverse engineering of flat-box furniture, we take the whole of Scripture apart; our goal is to discover what elements God is emphasizing in order to understand Scripture and more effectively reassemble it back into our life.

In Deuteronomy 1, God initiates a revolutionary idea to curb humankind's great appetite for violence and injustice. God makes the human race responsible for governing themselves. They will choose their leaders. They will choose the laws, and they will choose consequences for breaking those laws. God will give Israel his thoughts on these subjects, but the authority will be theirs to maintain or change their direction. A representative, bottom-up, consensus-based style of political power is born.

As we learned through Genesis, the consequence of sin, or separation from God, is death . . . always. We all die physically because sin came into the world. As God continues in Genesis, he hammers home that the fruit of sin is death. We begin with brother killing brother and continue until the entire human race is so violent that human life is endangered entirely. The flood and reset of human existence through Noah was God's just and merciful solution. But again humanity's descent into violence in Abraham's family is so rapid that in just three generations they have sunk to the near fratricide of Joseph and the genocide of the Shechemites. A 435-year generational sentence is imposed on Israel as a nation in order to create an understanding of the value of human life.

Now God liberates Israel and gives them the law. The judicial parts of the law are very clear. God is saying, If you knew what I know, you would purge these acts from your society, because they are the very things that will lead to increasing violence and loss of life.

In other words, in the law, God is telling us how to create safe, life-sustaining communities and is making us responsible to do it. The burden of justice is now on our shoulders. We are free to change the laws God has given, and we are free to evaluate the consequences, the fruit of our choices. Are we keeping our fellow citizens from violent deaths, or are violent deaths increasing?

CIVIL LAW VERSUS MORAL LAW

To rightly apply to our current events what we learn from the law of Moses and the history of Israel, we must understand the difference between two God-given authorities, the authority of civil law and the authority of moral law.

All "law" is moral in the sense that it says, "This is right and this is wrong." In setting a standard of acceptable behavior, we must judge what is "good" and "bad." But not all morality can be made a matter of civil law. By giving us responsibility to decide, God makes us look at the implications of our choices by examining their impact on the society in which we live and raise our children. Civil law, representing the people, will never be more moral than the majority of the people it represents. But a more moral people will seek a higher level of civil law. Therein lies the tension between a changed heart and a judicial system that deals with those who are unchanged.

Both civil and moral laws are given authority from God. But God has invested them with two different kinds of authority with two separate functions. One must have the will of the people behind it in order to have the authority and power to govern. The other must have the will of God behind it in order to have authority and power of God. One reveals the standards of the people, and the other reveals the standards of God. One must seek the support of the people or seek to change the thinking of the people in order to have authority. The other must ignore the thinking of the people and represent God alone in order to have authority. The two are divinely disagreeable in the purposes of God; we must have both to keep the kingdom tension of justice in human society. Those who write civil law must be continually committed to keeping both civil law and moral law safeguarded.

This is not just a dilemma, but divine tension.

If we ask the Bible the question, "What does loving my neighbor look like?" we could look at the Ten Commandments. If we ask, "Why are these Ten Commandments (prescriptive law) important, and how do I apply them?" we look at the whole of the Mosaic law for answers. If we ask, "What would happen to our society if we applied or if we moved away from these values?" we look at the prophets. And if we ask, "How might a community begin to move away from God's thinking?" we look at the history of Israel throughout the Old Testament (historical law).[1] The prescriptive laws[2] show us what God wants from Israel's political leaders and people. The historical law shows us what the leaders and people of Israel actually did.

For our purposes in this book, we look at the prescriptive and historical laws as they relate to civil law and justice, trying to draw out what is emphasized. We look at them independently from each other in Part II and Part III to see how they compare. But for the development of our thinking, we must see the prescriptive and historical laws as integrated and woven together, reinforcing each other. So, in effect, we dissect them to *analyze* and then put them back together to *understand* and *apply*. Both the prescriptive and historical parts of God's whole law teach us, and they shed light on each other.

For example, the prescriptive law says that adultery is illegal and punishable by death. But historically this was not applied when David committed adultery with Bathsheba (historical law). Why? Did Israel just not apply the law? Or was there more to "the law" than just the prohibitions? Was the right of the people to ratify and change civil law part of what the values of "the law" secured? When in John 8 the Pharisees brought Jesus a woman caught in adultery and encouraged him to stone her according to the law of Moses, Jesus encouraged them to stone her if their righteousness allowed them to stand as judge. Under Roman law, adultery was not illegal, and if they had stoned her, they would have been found guilty of murder. Perhaps this was their plan for trapping Jesus. Jesus dismisses the woman with the exhortation to "sin no more." Adultery is still immoral.

WORKING THE TEMPLATE

The law seems like a maze in part because of its circular storytelling style. We see themes rotating and weaving throughout, but they are difficult to grab hold of. Because I am dyslexic, it is essential for me to order information to retain it. So, as I often do, I used color to help me in this study of the law. I divided out the prescriptive parts of the law of Moses—those parts of the law that tell us to "do this but do not do this," like the Ten Commandments. These prescriptive portions are found in Exodus, Leviticus, Numbers, and Deuteronomy. Then beginning with Deuteronomy, because it is considered by Jewish and Christian scholars to be the "core book," I assigned each theme in the prescriptive law a color when it appeared in my reading and from then on used that same color each time that subject reappeared. Once I had used Deuteronomy to lay down the pattern, I then was able to see what God emphasized or added to these themes in the other three books of the law.

FIVE VALUES

To my surprise, I found that the entire prescriptive law builds on five core values that are repeated and supported in different circumstances and within different authorities. Here are the five values:

- Life is sacred.
- The material world is real, good, and essential for all of life.
- Words have power, and we are accountable for our words.
- Everything needs redemption and is redeemable.
- Any thinking that takes us away from God's truths and values will begin to curse us; in other words, idolatry will not bless us.

Of course each of these values supports the first: Life is sacred. And so all of them could be stated, "Life is sacred, therefore . . ."

FIVE ASSUMPTIONS

In chapter 6 we laid down five foundational truths on which the kingdom of God is built. These are the realities Scripture presupposes:

- God is, and is who he says he is.
- God is the Creator of the material universe, seen and unseen, and his creation is good.
- Human individuals, male and female, are created in the image of God and are his central purpose for all creation.
- Everything that God has created is damaged by the fall of man and sin.
- Everything that is damaged is redeemable through the blood of Christ.

Take a moment to compare these lists and notice the similarities between the five assumptions that all of Scripture supports and the five values of the law.

INSTITUTIONS OF AUTHORITY

In chapter 5 we looked at four institutions of authority created by God: the individual, family, government, and church.[3]

The sovereign individual, created in the image of God, is the foundational building block of the kingdom. The sovereign family of husband, wife, and children is crucial to the development of healthy and mature individuals. The sovereign government, empowered by the people being governed, is responsible for defining and enforcing God's delegated authority, rights, and responsibilities. And, finally, the sovereign church is responsible for rightly representing God and his standards.

Each of these institutions is given authority, jurisdiction, borders, rights, freedoms, and responsibilities that lay the foundational values base of civil law. These limited rights and borders, values of the law, do not perfect human beings or societies, but to the level they are established and reinforced they will create and sustain a more blessed society. When applied, these values and institutions reveal God to the human community. They work with the cross to reveal Christ the King, but they do not substitute for forgiveness and salvation through Jesus. They reveal the kingdom that is coming, but they cannot perfect that kingdom on earth. Established and used properly, these values produce a higher quality of life in all areas of life, but they will not finally perfect humankind or creation. We are back to the tension between issues of the heart and issues of civil justice.

We are beginning to identify the basic building blocks of God's kingdom and biblical thought. They overlap, weave, and repeat themselves over and over throughout Scripture. We must still add the themes of the prophets and of the New Testament writers, but the grid is taking shape. We have five assumptions on which God builds all his thinking, five values that are essential to uphold if these assumptions are true, and four institutional authorities that God gives us in order to preserve and perpetuate these truths and values for the purpose of blessing our lives and our communities.

TENSION

These biblical realities set up a tension of freedoms, rights, and responsibilities that must be maintained in order to preserve right order, or justice, and build healthy individuals, families, and communities. They cannot be "balanced." They must be mutually maintained.

Picture a tightrope. In order to be traversed, it must be rigid. If there is any give at all, the consequences can be catastrophic for the walker. The tightness of the rope is far more consequential than a set of scales that are just a few grams off. The acrobatic artist cannot survive a slack rope. He or she can only perform when there is perfect tension on the rope.

In political justice, if we err in one direction or the other, we distort God's order in his kingdom. God has made the individual free and sovereign. But since that is true of every individual, there are limits to any single individual's freedom. In order for every individual to be free, there have to be limits to all of our freedoms. Who has the right and responsibility to create and sustain those boundaries? God has created the family as the authority for and over children. The authority of parents is to love their children. If they are trying to murder their children, they are in violation of the sacredness and rights of the individual life. I have the freedom to believe what I like. Do I have the freedom to practice that freedom anywhere, anytime? If I believe in human sacrifice for my blessing, do I have a right to perform human sacrifice? Or is this an abuse of the rights of the one being sacrificed? Do we have rights as communities? How do we secure the rights of minorities, the rights of parents and children, and the freedom of faith while not destroying the rights of the community?

In every legal issue, we are asking these questions:

- To whom has God given rights and responsibilities?
- What rights and responsibilities has he given to each?
- What are the limits of those rights?
- How are violations of those rights to be dealt with?

Every system of governance has answers to these questions or is working on formulating answers. But are they biblical answers? We can know what God says about each question, and at any given time we can know whether our nation's laws and system of governance are blessed or in danger. This is the biblical template. But we must be willing to replace the thinking of the world, even when it has been called "Christian," with God's thinking, even when that is called "worldly."

As we move on, we will take up the areas the prescriptive law emphasizes more or less in order that they appear in Deuteronomy. We begin in chapter 9 with the form of government, including the formation of an executive and a judiciary, and with the overall purpose of government. Issues of land, refuge, and crime are discussed in the remaining chapters of Part II.

CHAPTER 9

CIVIL LAW

Formation and Form

As we left our study of Genesis in Part I, Abraham's descendants had devolved into violence, like the human race before them. Using the only symbol of righteousness God has given, circumcision, Jacob's sons plundered a tribe and destroyed life. This genocide of the Shechemites led to refuge in Egypt and finally more than three hundred years of slavery. It is interesting to note that the brother Jacob's son did not murder, but sold instead, was the instrument God used to save all of their lives.

The entire biblical history of Israel will refer back to these years of slavery during which they were without political or economic justice. When he sets them free from Egyptian bondage, God will constantly remind them of these difficult times and exhort them to remember not to do the same to others in the land he will give them.

Deuteronomy opens with the formation of Israel's first civil government in the wilderness.

THE FORMATION OF GOVERNMENT

Moses speaks to the gathered assembly:

At that time I said to you, "You are too heavy a burden for me to carry alone. The LORD your God has increased your numbers so that today you are as numerous as the stars in the sky. May the LORD, the God of your ancestors, increase you a thousand times and bless you as he has promised! But how can I bear your problems and your burdens and your disputes all by myself? Choose some wise, understanding and respected men from each of your tribes, and I will set them over you."

You answered me, "What you propose to do is good."

So I took the leading men of your tribes, wise and respected men, and appointed them to have authority over you—as commanders of thousands, of hundreds, of fifties and of tens and as tribal officials. And I charged your judges at that time, "Hear the disputes between your people and judge fairly, whether the case is between two Israelites or between an Israelite and a foreigner residing among you. Do not show partiality in judging; hear both small and great alike. Do not be afraid of anyone, for judgment belongs to God. Bring me any case too hard for you, and I will hear it." And at that time I told you everything you were to do. (Deut. 1:9–18)

THE AUTHORITY TO GOVERN IS AT THE BOTTOM

Because Deuteronomy is the "second writing" or summation of the law as a whole, I think we can assume that its order and emphasis is intentional. It is important to remember that Israel has been in Egypt for well over four hundred years, at least three hundred of which were in slavery, and the nation never formally governed itself. This passage in Deuteronomy 1:9–18 gives us a representative, consensus-based, decentralized, bottom-up system of governance.[1] The authority to govern a nation is in the people being governed. Practically, anyone seeking to govern a people must have some level of agreement from the people since the people, united, have the power to overthrow them. In other words, a government stands as long as enough people will support or tolerate it.

In 1776, Thomas Jefferson wrote in the United States Declaration of Independence: "Prudence, indeed, will dictate that Governments long established should not be changed for light and transient causes; and accordingly all experience hath shewn, that mankind are more disposed to suffer, while evils are sufferable, than to right themselves by abolishing the forms to which they are accustomed." In other words, until a people are willing to suffer the struggle and pain of freedom, they will suffer tyranny. Likewise, Gandhi said that the British would rule India as long as the Indians wanted them to. In other words, when a people are ready to be free, they have the power to free themselves. Each of these political leaders, in his own way, reiterated what God tells us in Deuteronomy. The authority to govern and the power to make it happen are in the people being governed. The kingdom of God builds on the authority and sovereignty of the individual.

At the time of Moses, the nations and tribes of the world had governance, and some had a form of rule of law. But there is a startling difference between God's revelation of authority in Deuteronomy and all other forms of government at the time. In every other political system, the power to govern was understood to be at the top.

FIVE HUMAN POLITICAL INVENTIONS

As we saw in chapter 2, five basic forms of political power emerge in human history. Each of these variations answers the question "Who has the authority or right to rule?"

1. We (or I) have the right to rule because we have the biggest military and we can make you obey.
2. We (or I) have the right to rule because we have the most money and can hire the biggest army and we can make you obey.
3. We (or I) have the right to rule because our father/mother ruled and they gave us the right.
4. We (or I) have the right to rule because god said we are to rule you.
5. We (or I) have the right to rule because we are god.

The sixth form of government is one conceived by God. God speaks for himself into human history and says, "You have the right to rule if the people being ruled give you that right." Governance is in the service of and is subservient to the people being governed; officials are literally "civil servants." Governments have the authority to enforce the laws that the people have ratified. The people are the authority behind both the form and the content of civil law.

INDIVIDUAL RESPONSIBILITY

Again and again in the books of Moses, the Lord pleads with Israel to remember what it was like to live as slaves, with no political or economic rights. He exhorts them to hold on to the blessing of freedom and self-rule he has secured for them. He warns them not to look to the cultures around them and copy them. Most specifically God warns them not to desire a king. This is not a warning against having a monarch or a political leader. This is a warning against giving away sovereign power to a monarch or political leader—in other words, moving power up and away from individual responsibility and local community systems. This is about putting too much power and authority in too few hands.

Like slavery, moving political power away from the people produces dependence rather than self-reliance. It weakens the very fiber of society, which is a strong individual with a community conscience. It allows the development of a culture of the needy. "We, the people, need the government to do this, that, and the other for us." It empowers the few, who are easily corrupted, to control the many, who are slow to change but less easily corrupted en masse. It allows governance to be the problem and the solution for every societal need. The population becomes increasingly powerless, waiting for *them* to fix it. Moving political power away from the people kills self-initiative and creativity and produces dependency and neediness. It ultimately destroys the image of God in the individual and makes us think of ourselves as victims.

These values are simple to grasp, but it is hard to get people to want to be responsible. The first generation of Jews in the wilderness wanted to go back to slavery. By their own testimony, they would have preferred to be slaves with guaranteed meals than free with responsibility. Anyone working in development will tell us that motivating people to change is the problem. This is the story God is telling us. The dilemma of nation building is to restore responsibility while maintaining freedom. This is not easy when raising a teenager to maturity, let alone when trying to mature a nation.

We, believers included, jump so quickly to faster solutions. "We will take over! We need a benevolent dictator! The people are not able to govern themselves! They are too poor, too uneducated. We will do it for them. Freedom is too messy, too violent, too chaotic! We need control!" None of these are kingdom ideas. But neither are they new ways of thinking.

WE NEED A KING: THE EXECUTIVE

While Israel is still in the wilderness, God understands that the people will tire of local responsibility and will want to move political power up; they will want to be like the nations around them. Fallen human nature wants *someone else* to be responsible while at the same time wanting to be significant. God in his great mercy anticipates this inevitability and lays down the criteria for a king if they are going to have one. They should at least seek God for his choice. The king should not be a foreigner, nor should he acquire many wives. The king should not accumulate great wealth and property and numbers of horses. He should know the law God has given Israel and read it all his life. Otherwise the king, along with the people, will return to the ways of the nations around them. The king is not to consider himself above the law.

> When you enter the land the LORD your God is giving you and have taken possession of it and settled in it, and you say, "Let us set a king over us like all the nations around us," be sure to appoint over you a king the LORD your God chooses. He must be from among your fellow Israelites. Do not place a foreigner over you, one who is not an Israelite. The king, moreover, must not acquire great numbers of horses for himself or make the people return to Egypt to get more of them, for the Lord has told you, "You are not to go back that way again." He must not take many wives, or his heart will be led astray. He must not accumulate large amounts of silver and gold.
>
> When he takes the throne of his kingdom, he is to write for himself on a scroll a copy of this law, taken from that of the

Levitical priests. It is to be with him, and he is to read it all the days of his life so that he may learn to revere the LORD his God and follow carefully all the words of this law and these decrees and not consider himself better than his fellow Israelites and turn from the law to the right or to the left. Then he and his descendants will reign a long time over his kingdom in Israel. (Deut. 17:14–20)

Of course none of the kings of Israel will fulfill all these criteria, not even those God actually indicated would be the better choice. This will become painfully clear when we look at the political history of Israel in future chapters.

"But why?" we ask. "Look at Israel under David or under Solomon." Yes, David whom God loved so much and Solomon to whom God gave wisdom—of all the kings, they were truly the best, but they still did not fulfill God's criteria. They had large numbers of wives and concubines, they had notorious stables full of horses, and they amassed great personal fortunes. Not to mention, they had grave personal issues.

"But," we say, "look at how well the country did under their rule. Israel enjoyed economic prosperity and greater peace and order!" All true. Three generations of kings did raise Israel to a level of development far beyond anything achieved in the thirteen generations of judges. But we must read on to the total destruction brought by the fourth king, Rehoboam. After just four generations of kings, the deterioration of Israel was amazingly rapid. They lost everything, and they never recovered.

Rather than a king, the executive God intended for Israel was a loose federation of tribal elders chosen by the tribes themselves, working together when there was a national crisis. In a time of national crisis, there was a need for a national leader to unite the strength of the tribes. When the crisis was over, the tribes would return to governance by the local elders. In a perfect world, they would not have a national crisis nor need a crisis judge, but God does not assume a perfect world. He assumes that fallenness and sin will corrupt and that trouble will arise.

Are we so busy looking at the best of the kings that we fail to see the point that God has been making throughout all the kings of Israel? Is it possible that we too want to see a triumphant king arrive on a stallion and vanquish all our enemies and solve all our problems? Could it be that we too, in this age of Christianity, are disappointed by a carpenter on a donkey and the message he brings?

WHY IS THIS SO IMPORTANT?

The kingdom of God builds from within and on the individual. It is with us—individuals created in the image of God—that God has chosen to place authority. Anything we do to strengthen and empower the individual builds the kingdom of God. Strong individuals need strong families. They need education and work. They need the right to earn and own and the responsibility for both. Individuals, in order to be strong, must be able to make choices and live with the consequences of those choices, learning from them, growing through them. People who are not allowed to make choices become weak and dependent. This is exactly what darkness is about—weakness and subservience. It is exactly the opposite of the kingdom of God—freedom and responsibility.

If we are not careful, we begin to see the church as a hospital, family as *the* building block, government as god, school as the parent, and individuals as powerless victims. All of these misappropriations of authority destroy the order God created.

THE GREAT DILEMMA

The great dilemma of the kingdom of God is not control but discipleship. Our goal is to get people to make good choices willingly. We know this in evangelism, where our task is to "win" people, bringing them to the place where they are able to make a choice. The more controlling our methods of evangelism, the less effective and fruitful they are. God does not totally change values when we work in the arena of civil governance. He does not suddenly strip the individual of all authority in society. We cannot beat a society into submission and obedience.

Jesus is a king. He makes that clear when Pilate asks him directly, "Are you the king of the Jews?" But he is not the king the Jews want. They want a king who will overpower and control the authorities while giving them power to do the same. But this is not the way the kingdom of God is built. God is not a top-down ruler.

In evangelism, we see the lost as the objective, the lost sheep that Jesus wants to find and save. When we move into the political arena, we often see the lost as the enemy, the ones to be defeated. But God's perspective does not change. They, too, are the lost Jesus seeks, who need to see and understand true political justice. Kingdom justice will reveal the King to them and give them a choice.

THE JUDICIARY

When Moses related the formation of government in Deuteronomy 1, he explained that Israel had become too populated for him to judge on his own. He had been following the traditional tribal system of "the chief" hearing all complaints. The people literally lined up all day long, waiting for their turn to be heard in this one-man court. Notice how Moses assumed that the most important function of governance was to arbitrate disagreements and disputes. In other words, justice is pursued primarily as prevention through conflict resolution and only secondarily as correction for wrongdoing or crime.

In this system, people in conflict were to work the issue out between themselves if they could, and if they couldn't, they were to bring their disagreement to the courts for arbitration rather than take the vigilante route of violence. This process puts heavy emphasis on individual and community responsibility and sees the courts as a fail-safe.

If we think back to what God has emphasized in Genesis, it is not difficult to see why the judicial role of governance is so important. The history of a fallen human race proves that humans, left to work out arguments by themselves, escalate rapidly into violence and mob law. Social order becomes survival of the fittest, and violent crime, the norm. Knowledge of the sacredness of life is lost, and human life rapidly loses its perceived value.

Through the biblical template, God is moving us toward community responsibility for the individual and individual responsibility for the community, so that we become mutually responsible to carry the burden for justice at the most basic levels of society. The scriptural model implemented by Moses with the consent of the people, in which an adequate number of judges was made available to hear the people, emphasizes that the legal system must be able to efficiently handle internal disputes.

RESOLUTION OF DISPUTES

Resolution of disputes is the primary objective of the courts in Scripture. This means finding guilt or innocence based on established law, but it goes beyond that to arbitration of grievances. The objective surpasses due process and seeks community harmony, part of the true meaning of the word *shalom*. This explains why judicial representation went from judges of a thousand all the way down to one judge for every ten people. The form of the biblical judicial system adapted to the population of the people and prioritized service and resolution.

As small as they were in relation to the wilderness, each tribe in Israel at the time numbered more than 100,000 people. When they settled in the land, the tribes were mandated to have judges in every town. In a village of one hundred people, there would have been ten judges. Clearly it was a simple matter to get a hold of someone to help with daily grievances before they escalated into violence. And perhaps that is part of God's point. Create a system that deals with disputes before a crime is committed.

The injunction to take grievances to court is very practical: "When people have a dispute, they are to take it to court and the judges will decide the case, acquitting the innocent and condemning the guilty" (Deut. 25:1). The people could follow due process.

Why the severity of the death penalty for contempt of due process in Deuteronomy 17:12? "Anyone who shows contempt for the judge or for the priest who stands ministering there to the Lord your God is to be put to death." Because disregarding due process would lead to violence and the degradation of human life, not only in the one case but ultimately on a much larger community scale.

Arbitration, rule of law, and due process are essential for protecting the sacredness of life. When we take justice into our own hands, we devolve into the violence of Genesis. Due process must be easily accessible to serve the needs of the community. And to be accessible, it must be community based.

APPEALS PROCESS

In Deuteronomy 17 the courts are instructed to create a system of appeals for all accusations. The passage stipulates that all legal matters, "whether bloodshed, lawsuits or assaults," are to be resolved. If people could not get satisfaction at one level of the judicial process, then they appealed to a higher judge. Under Moses were three levels of appeal— judges of ten, fifty, one hundred, and one thousand—before a person could appeal to the national leader. If one could not get satisfaction at any level of the judicial system, the final appeal went to the high priest of the day.

The point here is we must find a legal resolution to every dispute. If we cannot, we must appeal to God for his finding. And these findings must be binding. Why? Because they are perfect? No, but because as imperfect as they may be, rule of law is the only way to keep humanity from devolving into mass slaughter. We are not seeking perfection. We are seeking resolution that is impartial and uses all the evidence available. We are seeking the best outcome possible.

IMPARTIALITY

Deuteronomy also gives us a definition of *impartiality*. Chapter 1 instructs the judge to judge fairly and then goes on to define *fairly* as "impartial," meaning showing no regard for the status of the defendant, whether Jew or foreigner, man or woman, small or great. In other words, impartiality means seeing defendants as "equal" before God and the court. How might this impartiality be corrupted? Causes listed in other passages include intimidation of the judge, bribery of the judge, twisting the meaning of words, and ignoring evidence.

The cure for this perversion of justice is to see that the judge, the courts, and the process are all accountable to God. But, what sort of god are we talking about? We are talking about the God whose words always mean what they say. The God who made the material world that is real and can be known and gives evidence. The God who tells us we either saw it or heard it, or we did not, and our words must match the reality of our information or lack of it. We are talking about the God who does not value human life with partiality, according to nationality, social status, or any other criterion, including kingship. We are talking about the God who considers the value of every individual equally and therefore impartially.

Deuteronomy 25 defines *fairness* as closure to a case and a finding of guilt or innocence. Judging fairly means following the prescribed sentence for those found guilty. It also means that the prescribed sentence for the crime does not supersede the human integrity of the guilty. Fair judgment also means that the sentence is actually carried out, not given and then ignored. The biblical definition of a fair trial includes complete closure and implementation of the full sentence, no matter who you are.

THE MEASUREMENT

The measurement of a judicial system's impartiality and fairness is clear throughout Scripture. We measure the success of our judicial system by the quality of justice we deliver to the poorest of the poor, the bottom of the social ladder, the outcast, the powerless . . . what Scripture describes as the widow, the orphan, and the alien. In other words, God judges our political justice by the justice we demand for the least in our societies. The level of justice we will accept for the outcast or the disgusting is the level of justice God will attribute to us as a society. The New Testament continues this kingdom value with the injunction to do to others, no matter who they are, what we would have them do to us. In this sense, justice is measured by what we are "giving" as much as by what we are "getting," if not more so.

Once the judicial system is established in the wilderness, God begins to reveal the legislative instructions of the law. Deuteronomy and the other books of the Law focus on the justice issue of land distribution and ownership.

CHAPTER 10

LAND

Ownership, Rights, and Legal Boundaries

Does the Bible have anything to say about land?"

The man who posed this question was a former speaker of the house of parliament in his remote tribal island state. For security reasons, we were gathered as a small group in his home to discuss the future of their indigenous people within the greater development plan of the nation.

"The Bible has a lot to say about land," I answered. "In fact, if you color the word *land* on each page, you begin to think the Bible is a book about land." (There are more than fifteen hundred references.)

This man's question was important for the tribes because the national government had asked them to give up ownership of the tribal lands. The government felt that the tribes had done little to develop these valuable land assets. For the benefit of the tribes, as well as the nation as a whole, it was suggested that they give up their land rights.

What should they do?

Following the formation of government in Deuteronomy 1, the next passage of prescriptive law, found in chapter 4, deals with the division of the land among twelve of the thirteen tribes.

There is nothing more important to the life of a people than the land they inhabit. The only thing more devastating for the life of a people than the loss of their land is the loss of their language. Land, in part, defines a nation, and the story of land begins in Genesis 1.

A SHORT COSMIC HISTORY OF LAND

In Genesis 1, God creates the heavens and then the earth. Hebrew scholars draw out the symmetry of the first three days given to the creation of spheres—the sky, the waters, and then land—and the second three days given to the creation of the inhabitants—birds, fish, and finally land animals and man.[1] In physics it is understood that, in the origins of the cosmos, first there is space, then matter, time, and finally, life. Matter is not only the stuff *of* life, it is the stuff *for* life. If life is sacred, belonging to God, then so is the material world, including the land we live on, the air we breathe, the water we drink, and the food the land provides. We cannot live without the material world.

In the beginning, all the earth belongs to God. In Genesis 1 and 2, the Lord begins to delegate authority for the land to Adam. First, God develops a garden in the east and puts the first human beings there. Although all the earth is designated for humankind to rule, God begins with a garden. God gives the real estate very specific borders. In essence, this is the first land treaty and the first case of land boundaries. Notice that the boundaries of the garden are very specific and easy to recognize with the naked eye.

A river watering the garden flowed from Eden; from there it was separated into four headwaters. The name of the first is the Pishon; it winds through the entire land of Havilah, where there is gold. (The gold of that land is good; aromatic resin and onyx are also there.) The name of the second river is the Gihon; it winds through the entire land of Cush. The name of the third river is the Tigris; it runs along the east side of Ashur. And the fourth river is the Euphrates. The LORD God took the man and put him in the Garden of Eden to work it and take care of it. (Gen. 2:10–15)

BORDERS OF THE GARDEN

The geography of these border rivers is very interesting even today, and these borders will stay strategic throughout Scripture and history into our new millennium.

We still know where the Euphrates and Tigris are, even though they have deviated some from their ancient paths. Today the headwaters of these rivers form close together in the mountains of eastern Turkey. The Euphrates then flows through northeastern Syria and central Iraq, while the eastern border of the garden of Eden, the Tigris, meanders east of the Euphrates through Baghdad and eastern Iraq. The two rivers unite near Basra, Iraq, forming the Shatt al-Arab river before exiting into the Persian Gulf.

The two rivers given as western borders are more difficult to identify due to the shifting of continental plates. Farthest west is the Pishon, which is described as running through the entire land of Havilah. To its east, the Gihon is described as flowing through the entire land of Cush. Cush is generally accepted as being modern Ethiopia and running along the Red Sea. Havilah is generally accepted as the area at the southern end of the Red Sea extending west to the Nile River.

If you look at a satellite map of the region, it is not difficult to imagine that originally the eastern rivers ran from the Black Sea, through what is now called the Persian Gulf, to the Indian Ocean. The rivers on the western border of the garden are now what we call the Red Sea, also flowing to the Indian Ocean, and the Nile. Eden is most often thought to be near ancient Ur, southeast of Baghdad on the Euphrates River. This is where Abraham's family originated.

So, essentially, the garden of Eden may have constituted what today includes eastern Egypt, eastern Sudan, Eritrea, Ethiopia, Somalia, Uganda, Kenya, possibly Tanzania and Mozambique, the entire Arabian Peninsula, all of Palestine, Israel, Lebanon, Syria, Jordan, and most of Turkey and Iraq. Now that's a garden!

God gives title and authority over these defined lands to Adam, male and female. They are to have dominion over all creation, but for now over the garden. Boundaries and borders define responsibility and authority. No individual, family, tribe, or nation may own land until there is an established authority to officiate and secure that right. In Scripture that authority originates with God.

However, because of sin, the first family is banished from the garden (Gen. 3:23–24). The lifetime lease is rescinded. They have exceeded the authority of the terms of their contract. The promise is void.

Which direction did Adam and Eve go when they left the garden? The angel left to guard the border is stationed on the east side (Gen. 3:24). So it is possible they left in the direction that Abraham will return from, east of the Euphrates.

A SHORT HISTORY: LAND AND ISRAEL

Twenty generations after Adam and Eve are banned from the garden, God raises up a man named Abraham whose family roots are in Ur, a city south of Babylon on the Euphrates River. In Genesis 12, God calls Abraham to leave his ancestral home and people and travel west to a land where God will make him into a great nation. The land that God speaks to Abraham about is Canaan. It is on the western side of what was formerly called the garden.

Abraham and his family, including his nephew Lot, live as nomads in the land of Canaan. They are in the Negev south of the Dead Sea, or Salt Sea. In Genesis 13, when Lot's and Abraham's stock outnumber their ability to be sustained by the same land, the men negotiate a solution. Abraham gives Lot his choice of grazing lands. Lot takes the best of the land, the plain of the Jordan to the east. Abraham stays in Canaan, the land of promise, but evidently not the best land for grazing.

In Genesis 15, God speaks to Abraham again about the land he will give him and its boundaries. Abraham's land will run from the river of Egypt (possibly the Nile) to the Euphrates. No southern border is mentioned here, but this is all of the western border and much of the northern border of the garden of Eden. This territory covers most of today's Israel, Palestine, Syria, Lebanon, and western Iraq. But in this passage God makes it clear to Abraham that it will be half a millennium or more before his people take possession of these lands.

In Genesis 17, God promises to make Ishmael into a great nation and the father of twelve nations, in addition to his promises to Isaac. This will add territory to the land of Abraham's children, as Genesis 25:18 notes that Ishmael's descendants settle from Havilah to Shur. This covers much of the Arabian Peninsula up to the western Sinai.

We also learn that the six sons of Keturah, Abraham's second wife, move off to the southeast of the Jordan River, settling along the western border of the Arabian Peninsula. Lot settles in the hills outside of Zoar just south of the Dead Sea (Gen. 19:20–23). His daughters birth the fathers of the Moabites and Ammonites (Gen. 19:36–38). Esau, bereft of his inheritance through Jacob's deception, is blessed by his father to live "away from the earth's richness, away from the dew of heaven above" (Gen. 27:39). In other words, away from the promised land. He settles in the hill country of Seir, in what is now Jordan, east of the Wadi Arabah. Esau's descendants are the Edomites of what was then called Edom (Gen. 36). Esau marries the daughter of Ishmael, son of Abraham.

For some reason, few, if any, Bible aids map out the geography of these passages. You have to do the study and map it out yourself. As you do, you will begin to wonder whether the descendants of Abraham did, in fact, inherit most of the garden of Eden, as all of them had promises from God.

Here are two things I think we must see to understand God's view of land:

- *God gives land to all tribes and nations.*
- *Keeping those lands and the blessing of the land is dependent on the values the culture develops. God's promises are conditional.*

Therefore, throughout Scripture, from the garden of Eden on, we are dealing with shifting borders, nations gaining and losing land, nations dying and being birthed. God has a plan and purpose in all of it, as he does today.

LAND AND BOUNDARIES

When we have an overview of what God says in Scripture about land, it is clear that land is essential for a nation to exist and an economy to prosper. Distribution of land will be a key factor in whether or not economic development eliminates abject poverty in a society. In other words, all nations have wealth. That wealth is in the potential of the land and its people. A society's level of poverty is determined by where the wealth of the nation is held and how the people and the land are developed. In nations with crippling poverty, an elite few hold the land, while the masses remain without title to property, and the people remain woefully poor, their potential underdeveloped.

In the biblical discussion of land, there is an emphasis on boundaries, or rights and limits to land ownership. Deuteronomy 3:12–17 begins the process in Israel with very specific instructions for dividing the land among the twelve tribes of Israel. Other passages deal with the "land within the lands," the portion of the land of each tribe that was allotted to the Levitical priesthood (or ecclesiastical institution) and the king (or government). Each of these designations of land has very specific boundaries.

In contrast, in desperately poor nations today, land ownership is in the hands of the government, religious institutions, or a minority elite. Some nations' land is owned almost entirely by one or all three.

LAND IS FOR THE PEOPLE

Numbers 26:52–56 adds to our understanding of land boundaries. The boundaries God laid out for the tribes were based on the populations of the tribes. So more land was given to the large tribes and less to the smaller. I think we can assume that there was consideration for quality of the soil and the availability of water as well as what was most suitable for the tribe's occupation. This, by itself, would make a great study, especially for those needing to develop biblical criteria for land distribution and development.

Getting Israel to participate in land ownership was no easy task. These were nomadic herders like the Masai of Kenya or Tibetan mountain herders. Their entire culture was built around moving to greener pastures. The first challenge Israel faces is that they have to fight to free their land, necessitating putting their lives and the lives of their families on the line. The first generation is unwilling to do this, and so they spend forty years in the desert. They do not have the national will to form a military and fight for their borders.

Numbers 34 repeats in great detail the boundaries that God is now giving to Israel, along with the boundaries for all twelve tribal territories. It is important to note that the process of assigning the land is officiated by the head of government (Joshua son of Nun) and the head of the ecclesiastical institution (Eleazar the priest) with the help of one leader from each tribe. In other words, the distribution is ratified by the people, supported by God, and enforced by law.

In the book of Deuteronomy alone, the idea of occupying or "taking possession" of the land appears more than seventy times. Added to that is the injunction to make the land prosper, or develop it. Convincing and training these nomadic people with their slave mindset to develop the long-range planning and daily labor requirements necessary for this task, when their entire culture is built around short-term circumstantial factors, is no simple matter. It takes generations for the Jews in Scripture to integrate these values into their thinking. The shift in thinking from "move to the land that will prosper you" to "prosper the land where you are" is huge. But it is essential if a people are to be discipled. The process begins with owning land and with the consequences of that responsibility.

LOCAL AND FAMILY DISTRIBUTION

While tribal boundaries were designated at a national level and chosen by lot (Numbers 34), other passages note that the intratribal designation of land was done at the tribal level. When intratribal boundaries for families were decided within the tribe, we can assume the system supported the same values. And inheritance, while favoring eldest sons, was ultimately a family decision. All of this serves to push wealth, authority, and responsibility down.

NEGOTIATION AND PURCHASE

Throughout Genesis, the strategy for Abraham's use of land is "negotiation," and for acquiring land, "purchase." Abraham negotiates with Pharaoh in Egypt (chapter 12). He negotiates with Abimelek, king of Gerar (chapter 20), including for water rights in the land (chapter 21). Abraham negotiates and purchases land from the Hittites in order to bury his wife Sarah, acknowledging that he is a foreigner in a land that is rightfully theirs (chapter 23). While the strategy is clearly tainted by Abraham's use of his wife as leverage, "negotiation" and "purchase" were clearly the means God was using.

After the exodus God commanded the Israelites to drive out or destroy the people living in Canaan (Deut. 7:1–2). Would negotiation and purchase have remained God's strategy if the inhabitants of Canaan had not become irredeemably decadent in the centuries Abraham's clan spent in slavery in Egypt (Deut. 18:9–11; Lev. 18:25)? I think we can assume that, like the flood, the mandate to wipe out these tribes was a desperate redemptive measure on God's part. I think we can also assume that, as with the flood, it may have been a one-time event rather than a biblical strategy for redemption. The value is not the miracle or the means, but what God is accomplishing for the nation.

AMENDMENT OF LEGAL BORDERS

The first petition for change of tribal land assignments takes up the whole of Numbers 32. Two and a half tribes—the Gadites, the Reubenites, and the half-tribe of Manasseh son of Joseph—come to Moses to make an application to stay in the land on the east side of the Jordan rather than occupy the land they have been given on the western side. They are herders, and the eastern land is good for grazing. Moses is concerned that if these tribes receive land east of the Jordan, they will not help the other tribes of Israel take the territories west of the Jordan. In response, the two and a half tribes swear allegiance to the other tribes and commit their military support to taking all the lands. Moses, Eleazar the priest, and the tribal elders ratify the treaty for changing the designation of land with contractual conditions. The East Jordan tribes must fulfill their commitment to militarily support the other tribes in securing their land. If they fail to do this, they must take up residence in their assigned lands on the west side of the Jordan.

It is important for us to understand this transaction. The thirteen tribes of Israel have committed to God to secure and inhabit the land in Canaan that he has designated. They have all taken a vow to obey God and to support each other in this national movement. These are legally and morally binding promises and commitments. The two and a half tribes are a free people and have a choice. However, they do have a binding agreement they must fulfill before they are free to go their own way. Their individual tribal choices must not subvert the safety and good of the nation as a whole.

Jewish scholars comment, "Moses fears for the fate of Israel on account of the actions of Gad and Reuben; this verse assumes corporate responsibility, where a serious infraction by part of the nation endangers the nation as a whole."[2]

Moses reminds the Reubenites and Gadites of the rebellion in the wilderness, which cost an entire generation their inheritance in the promised land. He calls them a "brood of sinners" who make the Lord "even more angry" than the generation before had done. However, if they will fulfill their military responsibility to their brother tribes, helping their brother tribes capture and clear their tribal lands, then they will be released of their *legal* obligation. Still, there is no happy future for the eastern tribes, as the history of Israel will record.

On today's map, the land the eastern tribes settled is southern Syria and most of the nation of Jordan.

THE SECOND LAND AMENDMENT

The first appeal in Scripture regarding the interpretation of the law involves the inheritance of land within the family.

Found in Numbers 27, the specific question is whether daughters, in the absence of sons, have the right to inherit the land so that the father's inheritance is not lost to the family. Moses consults the Lord, and God answers, resoundingly, "Yes!"

An appeal of this law is recorded in Numbers 36. Here the men of the tribes argue that if the women inherit the land and then marry outside the tribe, the families will still lose their land. Moses consults the Lord again, and this appeal is also upheld. The new amendment states that if a woman inherits the family property, she must marry within the tribe so that the land is secured. (Apart from this constraint, she may marry whomever she wishes.)

Both the initial ruling and the appeal emphasize keeping ownership within the family. Likewise, in the fiftieth jubilee year, all leased land was returned to the owning family. This limitation on the outright sale of family land was also intended to protect the community from a monopoly of land ownership.

A land transaction was ratified before the community with the exchange of a sandal in the presence of the elders at the gate. Contractual agreements were to be witnessed, transparent, clear to the public, and legal in nature. I think we can assume this process safeguarded against deceit, theft, and violence. Again, God assumes that if we can be corrupt, some will be corrupt. Due process is intended to be a deterrent.

Blessings and Cursings: Losing the Land

From the promise of land to Abraham in Genesis to the distribution of land under Moses, and again in the times of the kings, several times God himself changes the boundaries of the land he has given Israel. When this happens in Scripture, it always indicates judgment on the choices of the nation. It is clearly not a blessing and indicates the degeneration of the culture. For example, in Deuteronomy 28, Moses tells the Israelites that if they do not obey the Lord and follow all the commands and decrees the Lord has made clear to them, they will be cursed:

> A people that you do not know will eat what your land and labor produce, and you will have nothing but cruel oppression all your days. The sights you see will drive you mad. The Lord will afflict your knees and legs with painful boils that cannot be cured, spreading from the soles of your feet to the top of your head.
>
> The Lord will drive you and the king you set over you to a nation unknown to you or your ancestors. There you will worship other gods, gods of wood and stone. You will become a thing of horror, a byword and an object of ridicule among all the peoples where the Lord will drive you. (Deut. 28:33–37)

In other words, they will lose the land and everything it provides.

God Gives and God Takes Away

We often focus on the land that God gives Israel in Canaan, land that is already occupied by seven other tribal nations. God is taking the land from those nations because their dissolute cultures are so lacking any redeemable virtue that there is no future for the people but destruction. They are slowly self-annihilating, and a swift end is the mercy of God.

But Israel was forbidden to touch the boundaries of any other tribe in the area. God clearly honors the boundaries of all nations and tribes with exceptions only in the most extreme cases. And what we need to remember is that the very same standards God applied to those seven tribes God later applies to Israel as they sink to the same level. They become, in the gravest sense of the word, a failed nation where life cannot be sustained.

We rarely highlight the numerous tribes and nations God forbids Israel to touch. God is not giving the chosen people a carte blanche to go for a land grab. He is very specifically taking land from degenerate cultures, doomed to self-destruct, and giving it to another tribe and nation. He is giving a new nation a chance.

God has a covenant with all tribes and nations. He is engaged in a redemptive process with all peoples. And that redemptive process includes the giving and the taking of land as a measurement of a people's values and a consequence of their own choices. Israel will finally lose their promised land for the same reason other nations lost their land.

The blessing and cursing of any people, tribe, and culture can be traced by contrasting the values they were applying when they were safe, secure, and prosperous and the values they were applying when they began to decline, devolve, and finally lose everything. Conquering peoples are not to be seen as the blessed victors. This is not good guys versus bad guys. Those in ascendance can be seen as the next peoples, tribes, and nations to whom God is giving a redemptive chance. How will they do? They will have to decide, and their choices will create their future, as the prophets make clear for Israel.

We seek to bless all nations and disciple them into making choices that will create a hope and a future. We seek to demonstrate to and through them the superior ways and values of God, that he might be seen. Part of discipleship is pushing land ownership down so that, increasingly, the people of the land hold the wealth of the land in large measure.

The next judicial issues addressed in the prescriptive laws are those of "cities of refuge" and "due process."

CHAPTER 11

CITIES OF REFUGE

Revenge versus Due Process

God understands that the "red thread of violence" that began in Genesis 4 will continue in the promised land with his chosen people. This, of course, does not surprise Moses, who has already murdered an Egyptian guard and fled the consequences for forty years. There is no idealism in God's thinking. Knowing our hearts and all that we are capable of, he moves on with his plan for redemption. He goes to great pains, however, to limit the damage of sin along the way. And so, after distributing the tribal lands, God sets aside land and cities in each of the tribal territories as cities of refuge, to be administrated by the priesthood.

Measures must be in place in any just society to mitigate the effects of violence. These measures ought to protect the community from the violent individual as well as protect the individual from violent communities.

One way we can measure a nation's judicial system against kingdom values is to assess whether due process is more or less accessible and efficient. Without a working system for due process, no nation can be just. The effectiveness of that system then becomes a way to evaluate the nation's level of justice development, highlighting what needs to be changed to create a more just society.

CITIES OF REFUGE: PROTECTION

The prescriptive law makes the need to provide protection and judicial process for violent crime the second priority after land ownership. Note that the emphasis is on protecting the *accused*. In other words, in this historical context, the greater danger seems to have been mob and community violence.

The assumption of these laws is that people will be killed, accidently or intentionally, and inflamed family and friends will seek revenge. Therefore, the community will need someplace where the accused can be protected until due process has run its course. Cities of refuge—God's solution—were to be strategically placed throughout the country and roads built so they were accessible. They were to be cities administered by the Levitical priesthood, and so, in essence, the priests would administer sanctuary and protection until trial. As the population of the territories increased, the law made provision for adding more cities of refuge, making sure the system served the needs of the population.[1]

DUE PROCESS

What constitutes due process from one culture to another can be vastly different. Again, if we are going to build God's understanding of justice into our societies, we must deal with the meaning of our terms. Does God provide a definition of *due process*? Does he give us a set of values we can apply today? He does! As God began to reveal in Genesis in the first trials of Adam and Cain, the biblical system of due process includes protection, evidence, motive, finding, judicial limits, sentence, and appeal.

JUDICIAL AUTHORITY

The law mandated a trial with judicial representation for every group of ten people. God left the Israelites no excuse for taking justice into their own hands. As we discussed in chapter 3, when we surveyed the trials of Adam, Cain, and the pre-flood human race, God modeled the elements of a trial for us in Scripture. Disrespect for judicial authority was held on par with disrespect for priestly and parental authority. The rejection of any one of the three was considered a crime punishable by death, as we will see in the next chapter.

A death penalty for disregarding judicial authority sounds unbelievably harsh at face value. But, in context, it is clear that God is speaking about something far more dire than a mere attitude issue. God is talking about restraining actions that lead to violence and the loss of human life. He is warning us that human beings who have no respect for any authority greater than themselves will become a destructive force, threatening the value of all life. We may not be able to require such individuals to *believe* in something, but society must make them *obey* something, or they will self-destruct, taking the community with them. God's earthly line of defense against mass destruction is civil law and judicial process. This is less about the rebellious teenager and more about the sociopath.

THE EVIDENCE AND WITNESSES

A second emphasis for due process is evidence. For evidence, the law required witnesses, not only one but at least two or three: "One witness is not enough to convict anyone accused of any crime or offense they may have committed. A matter must be established by the testimony of two or three witnesses" (Deut. 19:15). "Anyone who kills a person is to be put to death as a murderer only on the testimony of witnesses. But no one is to be put to death on the testimony of only one witness" (Num. 35:30).

The rules of evidence build on the five biblical presuppositions. If the material world, God's good creation, does not possess a reliable reality, there is no truth or evidence. If our words cannot be measured against the reality of that material world, there is no truth, witness, or testimony. If there is no truth to our actions, there is no guilt or innocence; guilt and innocence are ludicrous illusions at best. And if our words mean nothing, there is no justice, no promise, no contract, no commitment, no love, and no hope.

Our reality as human beings is conveyed through our words. Our words either measure up against the world around us or they do not. And so when it comes to evidence, it is testimony that is emphasized. In this way, God makes not only the accused responsible for their actions, but the community responsible for their own safety. The police and the courts can do very little if no one in the community will speak up. But in contrast, if there is a culture of truth and transparency, then due process becomes much easier. At a local level, someone almost always knows what happened. A community that will pay the price of openness will be safer than a community where no one will speak up.

The law also drives home the essentialness of a trustworthy community in dealing with malicious and false testimony. Deuteronomy 19:16–20 says that if it is proved that a witness has lied and conspired with the objective of false conviction, then the courts must convict that witness of perjury and pronounce the same sentence and consequences that the false witness sought for the innocent party. God is holding the community responsible for its own protection.[2]

THE MOTIVE

Accidents will happen, and people will die. Death is an unavoidable reality in a fallen world. In Numbers 35, God notes the difference between intentional and unintentional killing.

Was the incident a crime or a tragic accident? You can almost hear the ancient voices saying, "But what if they killed him with an ax, a stone, a piece of wood? What if they shoved him, threw something, hit him with their fist?" They are trying to judge intentionality by the instrument used in the killing. Today we could add our own list. What if they hit her with a car, gave her AIDS, or sold her fake pharmaceuticals? Can malice include indifference to life? By the time we get through the law of Moses, we'll see that the instrument is not the question of importance; rather motive is defined by why a person killed another and by the intent to kill.

> If anyone strikes someone a fatal blow with an iron object, that person is a murderer; the murderer is to be put to death. Or if anyone is holding a stone and strikes someone a fatal blow with it, that person is a murderer; the murderer is to be put to death. Or if anyone is holding a wooden object and strikes someone a fatal blow with it, that person is a murderer; the murderer is to be put to death. The avenger of blood shall put

the murderer to death; when the avenger comes upon the murderer, the avenger shall put the murderer to death. If anyone with malice aforethought shoves another or throws something at them intentionally so that they die or if out of enmity one person hits another with their fist so that the other dies, that person is to be put to death; that person is a murderer. The avenger of blood shall put the murderer to death when they meet. (Num. 35:16–21)

As in this passage in Numbers, Mosaic law emphasizes the distinction between intentional and unintentional killing. Intentionality is measured by "malice," an intent to do harm, and "aforethought," an understanding of the outcome ahead of time. Deuteronomy 19 provides a practical illustration of two workmen in the forest cutting wood when an ax head accidentally flies off, killing one. This constitutes "without malice aforethought," meaning the accused had "no intent" and "no prior knowledge" of consequences. The assumption is, if the workman had known, he would have stopped and fixed his ax head. And so if you cause a car accident while under the influence of alcohol, you may have no "malice," but you may have "aforethought" in that you knew your drunken driving caused danger to yourself and others. However, if you planned to run over an enemy and do him bodily harm, while under the influence or not, then you have "malice aforethought." This constitutes murder, a capital offense, requiring the death penalty.

Our court systems must be able to determine motive as well as action.

The Finding and the Appeal

The law emphasizes the importance of closure in issues of justice. Without closure, or a finding, the unresolved issue will continue to fester in the community, creating an environment for violence. A final judgment does not ensure perfect justice. But it does pronounce closure to the case, and the exhortation in Deuteronomy 17:11 to "act according to whatever they teach you and the decisions they give you" is a mandate to accept these findings and move on. Of course, the more corrupt the system, the harder this is.

The appeals process provided by the law recognizes the need for closure through a just finding. We saw the first appeal process in Genesis 4 when Cain asked God for protection of his life in exile. Later, in Deuteronomy 1, this process is built into the institution of governance when Moses establishes judicial representatives over ten, fifty, one hundred, and one thousand and then instructs that any case too difficult for this succession of judges be brought to the executive leader. He declares that a case that cannot be resolved even by the executive must then be presented to the high priest for finding.

Along with the importance of closure, the appeals process also emphasizes the importance of checks and balances in the judicial system. It is more difficult to corrupt six levels of appeals than to corrupt one judge.[3]

JUDICIAL CHECKS AND BALANCES

God's design for due process ensures that a system of checks and balances is in place. The national government creates the system, designates the locations, and builds the infrastructure. The priesthood provides refuge and sanctuary until trial, and the local courts have jurisdiction over the case unless there is an appeal.

This tension of authorities provides a better possibility of justice. Three judges are harder to corrupt than one, and two or three witnesses are harder to corrupt than one, just as three institutions are harder to corrupt than one. Therefore, in a fallen world, the more tension we have in due process, the safer our society is from corruption. Corruption will always be with us, but it cannot dominate a system with a strong balance of powers in place. Some feel that this balance of powers is the most important, and unique, contribution to judicial thought made by the law of Moses.

The objective of eliminating corruption altogether from our societies is like saying we will get rid of sin. We will not accomplish either of those objectives. God himself makes that clear. We are trying to limit the damage of sin—including corruption—and be a testimony to what perfect justice could look like and will look like when the King returns. We are working for the best judicial system possible.

JUDICIAL LIMITS

As with all other authorities, God places limits on the sentences applied by the judiciary. Three values are to guide judicial decisions.

Sentences must not degrade the value of the convicted's life. For example, leaving the body of an executed criminal hanging out all night is forbidden in the law (Deut. 21:22–23). Bodies were to be taken down and buried within a day or the land would be cursed, as it would with the same treatment of any body. In another example, the court was instructed not to exceed forty lashes, which was the acceptable limit for whipping. More than that degraded the convicted in the eyes of the public (Deut. 25:1–3).

No ransom may be offered for the life of a convicted murderer. "Do not accept a ransom for the life of a murderer, who deserves to die. They are to be put to death" (Num. 35:31). The value upheld here is the right of the community to be protected from those who have shown wanton disregard for human life.

The sentence for a crime may not exceed the consequences of the crime itself. The eye for an eye passages (Exod. 21:23–25; Lev. 24:20; Deut. 19:21) reinforce the innate equality of all human beings. No one's eye is worth two of another's eye. We must see these limits in light of the time. Remember, in Genesis 4, Lamech boasts that he has killed a man for slapping him and that the lives of seventy-seven people should be the vengeance for taking a single life (his). Nowhere in the known world at the time of Moses was the judiciary so limited in the amount of punishment they could mete out. One life does not have more value than another, nor does it have less.

JUDICIAL LIMITS IN CAPITAL CRIMES

The judicial limits set on the courts in the prescriptive law also cover capital crimes. The courts must make provision for protection of the accused until due process is complete (Deut. 4:41–43; Exod. 21:12–13; Num. 35:9–29). The courts must have at least two witnesses in order to find capital guilt (Deut. 17:6). The courts must provide a process of appeal (Deut. 17:8–13). The courts may not execute parents for a capital offense committed by their child or vice versa (Deut. 24:16), nor may the courts degrade the body of the executed felon (Deut. 21:22–23).

ACCIDENTAL DEATH AND THE VALUE OF A LIFE

The loss of a life is not only an immeasurable tragedy but also a measurable loss of relationships, time, and work contributing to the life of the family and community. There may be a no-fault death, but there is never a no-consequence death. The inherent value of the life, no matter the circumstances, is always relevant. But God also considers the value of the life of the defendant, the family of the deceased, and the community at large. There are consequences to death no matter what the circumstances. And the loss is not just that individual's loss of life. The loss of a life is also a loss to family and community, and when another person has contributed to this loss, this fact cannot be ignored.

Probably no passage illustrates these delicate dilemmas better than the instructions given in Numbers 35 detailing what happens pre-trial to protect the accused and post-trial when the accused killer is found "not guilty" of murder but "guilty" of accidental manslaughter.

> Then the LORD said to Moses: "Speak to the Israelites and say to them: 'When you cross the Jordan into Canaan, select some towns to be your cities of refuge, to which a person who has killed someone accidentally may flee. They will be places of refuge from the avenger, so that anyone accused of murder may not die before they stand trial before the assembly. . . . These six towns will be a place of refuge for Israelites and for foreigners residing among them, so that anyone who has killed another accidentally can flee there. . . .
>
> "If without enmity someone suddenly pushes another or throws something at them unintentionally or, without seeing them, drops on them a stone heavy enough to kill them, and they die, then since that other person was not an enemy and no harm was intended, the assembly must judge between the accused and the avenger of blood according to these regulations. The assembly must protect the one accused of murder from the avenger of blood and send the accused back to the city of refuge to which they fled. The accused must stay there until the death of the high priest, who was anointed with the holy oil." (Num. 35:9–12, 15; 22–25)

Now this is an interesting passage! Even when the accused are found "not guilty," they must not return to their hometowns. Why? Dropping the mandate to a values level will help us understand why. The answer must have to do the sacredness of life of all parties. The protection provided here is not for the community but for the accidental killers. They are not murderers and not dangers to the community. The concern here must be for the safety of the acquitted. The government cannot guarantee their protection from an entire community. As unfortunate as it is, there will be someone out there gunning for revenge, and God in practicality dictates that the accused relocate and live out their next years where they can be protected.

Perhaps the question for us is, "How do we judicially protect the one from the many?" The law's response seems to be that, ultimately, we cannot. Therefore, God provides an alternative for the protection of the one. But the choice is theirs: "But if the accused ever goes outside the limits of the city of refuge to which they fled and the avenger of blood finds them outside the city, the avenger of blood may kill the accused without being guilty of murder. The accused must stay in the city of refuge until the death of the high priest; only after the death of the high priest may they return to their own property" (Num. 35:26–28).

On the surface, this passage seems to permit murder without fault, but that would make nonsense out of the many other Scripture passages saying the opposite. So what are we dealing with here? Is it that the vindictiveness of the community is so great that there is no possible protection by the government if the acquitted returns? Is God also holding the individuals responsible to not put themselves in harm's way?

It is important to note that in the provisions of Numbers 35, as in the rest of the law, there is no assumption of human innocence; the presupposition of the law is that if there are not deterrents to violence, not only will individuals be violent, but also whole communities will devolve into vigilante law.

COMMUNITY RESPONSIBILITY AND UNSOLVED MURDERS

A passage in Deuteronomy 21 brings the idea of community guilt to the forefront and reinforces the community's responsibility to uphold the value of an individual's life. We are to create and maintain safe communities, and there is to be closure even to unsolvable murders. Death always has consequences.

> If someone is found slain, lying in a field in the land the LORD your God is giving you to possess, and it is not known who the killer was, your elders and judges shall go out and measure the distance from the body to the neighboring towns. Then the elders of the town nearest the body shall take a heifer that has never been worked and has never worn a yoke and lead it down to a valley that has not been plowed or planted and where there is a flowing stream. There in the valley they are to break the heifer's neck. The Levitical priests shall step forward, for the LORD your God has chosen them to minister and to pronounce blessings in the name of the LORD and to decide all cases of dispute and assault. Then all the elders of the town nearest the body shall wash their hands over the heifer whose neck was broken in the valley, and they shall declare: "Our hands did not shed this blood, nor did our eyes see it done. Accept this atonement for your people Israel, whom you have redeemed, LORD, and do not hold your people guilty of the blood of an innocent person." Then the bloodshed will be atoned for, and you will have purged from yourselves the guilt of shedding innocent blood, since you have done what is right in the eyes of the LORD. (Deut. 21:1–9)

We must drop to a values level to understand the message of this passage. The killing in this example happened in the open countryside with no known witnesses. It is expected that, if this had happened in a town, there would be witnesses and that those witnesses would come forward. The community was expected and pressured to support and help implement justice by being faithful neighbors.

The choice of town is in part random, in the sense that there is no way of knowing in which town the killer was resident. However, the choice of the closest town is not random at all in the sense that the town is responsible for the roads and territory where the murder took place. As a farmer is responsible for making sure his livestock are not a public danger, communities are responsible for making sure their territorial lands are safe. And it is the responsibility of the elders, or local government, to make sure these systems are in place.

Towns that neglect this responsibility pay a high price under the law. The cost of loss of life is always high. The price here is the loss of the full potential of a heifer that has never worked and never given birth and the pollution of prime land and a water supply that have never been used. In an agrarian economy, that is big money!

What is God's point? *There is no such thing as loss of life without consequences.* And those consequences are not invisible ideals that have no relationship to our daily lives. The consequences are economic and material, and they affect everyone in the community whether we know it or not. We are to be not only individuals who value life but also communities that protect lives, no matter who they are. We are communities who are responsible for what happens within our borders as well as for the borders themselves. The lesson: Keep the roads and the territory of your community safe!

CHAPTER 12

CRIME AND CONSEQUENCES

The Death Penalty

All sin is immoral. What should be illegal?

In addition to the form of governance, every nation must decide the content of law and the consequence of breaking law. Each must define what society will consider to be "a crime." So every culture has two value sets, one which its people believe you *ought to* live by and another that you *must* live by or face prosecution if you do not. The law of Moses has these same two distinctions: things you should or should not do and things you will be prosecuted for doing or not doing.

Our lack of biblical literacy leads to the impression that all or most of the laws in Scripture are to be upheld by the judicial process. But study does not verify that impression. In fact, out of the hundreds of admonitions in the books of Moses, only fifty or so injunctions have prescribed legal consequences.

In addition to defining which cultural values will be codified as law, justice systems all over the world debate what to do with the convicted. Are the consequences of crime to be punitive, corrective, or restorative? What do we want our penal systems to accomplish? What values do we want them, as institutions, to build on? In the absence of convictions based on Scripture, our prison systems will drift toward the values of the cultures surrounding us.

If God will judge our nations in part by the way we judge others, especially the poor, the foreigner, the oppressed, and the imprisoned, then the consequences we mete out for crime through our judicial systems are of grave concern to every believer. We must be able to give a biblical answer for the values embodied by our punitive system and work for a system based more fully on kingdom values.

WE WILL NOT OUTLAW SIN

We must start with the premise that we will never outlaw sin. If we were to attempt this, everyone would be in jail. Who would be the jailer? God is not idealistic but pragmatic when it comes to the condition of the lost world and the role of the believer in it. We will not perfect our societies, but we can improve them and move toward better justice rather than worse. The justice system faces a dilemma between the rights of the criminal and the rights of the community, both based in Scripture. We, as biblical thinkers, seek institutional tension between the two. We do not seek to choose between the two. Our question is, whose rights are being violated more, and what can we do to restore "right order," or justice?

Sin and rebellion have natural consequences. The natural consequence of any action, good or bad, are God's primary way of dealing with human choices. In other words, some consequences of disobedience or obedience are unavoidable. The blessing or the cursing is not a personal directive from God but the natural outcome of a cause-and-effect material world created by him. For the purposes of a discussion of crime and consequences via the civil court system, it is important for us to remember that, ultimately, God deals with all disobedience and sin. We are not to worry about this comprehensive task as a judicial issue.

THE VALUES BEHIND THE TEMPLATE

No one goes to prison in the books of Moses. Israel did not have any prisons yet. They will appear later in Jewish history. But for the time being, let's say that "prison" is an application of a value. The "death penalty" is an application of a value. But what is the value they seek to uphold? If we find the values behind God's thinking, then we can ask what application would be most appropriate for our nation and age. In this context, "most appropriate" means "upholding for the people of this society the same values as Scripture upholds." This is where the hard work of building the kingdom takes place.

WHAT IS CRIMINAL?

If we ask Moses two questions—"What was considered 'criminal' under the law?" and "What were the legal consequences in the law for this criminal behavior?"—we will get a clear sense of those things God deemed most destructive, leading to the greatest violence and loss of life. In other words, all sin will destroy the sinner, but some sins will destroy the nation or community as a whole and must be curbed by judicial boundaries.

Beginning with Deuteronomy, considered the core book of Mosaic law, I posed our two questions, isolating the prescriptive laws that had obvious mandatory sentences, and then went through the other four books of Moses to see what was repeated or added to the list.

The vast majority of the law addresses how we should choose to live and the blessings we will enjoy as a consequence of choosing that path, leaving us free to make our choice. But some of the laws mandate the community to take direct judicial action. The Jews were free to change these laws, and they did in biblical history, but God is warning them. He tells them in effect that these things have dire consequences within the community and are ignored at their own peril.

We will look at these judicial injunctions in two categories: in this chapter those actions deemed deserving of the death penalty, and in chapter 12 those actions assigned other consequences.

THE DEATH PENALTY

Capital punishment had a long history before Moses and the law. As we saw in Genesis, in dealing with murder God used both the "life sentence" and the "death penalty" with Adam, Cain, and finally a violent human race. He adds "generational exile" in his attempt to rid Jacob and his progeny of violence by removing their political and economic rights in Egypt. God is trying to curb the violence.

"Death sentences" were certainly not new to the nations surrounding Israel either. The Pharaoh of Egypt pronounces death for all Hebrew males at birth as an early form of population control for the working class. In the New Testament, King Herod seeks nearly the same sentence for a generation of two-year-olds in order to make sure he has killed the rumored baby king of the Jews. In these cases, the violence was simply used as a means of maintaining power.

THE HUMAN DILEMMA

The issue of death embodies the essence of the human dilemma. How does God save the human race from themselves while allowing them to live and be free? Eliminating the problem of violence is simple. Destroy the violent. But that same violent human race is the object of God's affection. How can humankind be saved from itself?

In the law, God makes that dilemma ours by making us responsible for governing ourselves. He tells us what should be a crime and what deserves the death penalty. These are not unclear scriptures. What is unclear is what we are to do with these scriptures today. Should we restore the death penalty? Eliminate the death penalty? Add to or subtract from the list of crimes deserving the death penalty? Modify the means of execution? What does a discipled nation look like in relation to crime and consequences? Good questions. Let's see what God gives us in the law.

CAPITAL OFFENSES

Remember what we have already covered in previous chapters. The entire purpose of the law is to build into our understanding the sacredness of all life. This is of dire importance to God because, left to our fallen selves, we almost immediately devolve into a tragic devaluation of human life and unnecessary death.

We can divide those offenses deserving of death in Mosaic law into seven basic categories: promotion of idolatry, premeditated murder, kidnapping, malicious testimony, willful destruction of another's family through adultery, specific destructive sex acts, and rejection of specific authorities. The serious destructiveness of all six of these crimes was observable in the seven tribes surrounding Israel in Canaan. These were not abstract scenarios but observable realities in practice in that day in those cultures.

Deuteronomy picks up this theme early in chapter 7 with the imperative to fully destroy the seven tribes in Canaan that God has named. If Israel does not destroy them, these tribes will turn future generations to their murderous, life-destroying ways. This is pandemic social destruction. They are no longer tribes with bad people, which is true of every tribe. They are tribes that have institutionalized life-destroying values that permeate every person, family, and institution within the system, like Sodom and Gomorrah, where not just a few come to rape the angels, but all the men do. The only mercy possible in this scenario is total destruction. Societies that uphold violence and the devaluing of human life as core cultural values will destroy themselves. The only way to curb this total annihilation is by upholding the values that diminish such thinking in society in general. The severity of a crime is valued by the destructiveness of its proliferation within society.

Therefore God warns clearly of the following categories of crime.

JEWISH IDOLATRY

The first capital offense emphasized in the law is the use of the religious platform as a means of promoting and spreading institutionalized apostasy and violence. In these passages, the law refers specifically to Jews promoting this path to fellow Jews. And it refers specifically to Jews encouraging Jews to follow the religious practices of those nations God has told them to destroy in order to get rid of the same violent practices they are now promoting.

Religious Leaders

Two passages deal with Jewish idolatry and the death penalty. Deuteronomy 13:1–5 and 18:17–20 relate to the prophets using their positions to promote the worship of other gods. Pretending to speak in the name of God, these leaders are openly encouraging the breaking of the covenant they and the people have made with God and each other by drawing the people into the beliefs that have destroyed the nations around them.[1]

Family

Deuteronomy 13:6–11 concerns those in the closest family relationships—brother, son, daughter, loved wife, or most intimate friend— who try to entice one to worship the gods of the peoples around them.

Community

Deuteronomy 13:12–16 exhorts the people to deal with any Jewish town or community that has turned to the worship of other gods from the covenant they have all made with God. The language used here is the language of war, and they are instructed to destroy all the people, cattle, and possessions of the town. Notice this is exactly what they were instructed to do with those who worshiped these gods in the land before them and what God did with Sodom and Gomorrah.

A final passage on idolatry and the death penalty is found in Leviticus 20:1–5. Here the people and the courts are to pursue the prosecution of anyone, Jew or foreigner, who sacrifices a child to the pagan god Molek, a common practice among the seven previous tribes in Canaan.

Due Process and Cases of Idolatry

Deuteronomy 17:2–7 tells the courts how to adjudicate a case of idolatry, requiring the use of thorough investigation, witnesses, and empirical evidence in order to prove guilt. Jewish scholars do not consider this passage an addition to the list of capital crimes, but rather instructions for the courts to deal with crimes of idolatry in the same way they would any other crime.[2] There is nothing mystical here. These are trials for religiously promoting human sacrifice and other practices that will lead to violence and destruction of human life. These practices and the religions that promote them are forbidden.

Notice the weaving of individuals, families, communities, and institutions in these texts. God is essentially saying, "As important as I have made the individual, the family, the community, and the priesthood, if any of these begin to draw you away from me and from the value of life, you must correct it. It is a cancer that will destroy everything in your society as it has in the tribes before you." Can you hear the heart cry of God here?

What Is the Purpose?

As in Genesis, God is clear about why Israel must prosecute these crimes, and his reasons continue to center on the rampant spread of death and violence.

"You must purge the evil from among you" (Deut. 13:5; 17:7). "Then all Israel will hear and be afraid, and no one among you will do such an evil thing again" (Deut. 13:11). God is pleading with the Jewish people to maintain the sacredness of human life above all other values. You cannot do that without a system of governance. You cannot do that without justice in land. You cannot do that without protecting due process. And you cannot do that and tolerate religious practices that grossly devalue human life through violence and human sacrifice.

There must be a tension between the authority of the individual, the authority of the religious institution, and the authority of the community represented by government. If any one authority is free to do as it pleases, all freedom will be destroyed by violence.

These idolatry passages are not written for the ignorant and unenlightened lost. God is shouting to *his people*, "If you would just stop these actions, you could LIVE!" But if they turn from the revelation in the law, if they turn from God, they will become like all other human beings: violent and with little concern for human life, or life in any form. And they do turn away, but that part of the story is for later.[3]

PREMEDITATED OR NEGLIGENT DESTRUCTION OF LIFE

Premeditated Murder

The next capital crime dealt with in Deuteronomy is premeditated murder. Deuteronomy 19 defines premeditated murder as the crime in which someone assaults and willfully seeks to take the life of another for his or her own reasons. "I thought about it. I planned it. I did it." In other words, this was not an accident. "But if out of hate someone lies in wait, assaults and kills a neighbor, and then flees to one of these cities, the killer shall be sent for by the town elders, be brought back from the city, and be handed over to the avenger of blood to die" (Deut. 19:11–12).[4]

Negligent Homicide

A number of passages in Exodus and Numbers deal with negligence that leads to death. In each case, the intent was not murder, but reckless behavior has led to loss of life. The penalty for negligent homicide is capital punishment.

The four passages in Exodus that treat negligent homicide address the use of excessive force to protect one's person and property, the beating of a male or female slave, the injury of bystanders in a fight, and the goring of another by one's wandering bull. In these examples, the value of a victim's life is not altered by social status, gender, the instrument of death, or the victim's criminal intent. Each human life is sacred.

The first of these Exodus passages involves the issue of unnecessary force: "If a thief is caught breaking in at night and is struck a fatal blow, the defender is not guilty of bloodshed; but if it happens after sunrise, the defender is guilty of bloodshed" (Exod. 22:2–3). There is no debate in the law that property owners have the right to defend their possessions. But, while allowance is made for a fatal blow that may have been accidental in darkness, in daylight the property owner is expected to use restraint and not equate the life of the thief with the value of the things being stolen. To take a life in the protection of personal property is vigilante law, and as we have seen before, vigilante law can lead only to escalating violence. This is a capital offense.

"Anyone who beats their male or female slave with a rod must be punished if the slave dies as a direct result" (Exod. 21:20). The life of a slave is no less sacred than the life of anyone else in society. I have not found passages on this type of offense allowing for the ransom of the owner's life. This is a capital offense.

"If people are fighting and hit a pregnant woman and she gives birth prematurely but there is no serious injury, the offender must be fined whatever the woman's husband demands and the court allows. But if there is serious injury, you are to take life for life" (Exod. 21:22–23). As with the life of the slave, the life of the unborn child is sacred. The sovereignty of the individual life and the contribution of this life to the community have been lost. This is a capital offense.

In the case of an owner's bull goring someone to death, the issue of past knowledge becomes important. If there is no knowledge of the bull being dangerous, then the death is treated as an accident. The bull is to be killed and its corpse destroyed. A human life has been lost, and no one should profit. If the owner has past experience and knowledge of the bull being dangerous and has not taken steps to protect the public, then the owner is guilty of negligent homicide. This is a capital offense. However, if the victim's family wishes to be compensated for their loss, the convicted can ransom his life and pay the compensation "of whatever is demanded." It does not matter *whom* the bull gored.

> If a bull gores a man or woman to death, the bull is to be stoned to death, and its meat must not be eaten. But the owner of the bull will not be held responsible. If, however, the bull has had the habit of goring and the owner has been warned but has not kept it penned up and it kills a man or woman, the bull is to be stoned and its owner also is to be put to death. (Exod. 21:28–32)

We will look at the concept of ransom more in the next chapter, but it is important to know that ransom may not be used to redeem anyone who has committed premeditated murder. "No person devoted to destruction may be ransomed; they are to be put to death" (Lev. 27:29).

What Is God's Objective?

Again, we have to ask and remember why God's law advocates such severe consequences. There is only one reason—to stop the escalation of violence and the arbitrary shedding of human blood.

"Show no pity. You must purge from Israel the guilt of shedding innocent blood, so that it may go well with you" (Deut. 19:13).

"Do not pollute the land where you are. Bloodshed pollutes the land, and atonement cannot be made for the land on which blood has been shed, except by the blood of the one who shed it. Do not defile the land where you live and where I dwell, for I, the Lord, dwell among the Israelites" (Num. 35:33–34).[5]

KIDNAPPING

Two passages of Scripture deal with kidnapping. The sentence for kidnapping was the death penalty regardless of whether the crime resulted in the death of the kidnapped.

> If someone is caught kidnapping a fellow Israelite and treating or selling them as a slave, the kidnapper must die. You must purge the evil from among you. (Deut. 24:7)

> Anyone who kidnaps someone is to be put to death, whether the victim has been sold or is still in the kidnapper's possession. (Exod. 21:16)

God is saying that life is more than breathing and surviving. Life is freedom and self-determination. Our God-given sovereignty as individuals means that we each have the right to make choices, determine our own destinies, and live out the consequences of our choices. For someone to steal that right from another is the same as killing him or her. It has the same weight as premeditated murder. This is a capital offense.

MALICIOUS TESTIMONY

Passages in Leviticus and Deuteronomy deal with false testimony, which includes both lying and refusing to testify.

> If a malicious witness takes the stand to accuse someone of a crime, the two people involved in the dispute must stand in the presence of the LORD before the priests and the judges who are in office at the time. The judges must make a thorough investigation, and if the witness proves to be a liar, giving false testimony against a fellow Israelite, then do to the false witness as that witness intended to do to the other party. You must purge the evil from among you. The rest of the people will hear of this and be afraid, and never again will such an evil thing be done among you. Show no pity: life for life, eye for eye, tooth for tooth, hand for hand, foot for foot. (Deut. 19:16–21)

If anyone sins because they do not speak up when they hear a public charge to testify regarding something they have seen or learned about, they will be held responsible. (Lev. 5:1)

When the results of these two types of malicious testimony lead to the death of the accused, the penalty for false testimony is capital punishment—the same penalty the false witness intended for the accused. When it comes to malicious testimony, both aggressive and passive disregard for human life are regarded the same as premeditated murder. The only difference here is that the weapon used is the court system.

You can imagine the words of the aggressive false witness: "But I never touched the guy! I wasn't even there!" True, but you testified that you were there and that you saw this other person do it. And, to spare your own life, or to gain a bribe, or because you didn't like this other person, or because you just felt like it, you lied with the intent of convicting this innocent person, knowing the consequence would be his death. You have sentenced yourself to death with your own value system.

Or the passive false witness might say, "But how could my testimony be malicious? I didn't testify! I refused. I was afraid." Exactly, and in protecting yourself, you condemned an innocent man to death with your silence and you gave a guilty man freedom, endangering other people's lives. In all ways, you understood a life would be taken. You knowingly collaborated in creating a community where fear has imposed a culture of silence and murder can be committed with impunity. Known killers roam safely, and innocent people fear for their lives.

Notice how the law emphasizes the obligation of community members to play their parts in safeguarding justice by speaking up, and speaking up truthfully. It is not enough for the judicial system to be committed to truth. If the individual citizen is not also actively engaged in the deterrence of crime, criminals will rule.

In Mosaic law, a citizen's obligation did not stop at speaking up but included active participation in executing justice: "The hands of the witnesses must be the first in putting that person to death, and then the hands of all the people. You must purge the evil from among you" (Deut. 17:7).

God is not only correcting and developing individuals; he is correcting and developing communities.

DESTRUCTIVE SEXUAL PRACTICES

Of the fourteen forbidden sexual practices listed in the prescriptive laws of Moses, about half were to be enforced by capital punishment. The remaining were not given judicial sanctions at all but left to community or consequential action. Here is the list that prescribed capital punishment: a man having sex with his mother or stepmother, his daughter-in-law, both a woman and her daughter, a man with a man, an animal, and consensual sex with or rape of another man's wife, before or after her marriage.

In order to grasp God's heart cry with these laws, we must keep in mind what God has been showing us since Genesis 3. Both before and after the flood our understanding of the sacredness of life degenerated rapidly into violence and the total devaluation of human life. Murder and genocide quickly became the norm.

Murder anywhere in the world has a very short list of motives, including property, vendetta, and crimes of passion or jealousy. If there is no monetary gain or history of aggravation found in a murder investigation, the police will focus in on close relationships, love interests, and sexual conduct. When we are slighted in matters of the heart, we are prone to kill. And no matters of the heart are more explosive than those having to do with our core family.

Look again at the list of destructive sexual sins with this in mind. God is trying to stop the violence. The rippling effects of these violations of love and trust will poison families for generations. Nowhere is this more graphically shown in Scripture than in the passages dealing with jealousy.

Deuteronomy 22:13–21 and Numbers 5:11–31 give us detailed accounts of due process in the case of alleged infidelities, suggesting to us that jealousy and betrayal will otherwise simmer into domestic violence, which will spill over into community violence. In Mosaic law, violations of love and trust are resolved and dealt with judiciously to decrease the violence.

Of course, all these laws will be challenged, changed, and ignored in biblical history. David commits adultery. David's son Amnon rapes his half-sister Tamar and then refuses to marry her, all without impunity. The simmering anger of this injustice builds in Tamar's brother

Absalom's chest until he strikes out and murders Amnon. This, also not dealt with, leads to Absalom's takeover coup of David's throne and Absalom having sex with David's concubines in public as revenge (2 Sam. 13–16). And the violence continues to compound. God's point is perfectly exemplified in biblical history.

There are two sex crimes on the list that fall outside this family dynamic: sex with animals and sex between men, both of which call for the death penalty. Again this makes no sense outside the context of what God is wrestling with. Sin is not sin because it is sin. God does not arbitrarily forbid behavior. If God says not to do something, it is because that behavior destroys our lives and ultimately the life of the community. If God gives the severest of penalties for doing something, it is because that behavior is more lethal than all the others. It is a small, imperceptible black dot of melanoma appearing in the community.

There is no such thing as "sex without consequences," and God is giving us fair warning. We only have to study the findings of virologists on the number of diseases that have been transferred to humanity from the animal kingdom. We can add to that the cumulative tragedies of venereal disease, incest, abuse of children, and rape—not only damaged minds but lost lives. The number of AIDS deaths alone surpasses already the total deaths from World War I and World War II. The idea of "sex without consequences" has perhaps taken the lives of more human beings than all wars combined. From God's perspective, this is violence.

I think it is worth noting two things here. One is the consistent emphasis on the responsibility of the men in these sexual laws (Deut. 22:18–29). It's not that the women involved are excused of any wrongdoing, but the laws are all directed at the male participant. And second, we must note the consistent emphasis on women and children as the abused.[6]

We will look at the sexual issues that do not require the death penalty in the next chapter.

ANARCHY AND REJECTION OF AUTHORITY

The foundations of kingdom thinking place great emphasis on the freedom and importance of the individual, so what are we to make of the scriptures that prescribe capital punishment for the rejection of institutional authority? The law includes strong exhortations to deal with those in the community who reject and rebel against the authority of parents, priests, and judicial leaders.

It is easy to isolate these passages and conclude that God wants us to obey authority absolutely, whether in the family, the church, or the government. That misguided conclusion is only one step shy of seeing these institutions as gods in our life, an understanding that would make nonsense out of the authority and importance of the individual and the limits to authority, placed by God, on each of these very institutions.

So where does that leave us?

We are left with the dilemma of human freedom. In a fallen world, unrestrained freedom will lead to some form of anarchy. As we have seen in human history, unrestrained anarchy will produce the greatest violence and loss of human life. The second greatest violence against humanity will come from the tyranny of unrestrained institutional authority. Therefore, in a fallen world, the best we can achieve is a tension of powers, a system of checks and balances among competing authorities and rights—"proper order."

This then is the most important task of civil governance: ensuring a proper tension between the rights and responsibilities of the individual and those of God's appointed social institutions. Law draws the line between the tyranny of the one and the tyranny of the many, between the individual and the community, whether represented by family, religion, or government.

The lines drawn by law must be very carefully placed. Draw the line too far one way, and you will destroy the nation with individual anarchy. Draw it too far in the other direction, and you will destroy the nation with institutional tyranny.

Scripture makes it clear that individuals can go too far in their freedom. When they do, the community must take action.

Priestly Authority

In the book of Numbers we are reminded that only the Levites may approach and do the work of the tabernacle. "Whenever the tabernacle is to move, the Levites are to take it down, and whenever the tabernacle is to be set up, the Levites shall do it. Anyone else who approaches it is to be put to death" (Num. 1:51; see also 3:10; 3:38; 18:5). God has chosen who will serve him in this capacity, and that choice must be respected. The individual does not have to believe, but he or she does have to respect the right of others to believe and order their belief.

Most or all of us are familiar with Jewish laws regarding work on the Sabbath. "Observe the Sabbath, because it is holy to you. Anyone who desecrates it is to be put to death; those who do any work on that day must be cut off from their people. For six days work is to be done, but the seventh day is a day of sabbath rest, holy to the Lord. Whoever does any work on the Sabbath day is to be put to death" (Exod. 31:14–15). The context of this passage is the building of the tabernacle. Jewish scholars indicate that this mandate may pertain to the work of building the tabernacle on the Sabbath rather than to work on all Sabbaths.[7]

The law also includes a very specific law pertaining to cursing God in the assembly of believers, using God's most holy of names[8]: "Say to the Israelites: 'Anyone who curses their God will be held responsible; anyone who blasphemes the name of the Lord is to be put to death. The entire assembly must stone them. Whether foreigner or native-born, when they blaspheme the Name they are to be put to death'" (Lev. 24:15–16).

A final passage can be understood only within the context of the reality of the unseen world of the dead and the fallen angels. "A man or woman who is a medium or spiritist among you must be put to death. You are to stone them; their blood will be on their own heads" (Lev. 20:27). Hebrew "tradition admits that this method of gaining knowledge of the occult is effective but places it strictly off-limits for Israelites."[9] The providers were to be executed, but the consumers shunned. Nothing blurs human responsibility more than allowing powers from the unseen world to access our daily lives. Anyone who has ever lived in cultures where this is common practice knows the death and violence that regularly results. Opening this doorway allows for increased violence and decreased understanding of human value while producing in the community a mindset of victimization.

Judicial Authority

One passage in the prescriptive law prescribes the death penalty for those who disregard judicial authority. The context is that of appeal to the priesthood, the final and highest appeal possible. This appeal was used when all other appeals through the court system had failed in a finding or the courts were failing themselves, most often in cases where there were no witnesses and inadequate evidence. But it was also used when the people were failing to respect the authority of the court system.

> If cases come before your courts that are too difficult for you to judge—whether bloodshed, lawsuits or assaults—take them to the place the LORD your God will choose. Go to the Levitical priests and to the judge who is in office at that time. Inquire of them and they will give you the verdict. You must act according to the decisions they give you at the place the LORD will choose. Be careful to do everything they instruct you to do. Act according to whatever they teach you and the decisions they give you. Do not turn aside from what they tell you, to the right or to the left. Anyone who shows contempt for the judge or for the priest who stands ministering there to the LORD your God is to be put to death. You must purge the evil from Israel. All the people will hear and be afraid, and will not be contemptuous again. (Deut. 17:8–13)

Showing contempt for the courts in this final appeal would deny the authority of due process, resulting in vigilante law and causing the community to spiral into violence and chaos. This cannot be allowed; it is a capital crime.

Parental Authority

Neither mainstream evangelical nor Jewish scholars hold these passages on parental authority to be strict legal pronouncements, but rather as strong exhortations to beware. For the Jews, parental authority was the cornerstone of social "order" (think justice) and all authority. In these passages, they saw God warning of "severe danger to society."[10]

> If someone has a stubborn and rebellious son who does not obey his father and mother and will not listen to them when they discipline him, his father and mother shall take hold of him and bring him to the elders at the gate of his town. They

shall say to the elders, "This son of ours is stubborn and rebellious. He will not obey us. He is a glutton and a drunkard." Then all the men of his town are to stone him to death. You must purge the evil from among you. All Israel will hear of it and be afraid. (Deut. 21:18–21)

Anyone who curses their father or mother is to be put to death. Because they have cursed their father or mother, their blood will be on their own head. (Lev. 20:9)

I think we would be closer to the mark to compare these scriptures to what we today would call sociopathy or antisocial personality disorder, defined in one source as a "condition in which a person's ways of thinking, perceiving situations and relating to others are dysfunctional—and destructive. People with antisocial personality disorder typically have no regard for right and wrong and often disregard the rights, wishes and feelings of others. [They] tend to antagonize, manipulate or treat others either harshly or with callous indifference. They may often violate the law . . . yet they show no guilt or remorse. They may lie, behave violently or impulsively, and have problems with drug and alcohol use."[11] Sociopaths, according to some sources, make up as much as 25 percent of a prison population.

The passage in Deuteronomy 21 emphasizes the responsibility of the parents to raise the alarm for the community and take the first legal action to curb their child's behavior. Also notice the community's responsibility to take action in supporting the legal finding. There are no passive observers here. There is a heavy emphasis here again on the destructiveness to the community from the destroyed family unit, and this is made all the more relevant given the mass of current statistics on the adverse effects of fatherless homes on individuals and society.

So what do we see in the way God uses the death penalty in the law of Moses? He does not use it for all sins. Therefore there is a logic to those things God deems necessary. What is he trying to tell us—that all sin ends in death, so the consequence for all sin should be the death penalty? No, we cannot outlaw sin. There would be no one to sit in judgment. However, we must put limits on human freedom or we will destroy ourselves. And so what is the value that God uses to decide what ought to receive the highest possible consequence? The actions that most directly lead to the highest level of violence, loss of life, and the loss of the value of life. As with the flood, God is trying to help us preserve life. The human dilemma stares us in the face again. How do we preserve freedom and sustain life simultaneously?

What all of the capital offenses in the law have in common is they directly or indirectly destroy life. God is not punishing the individual; he is correcting and warning the community: "If you do not address this, you will destroy yourselves."

It must not go unnoticed that God begins by dealing with his religious leaders who lead the people away from the life-giving thinking of God. He then turns to the believers themselves and deals with their own idolatry or thinking that is contrary to the teachings of God in the Law, undermining God's message altogether. God then deals with those individuals who actually kill, murder, kidnap, or lie with the intent of killing. And finally God addresses those who reject any, if not all, authority to put restraints on their freedoms, whether religious, judicial, or parental.

God is not saying any of these institutions are perfect in themselves. How their authority is used in our societies must always be up for question and correction. He is saying that the basic value of having some official limits to freedom in human society is essential if we are to survive as a human race . . . faulty as the limits may be.

Next we will look at those crimes with prescribed consequences other than the death penalty.

CHAPTER 13

CRIME AND CONSEQUENCES

Restitution, Fines, Retribution, and Lifetime Liability

O utside of capital offenses, all other crimes in Scripture are resolved with restitution, fines, retribution, or liability. The prescriptive law builds on the fundamentals of repayment and compensation with minimal use of punitive measures. We can divide the prescriptive passages dealing with non-capital offenses into five categories of crimes: destructive sexual conduct, bodily harm, property damage, theft, and malicious testimony. We can see that many of the categories match capital offenses, so why are the consequences different? Let's see what Moses gives us.

DESTRUCTIVE SEXUAL CONDUCT

Deuteronomy 22:13–19 prescribes due process for cases in which a wife has been accused of lying about her sexual status at marriage and the husband is seeking to get out of the marriage. *The Jewish Study Bible* points out that the husband may be trying to get out of the marriage without financial liability.[1] If proof is provided that he is lying about her conduct and has slandered the woman, he is to be punished (possibly flogged), fined one hundred shekels of silver (twice the fine for rape), and prevented from ever divorcing the woman, meaning he has lifetime financial responsibility for her.

What are we to make of these strong consequences? The consequences of this man's false accusations would have been far-reaching. The reputation of the woman's family would have been destroyed in the community, affecting every other endeavor they undertook requiring the trustworthiness of their word. If the false accusation were not discovered, the young woman could be prosecuted for adultery, which carried the death penalty. Normally the punishment for a false accusation resulting in death would be the death penalty for the false accuser. But in this culture, no one would marry an accused woman regardless of guilt, and so she would be left with no means to support herself. Therefore, rather than facing the death penalty as a malicious witness, the accusing husband must provide lifetime support by maintaining the marriage and its financial commitments.

Far from being condemned to a loveless marriage, the woman in this situation is being protected. These consequences safeguard her life by ensuring her lifelong right to financial means, security, and protection. The husband is responsible for fulfilling that commitment regardless of his like or dislike of the woman. He has made a lifetime commitment to her.

> If a man takes a wife and, after sleeping with her, dislikes her and slanders her and gives her a bad name, saying, "I married this woman, but when I approached her, I did not find proof of her virginity," then the young woman's father and mother shall bring to the town elders at the gate proof that she was a virgin. Her father will say to the elders, "I gave my daughter in marriage to this man, but he dislikes her. Now he has slandered her and said, 'I did not find your daughter to be a virgin.' But here is the proof of my daughter's virginity." Then her parents shall display the cloth before the elders of the town, and the elders shall take the man and punish him. They shall fine him a hundred shekels of silver and give them to the young woman's father, because this man has given an Israelite virgin a bad name. She

shall continue to be his wife; he must not divorce her as long as he lives. (Deut. 22:13–19)

Deuteronomy 22 also deals with cases of rape, which may have included consensual sex outside marriage, when the woman was not "pledged" to be married. The engagement of the couple was the legal part of Hebrew courtship, and the marriage was when that commitment was consummated. In cases where the woman is not pledged to another, the man is fined fifty shekels of silver, which is paid to the family (this would have been in addition to the negotiated bride price[2]), and he must marry her. If they are in love, this is not much of a problem and is a fairly light sentence, since both could have faced the death penalty if the woman had been engaged. However, the courts are not dealing with the couple's feelings for or against each other. The judicial process described in Deuteronomy 22:28–29 ensures that the woman is not left without a future and without financial support by holding the man responsible for life: "If a man happens to meet a virgin who is not pledged to be married and rapes her and they are discovered, he shall pay her father fifty shekels of silver. He must marry the young woman, for he has violated her. He can never divorce her as long as he lives." The value is that her life is not to be put in danger. He is to make lifelong compensation.

Apart from those sexual crimes assigned the death penalty, as discussed in chapter 12, the remaining situations involving irresponsible sexual behavior do not have judicial consequences. The five highlighted all involve immediate family members and are dealt with outside the judicial process: marrying a sister or stepsister, marrying your mother's or father's sister, having sex with an aunt by marriage, marrying your brother's wife, and having sex during a woman's period.

The consequences of each of these sexual sins were what the Jews called *kareth,* from the Hebrew verb *karat,* "to cut off." This punishment could include the ultimate extinction of a family line. In other words, one's family line would ultimately die off. This is not to be seen as excommunication or ostracism but rather as the consequences of the act itself affecting the health of the family line. The Jews would have seen this as a natural consequence of sin.[3]

If a man marries his sister, the daughter of either his father or his mother, and they have sexual relations, it is a disgrace. They are to be publicly removed from their people. He has dishonored his sister and will be held responsible.

If a man has sexual relations with a woman during her monthly period, he has exposed the source of her flow, and she has also uncovered it. Both of them are to be cut off from their people.

Do not have sexual relations with the sister of either your mother or your father, for that would dishonor a close relative; both of you would be held responsible.

If a man has sexual relations with his aunt, he has dishonored his uncle. They will be held responsible; they will die childless.

If a man marries his brother's wife, it is an act of impurity; he has dishonored his brother. They will be childless. (Lev. 20:17–21)

All sexual sins in the law of Moses have consequences, but they do not all have legal or judicial consequences.

One final passage can only be described as bizarre at first glance, standing out in contrast to all other categories of crimes and punishments: "If two men are fighting and the wife of one of them comes to rescue her husband from his assailant, and she reaches out and seizes him by his private parts, you shall cut off her hand. Show her no pity" (Deut. 25:11–12).

This text is easily misused. The consequences certainly seem to be beyond the spirit of an eye for an eye. Take a moment to imagine the context of this altercation: First, the action of the woman would have to have been specifically premeditated. Men wore loose clothing, and often long gowns; thus it would have been difficult, if not impossible, to grab a man's genitals by accident. Second, the woman's intent could only have been to damage, if not destroy, her victim's chance of future progeny, perceived by Hebrew culture as the greatest blessing anyone could have. In effect, the woman in this law is trying to destroy a man's entire future inheritance and family line for the much smaller offense of possibly causing her husband some bodily harm. With that in mind, the woman's crime is severe, she is trying to destroy future potential for creating life, and her punishment no longer seems to be as extreme. One has to at least consider that it was not a literal judicial punishment but a strong emotional plea for the sacredness of family and a future of children.

BODILY HARM

Exodus 21 gives us a list of five situations in which bodily harm results from fighting, beating, or injury from a domestic animal. Each case gives us a finding of liability and responsibilities based on benefit and loss.

Verses 18 and 22 describe injuries sustained during a fight. In the first case, two people are quarreling and one is injured but not killed: "If people quarrel and one person hits another with a stone or with their fist and the victim does not die but is confined to bed, the one who struck the blow will not be held liable if the other can get up and walk around outside with a staff; however, the guilty party must pay the injured person for any loss of time and see that the victim is completely healed" (Exod. 21:18–19).

In this situation, the injurer is liable for the injured's loss of income during recuperation and for medical costs until the injured is fully healed. We cannot support the sacredness of life without supporting the necessity of work and income to sustain it. The reality of the material world means that a realistic cost can be charged to irresponsible behavior. There are no punitive damages in this case, presumably because both parties were fighting.

The second scenario involves the injury of an innocent bystander; in this case a pregnant woman: "If people are fighting and hit a pregnant woman and she gives birth prematurely but there is no serious injury, the offender must be fined whatever the woman's husband demands and the court allows. But if there is serious injury, you are to take life for life, eye for eye, tooth for tooth, hand for hand, foot for foot, burn for burn, wound for wound, bruise for bruise" (Exod. 21:22–25).

This text is, perhaps intentionally, ambiguous about who is being injured, the mother or the child. The value upheld is clear, however. No distinction is to be made between the sacredness of the mother's life and the child's life. The damages in this case are punitive, presumably because the violence extended to the innocent bystander. And the punitive damages are to be at the discretion of the husband and the court—in other words, the amount required to restore community harmony.

The cases in verses 20 and 26 both relate to the bodily injury of a slave:

> Anyone who beats their male or female slave with a rod must be punished if the slave dies as a direct result, but they are not to be punished if the slave recovers after a day or two, since the slave is their property. . . . An owner who hits a male or female slave in the eye and destroys it must let the slave go free to compensate for the eye. And an owner who knocks out the tooth of a male or female slave must let the slave go free to compensate for the tooth. (Exod. 21:20–21, 26–27)

Slavery was universal in the world surrounding Israel. Outside of Israel, it was unheard of to consider the rights of slaves. Slavery came in two forms, that of chattel, or personal property, and that of indentured slavery. Indentured slavery acknowledged the value of a person's time and work as an asset to be used in the settling of a debt. Individuals could indenture themselves to work for a set period of time to offset monies owed. The limit for indentured servitude in Israel was seven years. Both kinds of slavery existed in historical Israel, but the law sanctioned only indentured slavery.

In these two cases, owners of a slave's debt lose their entire remaining investment if they cause permanent bodily harm. There are no punitive damages for the recovery time from an injury because the lost time is a loss to the owner. But the value statement is clear! No distinction is made between the worth of male and female slaves nor between the worth of slaves and free people. The law is blind to status and aware only of the sacredness of the life.

The final case of bodily harm involves injury caused by livestock. There was to be no benefit to anyone if an animal caused the death of a person. The animal was to be destroyed and not eaten. There were no punitive damages. In cases of unintentional homicide, if the family or owner preferred, ransom could be paid to spare the life of the owner.

The victim set the ransom and, we may assume, it was approved by the court. As in the case of the "rogue bull" in Exodus 21, the owner could redeem his life by paying what the family demanded.

In the case of unintentional or accidental death the accused was also to flee to the city of refuge and there were two possibilities in restoring order to the community. One was for the accused, now vindicated, to stay living in the city of refuge until the death of the high priest. This was meant to avoid vigilante justice in the home and community. And it presumably was the only way to assure protection of the innocent from community violence and the community from itself. The second was for the harmed party to accept ransom for the death, acknowledging that the wrong to them had been made right.

"Anyone who strikes a person with a fatal blow is to be put to death. However, if it is not done intentionally, but God lets it happen, they are to flee to a place I will designate" (Exod. 21:12–13).

In this final passage, the issue is the death of the slave by goring and the liability of the irresponsible owner. In this case the ransom is set at thirty shekels of silver by the slave's owner or, presumably, the maximum loss possible. That is, if the owner is willing to accept ransom. Capital punishment has already been established otherwise in previous texts.

"If the bull gores a male or female slave, the owner must pay thirty shekels of silver to the master of the slave, and the bull is to be stoned to death" (Exod. 21:32).

PROPERTY DAMAGE

The book of Exodus moves from prescriptive laws dealing with bodily harm to the subject of property damage. Four of the passages in chapters 21 and 22 deal with livestock, one with damaged crops, and a final with miscellaneous personal property.

Apart from land, livestock would have been the most valuable asset owned by the Hebrew public. Not only was there the intrinsic cost of the animal but also the value of its labor and reproductive potential. Damage or destruction of this property meant a major loss of income and livelihood and, therefore, could not be ignored if the value of human life was to be upheld.

The four cases dealing with livestock cover irresponsible land use, cattle injuring cattle, livestock injured while in another's possession, and livestock injured while being borrowed or rented by another. In each case, the liability is based on foreknowledge, responsibility, benefit, and the exact measurable value of the animal.

In the first case, someone has created an unsafe environment, and an animal is killed: "If anyone uncovers a pit or digs one and fails to cover it and an ox or a donkey falls into it, the one who opened the pit must pay the owner for the loss and take the dead animal in exchange" (Exod. 21:33–34). The one who has created the danger gets to keep the dead animal, which has some value, but must pay the cost of repurchase. There was unintentional negligence.

The second case involves one person's livestock killing another's: "If anyone's bull injures someone else's bull and it dies, the two parties are to sell the live one and divide both the money and the dead animal equally. However, if it was known that the bull had the habit of goring, yet the owner did not keep it penned up, the owner must pay, animal for animal, and take the dead animal in exchange" (Exod. 21:35–36). In this scenario, liability is based on foreknowledge. If the damaging owner had no previous experience of this animal being violent, then liability is a straight dividing of assets. They each take half the dead carcass and sell the living animal and split the money. There was no negligence.

A third case gives instructions for handling a situation in which something happens to an animal that has been left with someone for safekeeping. In this case, the caregiver swears before God that he has done nothing to the animal, which for a Hebrew would have been inviting God's punishment were he lying. That would settle the matter. However, if there was evidence, then the evidence would determine damages in keeping with the law.

> If anyone gives a donkey, an ox, a sheep or any other animal to their neighbor for safekeeping and it dies or is injured or is taken away while no one is looking, the issue between them will be settled by the taking of an oath before the LORD that the neighbor did not lay hands on the other person's property. The owner is to accept this, and no restitution is required. But

if the animal was stolen from the neighbor, restitution must be made to the owner. If it was torn to pieces by a wild animal, the neighbor shall bring in the remains as evidence and shall not be required to pay for the torn animal. (Exod. 22:10–13)

In the fourth livestock case, an animal that has been hired or borrowed is damaged or killed: "If anyone borrows an animal from their neighbor and it is injured or dies while the owner is not present, they must make restitution. But if the owner is with the animal, the borrower will not have to pay. If the animal was hired, the money paid for the hire covers the loss" (Exod. 22:14–15). In this scenario, the liability and damages depended on the presence of and the benefit to the owner. If the owner was present when the damage to a borrowed animal took place, he could have stopped it, unless the damage was accidental. So there is no liability to the borrower. If the owner was not present, then the borrower must replace the animal. If the animal was hired, the liability is split. The owner keeps the fee but loses the animal, and the hirer loses the productiveness of the animal, which he has already paid for.

In addition to the value of livestock, the law protects the value of crops, also vital to the Hebrew public. When crops have been damaged because of someone's negligent behavior, that person is liable. Damages are set at the value of the lost crops: "If a fire breaks out and spreads into thornbushes so that it burns shocks of grain or standing grain or the whole field, the one who started the fire must make restitution" (Exod. 22:6).

Finally, where small valuables have been left for safekeeping with someone and have gone missing, normal due process is to be followed if theft is suspected. If there is no evidence of misconduct, there is no liability. "If anyone gives a neighbor silver or goods for safekeeping and they are stolen from the neighbor's house, the thief, if caught, must pay back double. But if the thief is not found, the owner of the house must appear before the judges, and they must determine whether the owner of the house has laid hands on the other person's property" (Exod. 22:7–8).

And here the subject changes to theft.

THEFT

The eighth commandment—"You shall not steal" (Exod. 20:15)—lays the foundation for ownership, and ownership establishes the right to material possessions. In the Bible then, theft occurs when someone takes something from another that he or she has no right to take. All stealing is sin, but what stealing will we make illegal? This is the question every court system must answer, and the answer will reveal a portion of a society's values.

In cases of theft, the prescriptive law establishes punitive damages. Material property damages were double, and for livestock it is the value times two, four, or five depending on the livestock. Based on the overall teaching of the law, we can assume that the different values for livestock took into account future profits through work and reproduction. In other words, a thief stole from an owner both the animal and its future potential (Exod. 22:1, 7–9).

In Leviticus 6 it would seem that if the one who cheated or stole realized his guilt and "turned himself in" so to speak, his damages were the value plus one-fifth the value. It would seem he was a break. Nevertheless, the breach of trust within the community must be addressed.

> The LORD said to Moses: "If anyone sins and is unfaithful to the LORD by deceiving a neighbor about something entrusted to them or left in their care or about something stolen, or if they cheat their neighbor, or if they find lost property and lie about it, or if they swear falsely about any such sin that people may commit—when they sin in any of these ways and realize their guilt, they must return what they have stolen or taken by extortion, or what was entrusted to them, or the lost property they found, or whatever it was they swore falsely about. They must make restitution in full, add a fifth of the value to it and give it all to the owner on the day they present their guilt offering. (Lev. 6:1–5)

The law also settles disputed ownership, calling for both claimants to come before the judges: "In all cases of illegal possession of an ox, a donkey, a sheep, a garment, or any other lost property about which somebody says, 'This is mine,' both parties are to bring their cases before the judges. The one whom the judges declare guilty must pay back double to the other" (Exod. 22:9)

If stolen livestock are irretrievable, the convicted must pay the pre-assigned amount based on the type stock. "Whoever steals an ox or a sheep and slaughters it or sells it must pay back five head of cattle for the ox and four sheep for the sheep" (Exod. 22:1). If the stolen animal is found alive, the punitive liability is double the value of the stock. "If the stolen animal is found alive in their possession—whether ox or donkey or sheep—they must pay back double" (Exod. 22:4).

Thieves unable to pay restitution and damages are to work as inden-tured servants in order to pay their debt, whatever it is. "Anyone who steals must certainly make restitution, but if they have nothing, they must be sold to pay for their theft" (Exod. 22:3).

The law also considers it theft for owners to allow their stock to feed in a neighbor's field. Because the offense may be accidental, the liability is straight restitution. "If anyone grazes their livestock in a field or vineyard and lets them stray and they graze in someone else's field, the offender must make restitution from the best of their own field or vineyard" (Exod. 22:5). There are no punitive damages with the excep-tion that the best of the offender's field might be better than what the stock has wrongly eaten in the neighbor's field.

Finally, the prescriptive law discusses cases of theft in which the rightful owner of stolen property is dead. In that situation, inheritance laws apply, and the damages are to be paid to the closest relative, as ownership would have passed to that person. If there is no close rela-tive, damages are still owed by the guilty and are to be given to the temple as an offering. There are to be no unsettled damages when guilt has been assigned.

> The LORD said to Moses, "Say to the Israelites: 'Any man or woman who wrongs another in any way and so is unfaithful to the LORD is guilty and must confess the sin they have commit-ted. They must make full restitution for the wrong they have done, add a fifth of the value to it and give it all to the person they have wronged. But if that person has no close relative to whom restitution can be made for the wrong, the restitution belongs

to the LORD and must be given to the priest, along with the ram
with which atonement is made for the wrongdoer. (Num. 5:5–8)

MALICIOUS TESTIMONY

As we saw in the last chapter, retribution is used for all cases of false
testimony. In capital cases, in which the condemned would die, the false
witness must die. In other cases, retribution also matched the punishment faced by the accused.

> If a malicious witness takes the stand to accuse someone of a
> crime, the two people involved in the dispute must stand in the
> presence of the LORD before the priests and the judges who are
> in office at the time. The judges must make a thorough investi-
> gation, and if the witness proves to be a liar, giving false testi-
> mony against a fellow Israelite, then do to the false witness as
> that witness intended to do to the other party. You must purge
> the evil from among you. The rest of the people will hear of this
> and be afraid, and never again will such an evil thing be done
> among you. Show no pity: life for life, eye for eye, tooth for
> tooth, hand for hand, foot for foot. (Deut. 19:16–21)

The Hebrew use of "measure for measure" meant that the conduct
of the individual determined his or her fate.

FLOGGING

Just one passage in the law deals with the judicial use of flogging, and
that passage emphasizes limiting it. The punishment was to be administered in the court, and the judge was to be present. The number of lashes
was not to exceed the sentence, and the sentence was not to degrade the
guilty in the eyes of the people. These limits convey caution and reluc-
tance rather than a reliance on physical pain as punitive damages.

> When people have a dispute, they are to take it to court and the
> judges will decide the case, acquitting the innocent and con-
> demning the guilty. If the guilty person deserves to be beaten,

the judge shall make them lie down and have them flogged in his presence with the number of lashes the crime deserves, but the judge must not impose more than forty lashes. If the guilty party is flogged more than that, your fellow Israelite will be degraded in your eyes. (Deut. 25:1–3)

So there we are; that is the sum total of judicial actions actually mandated in the prescriptive law of Moses. What conclusions can we draw from the overview?

CHAPTER 14

MEASURING POLITICAL JUSTICE

How We Treat the Poor

Cursed is anyone who withholds justice from the foreigner, the fatherless or the widow. —Deuteronomy 27:19

The focus of social justice in Scripture, both Old and New Testaments, is the poor. *The Jewish Study Bible* commentary says it this way: "God is the ultimate patron of the powerless."[1] While many will measure the wealth of a nation by the quality of justice delivered to those at the top, God measures a nation's achievements by the quality of justice delivered to those at the bottom. It is assumed in the kingdom of God that the powerful will take care of themselves. Our strategic concern, as God's people, must be for those overlooked in our communities. Our society's true beliefs about the value of life will be revealed by the justice it demands for the least of us. Some will measure success by the well-known GNP—gross national product—but kingdom builders will measure by the other GNP—gross neglect of the poor.

The poor are defined in the law as the widow, the alien, and the orphan. These are people who, in Hebrew culture, lacked social or family protection and were vulnerable to exploitation. Of the fifteen or so prescriptive passages in the law of Moses dealing with the poor and political justice, the foreigner is mentioned eleven times, the widow and the fatherless four times. The significant emphasis on the alien stands out and is completely unique for the times. In Near Eastern cultures of the day, monarchs had sole discretion in the distribution of rights to foreigners residing in their realms. In contrast, the God of the Bible demands equal rights under the law for the foreigner and reminds Israel again and again that they should remember what it was like to be aliens and slaves in Egypt before he delivered them.

Likewise, God warns against overcompensating by showing favoritism to the poor and denying others their rights in court. Justice is "proper order," and proper order is a level playing field in interpreting and delivering justice regardless of the social standing of the defendant.

Only one political right was denied to foreigners. That was the opportunity to be appointed king. God exhorts Israel that when the time comes that they insist on having a king as the nations around them do, they must not appoint anyone from outside the Israelite community. We are to take responsibility for governing ourselves.

The prophets tell us much more about God's opinion of injustice to the poor, and what injustice looks like. Jeremiah makes this powerful declaration:

> "Woe to him who builds his palace by unrighteousness, his upper rooms by injustice, making his own people work for nothing, not paying them for their labor. He says, 'I will build myself a great palace with spacious upper rooms.' So he makes large windows in it, panels it with cedar and decorates it in red. Does it make you a king to have more and more cedar? Did not your father have food and drink? He did what was right and just, so all went well with him. He defended the cause of the poor and needy, and so all went well. Is that not what it means to know me?" declares the LORD. "But your eyes and your heart are set only on dishonest gain, on shedding innocent blood and on oppression and extortion." (Jer. 22:13–17)

God measures our justice systems, then, by what we demand for the least of these in our communities, not by what we demand for ourselves.

SOLOMON'S JUSTICE

In all of the Jewish history recorded in Scripture, God, the author and perfecter of his Word, chooses one illustration of political justice. The story begins in 1 Kings when God appears to Solomon in a dream and asks, "What shall I give you?" Solomon responds:

> "Now, LORD my God, you have made your servant king in place of my father David. But I am only a little child and do not know how to carry out my duties. Your servant is here among the people you have chosen, a great people, too numerous to count or number. So give your servant a discerning heart to govern your people and to distinguish between right and wrong. For who is able to govern this great people of yours?"
>
> The Lord was pleased that Solomon had asked for this. So God said to him, "Since you have asked for this and not for long life or wealth for yourself, nor have asked for the death of your enemies but for discernment in administering justice, I will do what you have asked. I will give you a wise and discerning heart, so that there will never have been anyone like you, nor will there ever be." (1 Kings 3:7–12)

The example of this "discerning heart to govern" follows in 1 Kings 3:16–28. The story is well known if not understood. It is the account of two women in a custody suit over an infant they both claim as their own child. The two women each had a child, and one child has died in the night. Both claim the living child as theirs and call the other mother a liar. It would seem that they have already been through the system of courts and appeals because they now have a Supreme Court appearance before the king.

Two poor and apparently husbandless women had the right to appeal to the king directly in a single child custody case! And what most readers fail to notice or remember is that these two women are prostitutes and yet they still have this right, plus the right to custody of a child.

Do I have to elaborate on why this is so mind blowing? And this is the example that God chooses for us? What are we missing in our understanding of God's definition of political justice and the rights he secures?

The poor of our communities and nations serve as a scale to measure the political justice of our system and help us understand whether God can bless it or not. When we look at each of the areas God emphasizes, we can gain insight by measuring from the poor.

THE FORM OF LAW

God intended that political power be held by the people being governed, empowering the individual—which in most countries of the world means "the poor."

How are we doing at engaging and mobilizing the masses to participate in governance? Is the value of the individual contribution held and celebrated? Do people vote?

In the judiciary the Jews were to have judges representing every ten people in the community. This is a massive effort to engage every level of society in due process and in the judicial process of dealing with disputes. The system was accessible to everyone and everyone had some level of responsibility to make the system work. Nowhere would this have a greater impact than in poor communities.

LAND RIGHTS

Distribution of land in Scripture had nothing to do with might and power. It was based on all the tribes and according to population and vocation. They were never to sell the land, and borders and leases were to be publicly documented and abided by. Who in society would most benefit from this? The poor.

CITIES OF REFUGE

Protection of the individual from the many until due process had been completed was to be provided by the priesthood and was free for all. It was a right, not a privilege. Again, who would most benefit from this protection in society? Those who have no one to protect them.

Due process was justice based on evidence and testimony, not on position and power; on fact, not on fortune. The value of life is sacred no matter whom it belongs to, and the consequences of crime are the same no matter who the victim is. Unsolved murders were a community responsibility no matter who was murdered. The gravity of the crime was not determined by who committed it or whom it was committed against. The gravity of the crime was based on facts of the act and the value of human life. Sentencing was without discrimination because the law was blind to the status of the lawbreaker.

So how do we measure up? Where are we failing? Where is our system drifting from God's values of political justice? Where have we never had those values? These are the questions God is asking as he evaluates our nation.[2]

Now we turn our attention to the historical law—God revealing his ways through how the Jews obeyed or disobeyed him as they moved in to establish the promised land. We need to take all the values of the law with us from the first five books, for those were the standards by which the actions of the succeeding generations of Jews were measured.

PART III

POLITICAL LESSONS
FROM JEWISH HISTORY

CHAPTER 15

ABRAHAM TO MOSES

The Tribal Beginnings

As it was for the Jews of the Old Testament, so it is important for us to distinguish religion from faith in the God of the Bible. Religion by definition includes a set of dogmas we believe in. Biblical faith is action we take because of what we believe. Belief and action cannot be divided in God's kingdom. Moral judgments are always situational, or applied in real situations; the Bible doesn't give us moral abstractions, or ideas that can be embraced without implication or application. In following God, we cannot just quote the sixth commandment, "You shall not murder," without defining what murder is and working to stop it. We cannot say "You shall not steal" without defining the right to own property and defending private ownership. So the laws of God are not abstract principles; they are principles and values applied in specific situations. The law of the Bible is a living law.

Theology, the study of who God is and how he relates to the world, cannot be understood in theoretical isolation. Biblically, for theology to be known and understood, it must be applied. The God of the Bible does not have the slightest interest in debating how many angels can stand on the head of a pin. The answer, if there is one, has absolutely no application in the real world God has created.

When we say that the Ten Commandments tell us not to murder, and we conclude or assume that this means we cannot be in the army or the police force, or defend our families or ourselves from attack, we have misunderstood. These conclusions are diametrically opposed to what the Bible teaches about military service and the right of protection. These conclusions draw on a very limited definition of death by violence, eliminating the broader biblical discussion of death by starvation because of greed, by poor building practices because of a lack of concern, by bad sanitation and health practices in the production of food, by lack of medical care, and so on. If we are to understand the law, we must understand the historical application of it in Israel through the lives of the kings and the message of the prophets.

The vast majority of the Old Testament focuses on political leadership. From Genesis to the Song of Solomon, fifteen of the twenty-two books primarily tell the story of what was happening in Israel in the political realm. In the prescriptive laws, God tells us what he wants from political leaders and the people. In the historical events, God tells us what the leaders and people of Israel did. The prophets add the consequences of those choices.

As we fly over this vast two-thousand-year landscape of political leadership, we are looking for God's emphasis. What is God telling us? Why does he include these details? What are we to take from this selected history of Israel and bring into our lives and work today? We are looking for the *meaning* of the history God gives us, in the form of eternal values and principles of the kingdom.

ABRAHAM, 2166–1991 BC (GENESIS 11–25)

Abraham is a good man. He builds altars and worships the Most High God. He gives the better land to his selfish nephew Lot when they part. He fights to free Lot from his political enemies and refuses any plunder from the war. He believes God will give him an heir late in life and is willing to offer this same child as a sacrifice if that is what God is asking. At ninety-nine, before he has had his miracle son, Abraham believes God and performs the first rite of circumcision on all the males of his clan, including himself. This patient man rescues his nephew a second time from the violence of Sodom and Gomorrah. He understands

God's heart to bless nations, and he pleads for all the mercy God is able to extend to a villainous people.

And yet this same man lies to two national leaders in order to protect himself and his wealth—the pharaoh of Egypt and King Abimelek of the Philistines. He eventually laughs at God's promise of a child in old age. It is Abraham who gives us the concubine solution, which produces his heir Ishmael, to whom God will also promise the blessing of a great nation through his sons. And these tribes will be at war with their cousins, the tribes of Isaac, all through human history.

As we discussed in chapter 10, the land God promises Abraham comprises most of what Genesis 2 describes as the garden of Eden. The land will never all belong to the heirs of Isaac, but most of it will be inhabited by the descendants of Abraham through Isaac's and Ishmael's sons and later the heirs of Jacob and Esau. Fast-forward to the twentieth century when, in the late 1940s, the king of Jordan is quoted as saying, "Let the Jews come back; they are our cousins and they will bless us."

Abraham dies at 175 years of age.

ISAAC, 2066–1886 BC (GENESIS 17–35)

Isaac is a miracle child born to parents more than one hundred years old. He inherits Abraham's promise from God that his descendants will become a great nation that will bless all the nations of the world. He grows up among the Hittite people from whom his father has bought land. He settles on what would now be the southernmost border of Israel. God miraculously provides a wife for Isaac from his father's people near Harran, in the land of the Amorites. Rebekah is Aramean, and she is told that she will give birth to two nations and that the elder, Esau, will serve the younger, Jacob.

In spite of all this great blessing, Isaac lies, as his father did, to Abimelek, king of the Philistines. He breaks the treaty his father has made with Abimelek and then makes a new one, fearing God is unable to protect him. His beautiful wife proceeds to poison their son Jacob with the need to manipulate and deceive his father in order to get the blessing God had already promised him. On the other hand, Isaac was going to give Esau the blessing God had promised Jacob, in spite of what God had already told them about Jacob's leadership. The descendants of these two great tribes will feud through all of history.

Isaac dies at 180 years of age.

JACOB, 2005–1859 BC (GENESIS 25–49)

Jacob has an impressive beginning. While he is still in his mother's womb, God chooses him to lead his tribe, and later, Jacob gets a double blessing from his father, Isaac. On Jacob's way to his mother's family in Harran, God sends him angels in a dream and appears himself in the dream to promise that Jacob's descendants will multiply greatly and that through them God will bless all the peoples of the earth. Jacob works very hard for fourteen years to obtain his uncle Laban's daughters in marriage, and God blesses both Leah and Rachel with children. Jacob's own business prospers as does the uncle he serves. When Jacob returns to Canaan with his family, God sends an angel for a second time to wrestle with and bless him. Jacob is crippled in the encounter, but he is also changed and God gives him the name Israel. He reunites with Esau on his return and buys land from the Philistines in Shechem and settles there.

As blessed and called of God as Jacob is, many areas of his life are a disaster. He lies to his father and steals his brother's birthright and blessing. His wife Rachel lies to her father and steals his idols, hiding them and taking them to Canaan. Leah and Rachel fight constantly, and his sons are a mess. They are jealous, selfish, treacherous, and violent. They plot to murder their little brother Joseph but decide selling him would be more profitable. They lie to the Shechemites and then commit genocide of the male population in order to build their own wealth. Jacob astutely understands this will turn all the tribes in Canaan against them and flees to Bethel, the place where God first spoke to him.

Jacob dies at 147 years of age.

JOSEPH, 1914–1805 BC (GENESIS 37–50)

God singles out Joseph early on to lead his people. Joseph is adored by his father as the son of his first love, Rachel. He is a diligent and honest worker. Although sold by his brothers into slavery, he keeps his trust in God, and God exalts him in his work. He is honorable when solicited by his boss's wife but is thrown in prison anyway. He keeps serving God and is blessed again in his work in prison. Because of his relationship with God and the blessing of fellow prisoners through his care and wisdom, he is singled out by Pharaoh to interpret a dream. Not only does God tell him the dream and the meaning, but Joseph is successful in saving the lives of all the pagan magicians. Pharaoh makes him second in state and puts him over all his affairs, including disaster relief.

Joseph is used by God to save the nations of Egypt and Israel from financial ruin and starvation. Because of Joseph, his people are protected and blessed in Egypt for more than one hundred years. His two sons are given equal status with his brothers and are founders of two of Israel's twelve tribal nations, Manasseh and Ephraim.

Joseph does not lie, cheat, steal, or dishonor others until his brothers come to Egypt for financial help. Joseph becomes unrecognizable with displays of emotion that alert the whole palace. He manipulates to get his brothers and father back to Egypt. He has no idea that the fruit of his actions will result in more than four hundred years of slavery. Though innocent, Joseph is a convicted sex offender who has spent thirteen years in prison. And he nearly rejects God's chosen leader in Ephraim, his younger son, preferring his elder son, Manasseh.

Joseph dies at 110 years of age.

MOSES, 1526–1406 BC (EXODUS 2–DEUTERONOMY 34)

Toward the end of Israel's slavery in Egypt, God miraculously spares Moses from the genocide of his generation and raises him up as political liberator and leader. Pharaoh's daughter rescues him from a basket in the Nile and raises him in Pharaoh's palace. Moses is a natural leader. He brings all of Israel, along with other slaves, out of Egypt to freedom with no army or formal government to back him. He receives the law from God and builds the foundations for discipling nations. He forms Israel's first government and priesthood. He builds the tabernacle. He sees God face to face and performs dramatic miracles that provide food and water for more than three million refugees in the wilderness. Beginning at eighty years of age, he leads his people for forty years in the wilderness with no outside support system. And in Matthew 5, Jesus says that Moses laid the foundation for his message.

Before he accomplishes all this, Moses commits murder, flees to political asylum, and marries a Midianite whose father is a pagan priest. Moses nearly dies because he has failed to circumcise his sons. His step-brother Pharaoh and the elders of Israel reject him as the leader for years. The plagues will destroy millions of lives, and billions in property value will be devastated in Egypt under his leadership. He fears failure, and he fears public speaking. Later, when he sees Israel build the golden calf under his brother Aaron's leadership, he responds in such anger and frustration, taking credit for a miracle God performed, that God forbids him to enter the promised land.

Moses dies at 120 years of age.

As we finish this overview of Israel's political history from Abraham to Moses, what stands out?

- Each of these leaders was chosen and called, and they each showed personal commitment and accomplished great feats of faith. But they all had formidable faults and made grave errors as well. They all had major family issues and family patterns which were destructive and generational.

- While history has judged them well and God clearly used each of them in important ways, they all brought very difficult times upon their people. They all had skeletons in the closet. Is it possible they would all have a hard time being elected to office today? And yet God chose and used each of them at this point in the development of the nation.

- Have we developed a romanticized concept of leadership that makes us vulnerable to deception? Are we looking for that knight in shining armor who will ride in and take our nation to perfection? Is it possible that none of that is God's perspective? That rather God always has an imperfect candidate on the sidelines who is the best possible leader he can find but never a perfect one? That God may actually choose a leader who will take our nation into difficult times? Is it possible that while having a leader in mind, the emphasis of God is not on national leadership at all, but on something else going on in the community?

Let's see what we find as we look at the history of Joshua and the judges.

CHAPTER 16

JOSHUA AND THE JUDGES

With the reading of the law, the renewal of the covenant with God, and the appointment of Joshua, Israel crosses the Jordan River. Moses gave them the law. He interpreted the law for them for nearly forty years. He led them in two decisive military victories. Moses was shown the promised land from Mount Nebo. Now he stays on the wilderness side of the Jordan, and we will never fully know what happened to him. Why this mysterious ending? Surely part of God's intent was to keep Israel from making a god of Moses. Even so, they begin worshiping Moses's shepherd's staff centuries later.

JOSHUA, 1355–1245 BC

Joshua has been at the right hand of Moses from the very beginning of the wilderness journey. He, along with eleven others, is sent to spy out the land of Canaan soon after crossing the Red Sea. Only he and Caleb report that it is a wonderful land. Yes, there are giants there, but the giants will not be able to stand against God. They believe that God will fight for Israel. The other spies view their nation-forming task as impossible and themselves as grasshoppers. While those men do their reconnaissance purely from the human perspective of what they thought they could accomplish on their own, Joshua and Caleb are called men of a different spirit, men after God's own heart.

Now, at eighty years of age, Joshua is still seeking God's perspective and looking to God for strength. He now leads Israel into the promise of God that has been waiting more than eight hundred years for fulfillment.

God gives Israel a second great miracle of liberation by dividing the waters of the Jordan for the people to cross into Canaan. Joshua builds an altar, and although they are in enemy territory, he has all the males circumcised at the word of the Lord. While the sons of Jacob once made the enemy vulnerable by circumcising the Shechemites, God now makes Israel vulnerable to the enemy by circumcising them.

At Jericho, Israel's first military victory in Canaan is won by radical obedience as Joshua obeys God's detailed instructions for circling the city with the army, the ark, and seven priests with trumpets. In Ai, Joshua deals with idolatry. At Mount Ebal, he and the people renew their covenant with the Lord. Joshua defeats the five united kings of the Amorites, and in response to Joshua's prayer, the sun stands still for an entire day. Joshua goes on to lead Israel in conquering the northern and southern kings, for a total of thirty-one defeated kings. All twelve tribes inhabit their lands, although not all of the former resident tribes are gone. Joshua establishes the cities of refuge according to the law, and he divides out the land in each tribe to be given to the Levites. Before he dies, Joshua has all the people, again, renew the covenant with God at Shechem.

Joshua is nearly faultless in his leadership. But even with all his great strengths, it is Joshua who is deceived by one of the Amorite peoples, the Gibeonites, into making a peace treaty contravening the word of the Lord to destroy all the tribes. This peace treaty will be broken by Saul fourteen political generations later, and its consequences will reach into Israel's history under David, who executes seven of Saul's sons in order to placate the Gibeonites for the broken treaty.

Joshua dies at the age of 110.

JUDGES, 1350–1100 BC

The major military challenge of possessing the land is complete. Now Israel begins the system of decentralized government outlined in

Deuteronomy 1. Tribal leaders will govern the tribal lands. They will all come together for worship, and the Levites are given land in every tribe to provide access to God and the services of the priesthood. Sacrifices will be offered only at the tabernacle, and a national leader will be needed only when there is a national crisis.

This system will keep maximum authority at the grassroots level of governance. It will make the people of each tribe more responsible for their own governance through local interpretation of the prescriptive law of Moses and local formulation of specific laws and consequences. It will make unity a choice, and it will assure diversity in the interpretation and application of law—principles that seem important to God throughout Scripture.

Israel begins well. They serve God throughout the lifetime of Joshua and the tribal elders of his generation. As a people they ask God for direction in the next phase of military conquest—clearing the land. The various tribes begin to obey God and work together to take their lands.

Then we read these devastating words in Judges 2:10–15:

> After that whole generation had been gathered to their ancestors, another generation grew up who knew neither the LORD nor what he had done for Israel. Then the Israelites did evil in the eyes of the LORD and served the Baals. They forsook the LORD, the God of their ancestors, who had brought them out of Egypt. They followed and worshiped various gods of the peoples around them. They aroused the LORD's anger because they forsook him and served Baal and the Ashtoreths. In his anger against Israel the LORD gave them into the hands of raiders who plundered them. He sold them into the hands of their enemies all around, whom they were no longer able to resist. Whenever Israel went out to fight, the hand of the LORD was against them to defeat them, just as he had sworn to them. They were in great distress.

Israel's political problems resulted from their own disobedience to God. These difficulties did not come because of the devil or because of the evil in the cultures around them. The power to be attacked and defeated came from God's people themselves turning away from God. God's people were the reason for their own defeat. In their defeat, God is not emphasizing the power of their leaders, their enemy, or even the lost. He is emphasizing the devastating power of his people to curse themselves through the consequences of their choices.

Judges 2 continues:

> Then the LORD raised up judges, who saved them out of the hands of these raiders. Yet they would not listen to their judges but prostituted themselves to other gods and worshiped them. They quickly turned from the ways of their ancestors, who had been obedient to the LORD's commands. Whenever the LORD raised up a judge for them, he was with the judge and saved them out of the hands of their enemies as long as the judge lived; for the LORD relented because of their groaning under those who oppressed and afflicted them. But when the judge died, the people returned to ways even more corrupt than those of their ancestors, following other gods and serving and worshiping them. They refused to give up their evil practices and stubborn ways. (Judg. 2:16–19)

Each time the tribes of Israel move toward destructive idolatry, God raises up a political enemy. When Israel has a political enemy, the tribes must unite under a national leader, and God raises up such a leader to deliver them. In this context, the need for strong national political leadership is not an encouraging marker of a nation's health.

Let's see what God chooses to highlight in his Word about the political leadership of the judges.

OTHNIEL: TRIBE OF JUDAH

Judges 3:7–9 says: "The Israelites did evil in the eyes of the Lord; they forgot the Lord their God and served the Baals and the Asherahs. The anger of the Lord burned against Israel so that he sold them into the hands of Cushan-Rishathaim king of Aram Naharaim, to whom the Israelites were subject for eight years. But when they cried out to the Lord, he raised up for them a deliverer, Othniel son of Kenaz, Caleb's younger brother, who saved them."

It takes Israel eight years to get desperate enough to cry out to the

Lord. The leader Othniel comes from good stock. He is the nephew of Caleb, the only spy who along with Joshua gave a faithful report of God's ability to help them enter the promised land. Othniel's wife is Caleb's daughter. The Spirit of the Lord comes upon Othniel, who is raised up to lead Israel in the military defeat of the king of Aram.[1]

Israel then has peace for forty years.

EHUD: TRIBE OF BENJAMIN

Once again "the Israelites did evil in the eyes of the Lord, and because they did this evil the Lord gave Eglon king of Moab[2] power over Israel. Getting the Ammonites[3] and Amalekites[4] to join him, Eglon came and attacked Israel, and they took possession of the City of Palms. The Israelites were subject to Eglon king of Moab for eighteen years. Again the Israelites cried out to the Lord, and he gave them a deliverer—Ehud, a left-handed man, the son of Gera the Benjamite. The Israelites sent him with tribute to Eglon king of Moab" (Judg. 3:12–15).

This time it takes Israel eighteen years to become desperate enough to call out for God's help. The Israelites send Ehud with tribute to the king of Moab as a ruse to assassinate him. After killing the king, Ehud calls for the Ephraimites to join him, and they defeat and kill ten thousand capable Moabite troops.

Then Israel has eighty years of peace.

SHAMGAR: TRIBE OF NAPHTALI

"After Ehud came Shamgar son of Anath, who struck down six hundred Philistines with an oxgoad. He too saved Israel" (Judg. 3:31).

That is all we know about Shamgar. But we can assume that the theme uniting the judges continues: Israel does evil, God raises up an enemy, Israel cries out to God, and God helps them by raising up a political leader.

DEBORAH: TRIBE OF EPHRAIM

"Again the Israelites did evil in the eyes of the Lord, now that Ehud was dead. So the Lord sold them into the hands of Jabin king of Canaan, who reigned in Hazor. Sisera, the commander of his army, was based in Harosheth Haggoyim. Because he had nine hundred chariots fitted with iron and had cruelly oppressed the Israelites for twenty years, they cried to the Lord for help" (Judg. 4:1–3).

Israel's insensitivity to suffering is increasing; this time it takes twenty years for them to cry out for help. This time God raises up a woman who has already been functioning as a judicial leader in her tribe.

Deborah calls on Barak of Naphtali to raise an army of ten thousand from the tribes of Naphtali and Zebulun to attack Jabin's army. Barak refuses to go unless Deborah leads the army with him.

Deborah is full of faith in God. Barak defeats Jabin's army in spite of being completely out-armed. Sisera, the commander of the army, eludes capture and is killed by a woman while seeking refuge in her tent. As Deborah had prophesied, the victory is assigned to the woman. The Lord continues to give the Israelites strength, and they completely defeat King Jabin and the Canaanites.

GIDEON: TRIBE OF MANASSEH

The Israelites did evil in the eyes of the LORD, and for seven years he gave them into the hands of the Midianites.[5] Because the power of Midian was so oppressive, the Israelites prepared shelters for themselves in mountain clefts, caves and strongholds. Whenever the Israelites planted their crops, the Midianites, Amalekites and other eastern peoples invaded the country. They camped on the land and ruined the crops all the way to Gaza and did not spare a living thing for Israel, neither sheep nor cattle nor donkeys. They came up with their livestock and their tents like swarms of locusts. It was impossible to count them or their camels; they invaded the land to ravage it. Midian so impoverished the Israelites that they cried out to the LORD for help.

When the Israelites cried out to the LORD because of Midian, he sent them a prophet, who said, "This is what the LORD, the God of Israel, says: I brought you up out of Egypt, out of the land of slavery. I rescued you from the hand of the Egyptians.

And I delivered you from the hand of all your oppressors; I
drove them out before you and gave you their land. I said to
you, 'I am the LORD your God; do not worship the gods of the
Amorites, in whose land you live.' But you have not listened to
me." (Judg. 6:1–10)

This time the enemy is so oppressive that the Israelites live in caves,
their communities and economies devastated. For the first time, God
sends a prophet before he raises up a deliver. The prophet tells the people clearly that they are the cause of their own suffering. The simple
diagnosis? God's people no longer listen to God.

Gideon is fearful, self-conscious, and indecisive, but God uses him
to rout the Midianites using an army of just three hundred men. "The
Lord turned to him and said, 'Go in the strength you have and save
Israel out of Midian's hand. Am I not sending you?' 'Pardon me, my
lord,' Gideon replied, 'but how can I save Israel? My clan is the weakest
in Manasseh, and I am the least in my family'" (Judg. 6:14–15).

It would seem that not only are the people of Israel more and
more idolatrous, but also the best leadership God can find is declining
in quality. Where will a leader come from but from the people being
led? As the culture declines, so does the quality of those who may lead.
First, under Deborah, we have a skeptical military leader in Barak. Now
Gideon, the leader God is calling, is skeptical of God's ability to save the
nation. Watch the decline! God raises up political leaders to help Israel.
Then as the leaders are of lesser caliber, God raises up prophets. With
Gideon, God sends a prophet, an angel, and miracles to convince this
political leader that the Lord is able to help the Israelites. The presence
of this prophet, the angel, and the miracles is not a good sign. It means
Israel is getting more and more hard of hearing.

In obedience, Gideon does tear down his father's altar to Baal and
his Asherah fertility pole. As instructed, he then builds an altar to God
and uses the wood from the pole in a burnt offering of a bull. When the
people see this, they are so angered at this affront to their Jewish idolatry that they want to kill Gideon.

The Midianites, Amalekites, and all the other eastern peoples cross
the Jordan en masse, intending to destroy Israel. God stirs Gideon,
and Gideon calls out an army from Manasseh, Asher, Zebulun, and

Naphtali. God whittles down the army to just three hundred soldiers, making sure Gideon cannot be given credit for the victory. The invading armies are so terrified by the sounding trumpets of the three hundred men that they rise up in confusion and begin to kill each other. As they retreat, the rest of Gideon's army pursues them, calling in more recruits from the tribe of Ephraim and defeating the Midianites.

After this astounding military victory, Israel wants to create a dynasty from Gideon and his son. The desire of the tribes for a king begins to rumble. But in true humility, Gideon refuses this temptation and replies, "I will not rule over you, nor will my son rule over you. The Lord will rule over you" (Judg. 8:23).

However, after showing such godly wisdom, Gideon asks for tribute from the plunder. From forty-three pounds of gold, he makes a sacred ephod and places it in Ophrah, where the people begin to worship it. Why an ephod? Gideon is not a Levite. Why Ophrah? It is not a Levitical city. God clearly outlines in the law of Moses that the priests are to wear the ephods. But Ophrah is where the angel met with Gideon and called him to lead Israel in the military action against the Midianites. The ephod seduces Gideon and his family, along with the people.

Israel has peace for forty years in the time of Gideon.

ABIMELEK: TRIBE OF MANASSEH

Born to Gideon's concubine, who lived in Shechem, Abimelek is one of Gideon's scores of sons. Abimelek clearly thinks his father has made a mistake in declining the role of king. He goes to his mother's clan and proposes that they appoint him king, telling them that they will otherwise be ruled by the seventy sons of Gideon's wives. Reasoning that he is their relative, the tribe agrees to make him king. The people had turned back to worshiping Baal as soon as Gideon died, and now they take seventy shekels of silver from the temple of Baal and give it to Abimelek to hire an army—Israel's first non-volunteer army. Abimelek immediately goes to Ophrah and assassinates sixty-nine of his brothers, all except Jotham, who escapes. "Then all the citizens of Shechem and Beth Millo gathered beside the great tree at the pillar in Shechem to crown Abimelek king" (Judg. 9:6).

With Abimelek, we are back to fratricide!

This is the first time God has had no involvement in the selection of a political leader and the first time Israel has appointed a leader in the absence of a national military crisis. It is the first time finances for government have been taken from a temple, and a pagan one at that. It is also the first time political leadership has been seen as a family inheritance in Israel. On top of all this, in killing his brothers, Abimelek has orchestrated the first national political assassination in Israel, but this first assassination will not be the last.

Gideon's youngest son, Jotham, who hid and escaped his murderous brother, rises up and says the Shechemites will be accountable to God for the way they have treated his father and family and the godless way they have chosen a leader. Judges 9:19–20 says, "So have you acted honorably and in good faith toward Jerub-Baal [Gideon] and his family today? If you have, may Abimelek be your joy, and may you be his, too! But if you have not, let fire come out from Abimelek and consume you, the citizens of Shechem and Beth Millo, and let fire come out from you, the citizens of Shechem and Beth Millo, and consume Abimelek!"

Jotham flees for his life, and Abimelek leads for three years. God sends an evil spirit between Abimelek and the people he leads because of the role of both parties in shedding the innocent blood of Gideon's sons. The people take authority back from their appointed king.

During the Baal Harvest Temple Festival, in a scene that rivals the violence of Genesis, an adversary raises himself up as Shechem's political solution to Abimelek. In secret, the city's governor sends a message to Abimelek to attack while his detractors are in the city, which he does with a vengeance, running off the competition. But then the next day, Abimelek's troops attack the citizens when they go to the fields, slaughtering them and razing and salting the city. Abimelek sets fire to those citizens who have fled into the tower of Shechem to seek refuge, burning more than a thousand men and women alive. He then attacks those citizens who have fled to the city's tower for safety. One of the women in the tower drops a millstone on Abimelek's head, severely wounding him, and he commits assisted suicide with the help of his armor-bearer.

This is the first intratribal civil war and the first time an Israeli army turns on its own people. "Thus God repaid the wickedness that Abimelek had done to his father by murdering his seventy brothers. God also made the people of Shechem pay for all their wickedness" (Judg. 9:56–57).

We are back to the "red thread of violence." Israel is descending into a total disregard for God as demonstrated by their disregard for human life. The result is wholesale murder as in the days before the flood. The tribes of Israel have political freedom. They have the thinking of God in the law. God sends prophets to warn them and miracles to inspire their faith. But they refuse to listen. God holds both the people and their leader responsible.

TOLA: TRIBE OF ISSACHAR

"After the time of Abimelek, a man of Issachar named Tola son of Puah, the son of Dodo, rose to save Israel. He lived in Shamir, in the hill country of Ephraim. He led Israel twenty-three years; then he died, and was buried in Shamir" (Judg. 10:1–2).

There is no mention of the people crying out to God for help. There is no mention that God raised up Tola as a deliver. There is no mention of what Tola rose up to save Israel from. Is it possible that Israel is now their own worst enemy?

JAIR: TRIBE OF MANASSEH

"He was followed by Jair of Gilead, who led Israel twenty-two years. He had thirty sons, who rode thirty donkeys. They controlled thirty towns in Gilead, which to this day are called Havvoth Jair. When Jair died, he was buried in Kamon" (Judg. 10:3–5).

God no longer features in the people's choice of a leader, nor does he appear to influence the leader himself. Judges are no longer chosen to lead only during a national crisis. They are in power all the time. In effect, Israel, while not instituting the title, has shifted to a top-down governance of kingship, while still using the term *judge*.

JEPHTHAH: TRIBE OF MANASSEH

"Again the Israelites did evil in the eyes of the Lord" (Judg. 10:6).

Again the people of Israel give themselves to foreign gods. They worship Baal and the Ashtoreth goddesses; they worship the gods of Aram, Sidon,[6] and Moab and the gods of the Ammonites and the Philistines.[7] God raises up the Philistines and Ammonites as enemies, subjecting the Israelite tribes east of the Jordan to eighteen years of slavery at their hands. Then the Ammonites cross the Jordan to invade the tribes of Judah, Benjamin, and Ephraim, too. At this, the Israelites cry out to the Lord, seemingly for the first time in sixty-three years.

Listen to God's response:

> "When the Egyptians, the Amorites, the Ammonites, the Philistines, the Sidonians, the Amalekites and the Maonites oppressed you and you cried to me for help, did I not save you from their hands? But you have forsaken me and served other gods, so I will no longer save you. Go and cry out to the gods you have chosen. Let them save you when you are in trouble!"
>
> But the Israelites said to the Lord, "We have sinned. Do with us whatever you think best, but please rescue us now." Then they got rid of the foreign gods among them and served the Lord. And he could bear Israel's misery no longer. (Judg. 10:11–16)

The Ammonites have crossed the river and are poised to attack the western tribes. The people are looking for a warrior to lead their defense. Jephthah is a mighty warrior, son of the patriarch of the Gileadites. His mother was a prostitute, and his half-brothers have run him out of the family, leaving him with no inheritance. He has raised up an ad-hoc army and lives in Tob. With the Ammonites and Israelites encamped for battle in Gilead, the people ask Jephthah to lead them. He is hesitant, but when promised by the elders of Gilead that they will make him their leader permanently, he agrees to return.

Jephthah sends diplomats to find out why the Ammonites are preparing to attack. They respond that it is because the Israelites took the Ammonite lands when they came out of Egypt. Jephthah responds with an astute retelling of the facts. Israel had not taken their lands until the kings of Moab and Edom[8] had refused them compassion and passage through their lands as they fled Egypt. Then they asked Sihon king of the Amorites for safe passage, and he denied them as well. But unlike the other kings, Sihon marshaled his troops against them and attacked. Israel defeated them and took their land. They have now lived there for three hundred years. Jephthah tells the Ammonites, "I have not wronged you, but you are doing me wrong by waging war against me. Let the Lord, the Judge, decide the dispute this day between the Israelites and the Ammonites" (Judg. 11:27).

Jephthah then appears to make a vow before the Lord, saying that if he gets victory, he will sacrifice whatever first comes out of his house on his return home. He wins the battles and defeats the Ammonites. On his return home, his only child, his daughter, comes out to meet him, dancing with a tambourine to welcome him home. And he sacrifices her.

This is the first account of human sacrifice in Israel. Of course Jephthah is not relying on the God of his forefathers; Israel's faith in the God of Moses is long gone. He is using the language of his ancestors, but he is talking to the new gods of Israel, the gods who gladly accept human sacrifice.

Following the victory over the Ammonites, an old feud with Ephraim rises up again. The forces of Ephraim come to Jephthah ready to fight. Why has Jephthah not asked them to help fight the Ammonites? The Ephraimites and Gileadites proceed to fight Israel's first civil tribal war. The decline continues.

Jephthah led Israel six years. The next three judges don't take up much space in the history of the judges.

IBZAN: TRIBE OF JUDAH (POSSIBLY ZEBULUN)

"After him, Ibzan of Bethlehem led Israel. He had thirty sons and thirty daughters. He gave his daughters away in marriage to those outside his clan, and for his sons he brought in thirty young women as wives from outside his clan. Ibzan led Israel seven years. Then Ibzan died and was buried in Bethlehem" (Judg. 12:8–10).

ELON: TRIBE OF ZEBULUN

"After him, Elon the Zebulunite led Israel ten years. Then Elon died and was buried in Aijalon in the land of Zebulun" (Judg. 12:11–12).

ABDON: TRIBE OF ASHER

"After him, Abdon son of Hillel, from Pirathon, led Israel. He had forty sons and thirty grandsons, who rode on seventy donkeys. He led Israel eight years. Then Abdon son of Hillel died and was buried at Pirathon in Ephraim, in the hill country of the Amalekites" (Judg. 12:13–15).

We are not yet at the bottom of the decline in Israel. The sin in Israel increases even more, and God raises up an enemy, a very familiar one by now, the Philistines: "Again the Israelites did evil in the eyes of the Lord, so the Lord delivered them into the hands of the Philistines for forty years" (Judg. 13:1).

SAMSON: TRIBE OF DAN

We finally arrive at the most memorable of the judges. Samson is born for the job. He is born for it, quite literally, because there is no one living in Israel, man or woman, whom God can use to lead the people. The moral fiber of the nation is so destroyed from within that there is no leader for God to raise up to deliver them. (We will soon see the same desperate situation in the call of a two-year-old boy named Samuel.)

God has delivered Israel into the hands of the Philistines. The angel of the Lord comes to the wife of a man named Manoah of the tribe of Dan, telling her that even though she is barren and childless, she will conceive a son who will lead the deliverance of Israel from the Philistines. The mother is not to consume wine nor eat anything unclean, for their son will be born a Nazirite, "dedicated to God from the womb" (Judg. 13:5). The boy, Samson, is born. "He grew and the Lord blessed him, and the Spirit of the Lord began to stir him" (Judg. 13:24–25).

In spite of the miraculous nature of Samson's conception and birth, in spite of the dedication of his parents to obeying God, in spite of the blessing of God, Samson has issues. Most of his issues revolve around women.

In spite of his parents' advice, Samson wants to marry a Philistine, a young woman he has seen down in Timnah. When it comes time for the marriage rituals, Samson and his parents go to Timnah, and he throws the customary feast. The people there choose thirty Philistine companions for him. He gives the men a riddle and promises that he will give them thirty sets of garments as a prize if they guess the meaning. They cannot, so they coax the bride into weaseling it out of Samson. Samson is furious and murders thirty Philistines, giving their clothes to the companions who answered the riddle. His wife is given in marriage to one of the Philistine companions, the one who had been best man.

Samson seeks revenge by destroying the Philistines' harvest of grain, vineyards, and olive groves. The Philistines then burn the ex-wife and her father for bringing this terror on their community. Samson responds by slaughtering many and then hides in a cave. Three thousand men from Judah come to get him to turn him over to the Philistines because he has caused them so much trouble with their oppressor. They swear they won't kill him, then tie him up, take him to the Philistines, and hand him over. But "the Spirit of the Lord came upon him in power" (Judg. 15:14). The ropes break. Samson picks up a fresh donkey jawbone and kills a thousand Philistines. He is very thirsty, and at his prayer, God provides water from a rock and he is revived.

Samson's next escapade finds him in Gaza in bed with a prostitute while the place is surrounded by Philistines tipped off to his presence. He escapes, only to later fall in love with Delilah. Delilah is co-opted by the Philistines to collaborate in finding out the source of Samson's great strength. For this knowledge, they will pay her the value of 275 slaves. The plot goes back and forth until Samson finally succumbs to Delilah's pleading. His hair is cut, and he is captured, tortured, and put on display in the temple of the Philistine god. The God of Israel pours strength through Samson again, and Samson pulls down the pillars of the temple, killing himself and everyone inside—more than three thousand Philistines, including the Philistine rulers. Thus Samson killed many more people in his death than he killed during his life.

Samson ruled Israel for twenty years.

WHAT NOW?

Good heavens! What does this all mean? God has selected these terrible accounts of Israel's history and preserved them for more than three millennia to teach us what? This is the history of Israel's political leadership thus far. God is not making the stories up. God is telling us what happened. What are we to see, understand, and apply? What on earth does this have to do with civil governance and justice in the twenty-first century?

As we finish this era of political history in Israel, let's look at what stands out.

THE PEOPLE

The moral decline of the people seems to precede the moral decline in their political leadership. For the first four generations, we are told that Israel had a political enemy because "the Israelites did evil in the eyes of the Lord." Only because they had, as a culture, moved toward idolatry were they in need of God's intervention through a political leader. And only after they, the people, had cried out to God did he raise up a defending national leader for them. It takes the people longer and longer to turn to God.

As the decline continues throughout the time of the judges, we see that the people and then the leaders themselves contribute to the nation's demise. And the people and their leadership both continue to accelerate that demise. The idolatry of the people builds from worship of other gods to human sacrifice, assassination, civil war, and violence as a means and solution.

In the beginning Israel's decline is the result of the people and the culture at large; the Jews themselves move away from God. Is this where some believers in history got the concept that we get the political leadership we deserve?

THE POLITICAL LEADERS

It is interesting that the judges come from nine of the twelve tribes of Israel. Perhaps it would have been twelve if Manasseh had not begun to hog the stage. God is clearly spreading the leadership around. This builds the value of "representation," but it does something else as well. As the culture declines, it reveals that no matter where the leaders come from, they are less and less able to represent God—even when they are the best God can find and are raised up by him.

The first four judges do a pretty good job with the brief task God gives them. They deal with the enemy, reinstate peace, and return to their daily lives. By the time we get to Gideon, the best leader God can find is not sure God can do the job. (It is fitting that God defeats the enemy with only three hundred soldiers.) God gives Gideon victory, but when it is all over, Israel wants to make Gideon a king and dynasty. They give credit for the victory to the man rather than God.

Gideon still has enough wisdom to turn them down. But his son Abimelek does not. This conspiracy to rule all of Israel will plague Israel's politics for the rest of biblical history. And as we will see in the days of the kings, it is the beginning of the divided kingdom and the final dispersion. The quality of Israel's leadership has entered free fall.

THE ENEMY

Every time Israel has a political enemy in the book of Judges, God has raised up that enemy. Each time God raises up a political enemy, he does so to show his people that they are drifting from him. God's emphasis is not on the foreigner in Israel or the foreign invader. God's emphasis is on God's people ceasing to be God's people. When God's people turn back to God, he delivers them.

As in the history of the believers in the New Testament epistles, the gravest danger comes from within the community, not from without. But we will get to that in Part IV.

GOD

For God's part, he does nothing but increase his efforts to get Israel to listen. He reminds them of his laws, he warns them, he raises up leaders when the people cry out to him, he sends prophets, he performs miracles to get their attention, he calls leaders from birth to circumvent the moral decline of the culture. And? God's people listen less and less!

This is a very heavy history. Nothing speaks to me more of the inspiration of the Bible than the fact that, left to themselves, no nation would choose to document this history of themselves. It is too awful.

But we are not done yet! Are you willing to suffer God's pain for generations more? Are you willing for God to tell his story his way and prepare our hearts for what is to come?

CHAPTER 17

SAMUEL AND THE WANDERING PRIESTS

"In those days Israel had no king; everyone did as they saw fit." —Judges 17:6

So, where are the priests? In the history of the judges, they are almost entirely absent. Are they not important to the history of the country? Surely they are, but why are they so quiet then? The way the book of Judges concludes and 1 Samuel begins may provide clues. The book of Judges ends with two rather bizarre stories that, at first, seem out of place. The subjects in these two stories are priests of the Levitical tribe.

MICAH AND THE WANDERING PRIEST

In the first story, found in Judges 17, we are told of a man named Micah in the tribe of Ephraim who has stolen a great quantity of silver from his mother, about twenty-eight pounds or thirteen kilos. He confesses because his mother has put a curse on the thief. He gives the silver back to his mother, and she in turn consecrates it to the *Lord* and encourages Micah to make idols from it. Micah already has a shrine and uses the silver to add new idols and an ephod. He then installs his son as priest.

We must wonder at this point, "To what *Lord* they are consecrating these things?" Everything they do breaks the law of Moses. They are not to have idols, they are not to curse in God's name, and they are not to build shrines. Ephods are to be worn only by the priests, and the priests are to be Levites.

The picture God is painting for us is one of total disregard for what God has taught Israel about worship. The people are in rebellion, worshiping the gods of the nations around them, all the while still using the name of the Lord as though they are worshiping him.

A priest of the Levitical tribe enters the scene. He is from Bethlehem and has wandered off looking for another home. We don't know why he does this, but we do know that the clans of the priests have all been assigned homelands. The wandering priest comes across Micah in Ephraim, and Micah makes him an offer: Live with his family, become his priest, wear his new ephod, and represent his family in their idol shrine. Micah will pay the priest an annual sum and give him food and clothing. So Micah installs the wandering Levite as priest, noting that now he knows "the Lord will be good to me, since this Levite has become my priest" (Judg. 17:13). What *Lord*?

If we do not read the Bible with the law of Moses in mind, we will miss the point here. Mosaic law lays down the template by which we understand everything else that happens in the history of Israel, including the prophets, the coming of Christ, and the expansion of the gospel to the Gentile nations. God does not start from scratch in each book of the Bible. The books build progressively, and the one before helps us understand the ones that follow. Everything everyone does in all of Scripture is to be measured by what God has already told Israel in the law. Without this measurement, we will distort the meaning of the history of Israel and distort God's message.

God is showing us through the life of this priest and Micah's hiring of him that the Israelites have no regard for God's law at this time in their history. Everything the priest and Micah do here is in direct violation of God's instructions. However, they still want the God of the law to bless them! The deterioration of Israel has come from within the Jewish community.

The story of Micah's wandering priest continues and gets worse! The Danites are looking for a place to move, and they come across

Micah and his young Levitical priest. God, Moses, and Joshua have all assigned the tribes to specific tribal lands with detailed borders, and yet we have a wandering tribe. We don't know the exact story, but the Danites have not been able to take their assigned land. In fact, they have been run out. It appears that none of the tribes have come to their brothers' rescue.[1]

The Danites ask Micah's priest to inquire of the Lord whether their mission to find a new home territory will be successful, and the priest assures them that the Lord approves their mission. Does he? They find a beautiful, prosperous land, where they attack "a people at peace and secure" (Judg. 18:27), destroying them and burning down their city. Is this one of the seven tribes they were told they were to destroy, or is this now just wholesale genocide?

The army of Dan returns to Ephraim, steals the idols and ephod, and makes the priest a better offer. Why be a priest for a family when he can be a priest for a whole tribe? The Danites rebuild the burnt city of Laish and rename it Dan. "There the Danites set up for themselves the idol, and Jonathan son of Gershom, the son of Moses, and his sons were priests for the tribe of Dan" (Judg. 18:30). The tribe that has just sought God sets up idols. Who are they seeking and worshiping? The wandering priest is the grandson of Moses![2] The idolatry set up in the city of Dan will plague Israel for the rest of their history.

Well, there we are! Not only is there political corruption in Israel, but it would seem the priesthood is in a very bad state as well.

Now we come to the second story of a priest, the last in the book of Judges.

THE LEVITE AND HIS CONCUBINE

Another priest from the hill country of Ephraim takes a concubine, a lesser wife, from Judah to live with him. We are not told why, but she runs away from him and returns to her father's house. The priest comes looking for her and is hosted by the father for days as he delays their leaving.

At last, quite late in the day after more delays, the priest and his concubine leave for home. Careful not to stop in non-Jewish towns along the way where they will not be protected, the Levite decides to stop for the night at Gibeah in the Benjamite territory. They wait at the town square as was customary for travelers looking for lodging for the night. No one helps them until evening, when an old man from Ephraim who lives in Gibeah graciously takes them in and provides for their needs.

We hear echoes of Sodom and Gomorrah when, while the travelers are eating, wicked men from the town come, demanding that the old man give up the priest for them to have sex with. He pleads with them, attempting to shame them by offering his own virgin daughter or his guest's concubine. The men of Gibeah won't listen, and finally the Levite forces the concubine to go out to them. They rape her all night long, and in the morning she lies dying on the threshold of the house. The priest lays her across his donkey, and when he reaches his home, he cuts her body into twelve pieces and sends one to each tribe of Israel as a message. How can such a thing happen in Israel?

The tribal response is unanimous: "Such a thing has never been seen or done, not since the day the Israelites came up out of Egypt. Just imagine! We must do something! So speak up!" (Judg. 19:30).

The Jews seem to be astounded by their own wickedness. And when this one priest finally calls them to accountability, they respond. The tribes come together with 400,000 soldiers. They hear the priest's testimony and determine to bring judgment on the Benjamites. They ask for the surrender of the guilty men. The Benjamites refuse and amass more than 26,000 soldiers of their own and go to war with their brothers. Neither tribal accountability nor accountability to the law of Moses moves the Benjamites.

In the first day of fighting, the Benjamites kill an astounding 22,000 soldiers from the other tribes. The next day 18,000 are killed. Weeping and inquiring of the Lord, the eleven tribes fight another day. On the third day of civil war, the eleven tribes kill 25,100 of the 26,000 Benjamite troops and destroy their towns and livestock.

The loss to the Benjamites is so great that, if the tribes had not helped them, they would have become extinct. And the book of Judges closes out: "In those days Israel had no king; everyone did as they saw fit" (21:25).

There is no victory here. There is some level of justice and retribution. There is some course correction in the moral decline of the Jewish people. But these stories at the end of Judges show that even with all that

God has done for his chosen people, they are still as bad, if not worse at times, than the pagan nations surrounding them. Their religious leaders are full of idolatry, and their political leaders are morally spent.

The red thread of violence continues its destructive flow through God's chosen people. Through Israel, God has wanted to reveal his values for nation building—values for all nations. But Israel is going backward.

> Therefore the LORD was very angry with Israel and said, "Because this nation has violated the covenant I ordained for their ancestors and has not listened to me, I will no longer drive out before them any of the nations Joshua left when he died. I will use them to test Israel and see whether they will keep the way of the LORD and walk in it as their ancestors did." The LORD had allowed those nations to remain; he did not drive them out at once by giving them into the hands of Joshua. (Judg. 2:20–23)

Israel has enemies because God is using conflict to get their attention. In the two-hundred-plus years since the time of Joshua, the character of Jewish justice has deteriorated dramatically. It is time for change.

SAMUEL, 1060–1020 BC

As we enter the book of 1 Samuel, the writer begins with the condition of the priesthood. We are told that Eli the priest and his sons are wicked. His sons steal from the Lord and use temple prostitutes. God says he is going to destroy the family and raise up a new leader.

In God's search throughout all of Israel, he can find no one able to lead the nation. They have reached the cultural bottom. Both the political leadership and priesthood are in serious trouble. Still, there is faithfulness in Israel beyond the institutions. We are told of a faithful woman and her husband who, while all of Israel runs headlong into paganism, stand firm in their commitment to God. The husband, Elkanah, is an Ephraimite with two wives, Hannah and Peninnah. Peninnah has children, but Hannah is barren.

Every year this faithful man goes up to Shiloh, where Eli and his sons are priests, to worship and offer sacrifices for all his children and both wives. Year after year, when they are in the house of the Lord, Hannah is inconsolable because she is childless. One year, as she cries out for God's help, she is so fervent in her prayer that Eli thinks she is drunk. Denying it, she puts her petition for a child before Eli. He blesses her and asks God to grant her request.

Back home, God does answer Hannah's prayer. Elkanah lies with Hannah, and before long she conceives. She names the child Samuel because "I asked the Lord for him" (1 Sam. 1:20).

As soon as the boy is weaned, Hannah takes him up to Shiloh, where she offers him to the service of the Lord for the rest of his lifetime. After sacrificing a bull and worshiping God, Hannah leaves this precious gift-child under the supervision of these awful priests. Her trust is in the Lord, not the system.

God says, "I will raise up for myself a faithful priest, who will do according to what is in my heart and mind. I will firmly establish his priestly house, and they will minister before my anointed one always" (1 Sam. 2:35).

When God speaks of raising up a faithful priest, is he speaking of Samuel? Many times in Scripture thus far God has spoken of raising up a faithful leader. But who is he talking about? Certainly, Samuel will give faithful leadership for a generation and will improve Israel's state. However, Israel will decline again. What is God saying? It is not yet clear.

Beginning with a child, God turns his attention to a new generation, as he did in the wilderness with Moses. His desire is to use every generation, but there comes a time when it may be too late for a generation to change, and he must start again with the younger generation.

God begins to prepare Samuel. "In those days the word of the Lord was rare; there were not many visions" (1 Sam. 3:1). But Samuel hears God speak from an early age, and Eli is righteous enough to understand that it is the Lord Samuel hears. Samuel grows in maturity and does not forget anything God has said. He is recognized throughout Israel as a prophet of God.

Israel's nemesis, the Philistines, are as feisty as ever. They raid Israel, defeat the army, and steal the ark of God. Smart enough to know that the ark has power, the Israelites have brought it to the battlefield. But they are too far from the truth to understand that God will not bless them. The Philistines are smart enough to be afraid of the presence of the ark because they know the God of Israel is powerful. But they win anyway and capture the ark. Hophni and Phinehas are killed in battle, along with thirty thousand others. Eli drops dead when he hears of the death of his sons and the loss of the ark.

Meanwhile, the Philistines have a terrible time with the ark. They place it in the temple of Dagon, their god. The people experience a pandemic of tumors, and the statue of Dagon keeps falling over before the ark. The Philistines finally decide to return the ark to Israel.

Twenty years go by, with all the people crying out to God. When "all the people of Israel turned back to the Lord" (1 Sam. 7:2), Samuel tells them what they must do if they are truly returning to the Lord with all their hearts. He leads them in giving up their pagan worship of gods and coming back to the God of Israel. Then, like the judges of old, he leads them into war with the Philistines at Mizpah, the same battlefield where the tribes and the Benjamites fought the devastating civil war. Is that a coincidence?

The Philistines are defeated, Israel's land is restored, and there is peace. Samuel goes back to his home in Ramah and judges Israel from there, riding like a circuit judge from tribe to tribe. It seems he has ceased to function as priest.

But Samuel is a priest, though not a Levite; he is a prophet and political leader, though not a traditional judge. He is a transitional leader God uses in unconventional ways. Like Moses, who was a Levite but gave Aaron the priesthood while he retained political leadership, Samuel does not fit God's norm for institutional authority. Samuel is essential to get the nation back on track, but he is not the template of leadership.

As Samuel gets old, we read, "He appointed his sons as Israel's leaders" (1 Sam. 8:1). But his sons do not walk in integrity before God as Samuel has. They accept bribes, and they pervert justice. And the people reject them. Israel wants a king to lead them.

God has said he will establish the house of Samuel in leadership over Israel. But as with Eli and his sons, this promise is conditional. The character of the sons is unacceptable to God and the people. Samuel was the messenger who brought this word of the Lord to Eli. So why does Samuel now think that God will use his sons regardless? We are not told why. God does not elaborate for us. But this disregard of fathers for the character of their sons will plague Israel throughout its history, from David to the last of the kings.

Now we begin the history of Israel's kings. The next several hundred years will bring us to the greatest heights, as well as to devastating valleys, in Jewish history. God requires us to read through tragedy after tragedy for hundreds of pages with only a few points of historical encouragement. Why? What are we to learn from all this? What will we miss in the message of Jesus if we do not understand this history? Jesus mastered these events. He understood them, and he knew what the Father was saying in them. So must we.

CHAPTER 18

THE KINGS IN ASCENT

As we begin looking at the kings of Israel, we must work from 1 and 2 Samuel, 1 and 2 Kings, and 1 and 2 Chronicles together, since they overlap in telling the history of the political leaders. Some books list different details, which I have tried to harmonize into a single overview. We are given a lot of detail about the first three kings, but then history and the scriptural record settle down into repeating patterns of information. God is not telling us everything from each political leader's life. He tells us what he considers significant for our learning of the political history, and he gives us principles for the growth and destruction of a nation. How many generations does it take to see a blessing? How many generations does it take to destroy the fiber of a nation? What are the signposts along the way?

As recorded in 1 Samuel 8, the people come to Samuel requesting a new form of government. They want a king like the other nations have. As the nations around them do, they want to give more power to a national leader who will lead them all the time. Previously, political power rested in the individual tribes, and a national leader was appointed when there was a national crisis. Generations have progressively modified the executive institution, creating a more permanent leadership. Now Israel wants a constitutional change in how they are governed.

Samuel consults God. God tells Samuel to tell the people why this is a bad idea. In short, God says having a king will divert the nation's prime resources. Prosperity will be traded for less responsibility, and reliance on a king for security will replace reliance on God. So far, when the people have turned away from God by worshiping pagan gods, forcing God to turn his back on them, God has always raised up a leader and an army when the people turned back to God. Now the people want a layer of protection in their system that will compensate for their idolatry and lessen their need to return to God. They want a king who will protect them all the time, even when they turn away from God.

God makes it clear that this new executive will be very expensive. Their sons will spend their youth in full-time military service as the king creates a professional military. Likewise, the king will need to create a professional service to provide for the needs of state, and their daughters will be taken into this bureaucracy to work as servants—as perfumers, cooks, and bakers. The system will require the best of their economy, and the king will institute taxation to support it. He will take the best of their workforce and the best of their livestock and harvest and tax them on what remains.

"But the people refused to listen to Samuel. 'No!' they said. 'We want a king over us. Then we will be like all the other nations, with a king to lead us and to go out before us and fight our battles.' When Samuel heard all that the people said, he repeated it before the Lord. The Lord answered, 'Listen to them and give them a king'" (1 Sam. 8:19–22).

As described in Deuteronomy 1, God gave the people the right to choose how, by whom, and over what they would be governed. He then told the people how they should do it. But the choice is theirs. And Israel makes their choice. They want a king!

As Samuel steps down from political leadership, he calls all the people together. His final speech is purposeful. He reminds the nation that because they have demanded a king, he has provided a process for that transition. As he steps down, he asks two questions and requires them to be witness to the answers. Who has he cheated or oppressed? If they know of any incident in which Samuel has stolen, bribed, or turned a blind eye to pervert justice, they are to stand up and speak now. The people unanimously agree that he has not done any of these things.

Interesting to have a vote of confidence for an outgoing leader. What concerns Samuel? Is he afraid of retribution by the incoming power, or does he anticipate revenge when the people become discontent with their political choices? Whatever it is, in spite of the fact that God will honor the choices of the people, Samuel is distancing himself from the direction that Israel has taken in appointing a king. He tells them, "Now here is the king you have chosen, the one you asked for" (1 Sam. 12:13).

Samuel reminds the people that God is ready to bless them and their king: "If you fear the Lord and serve and obey him and do not rebel against his commands, and if both you and the king who reigns over you follow the Lord your God—good! But if you do not obey the Lord, and if you rebel against his commands, his hand will be against you, as it was against your ancestors" (1 Sam. 12:14–15).

God's requirement of obedience for blessing hasn't changed now that they have a king. However, now that they have added another layer of authority, they have added another layer of requirement—the agreement of their king.

When the people are fearful for having "added to all our other sins the evil of asking for a king" (1 Sam. 12:19), notice Samuel's emphasis on the choices of the people:

"Do not be afraid," Samuel replied. "You have done all this evil; yet do not turn away from the LORD, but serve the LORD with all your heart. Do not turn away after useless idols. They can do you no good, nor can they rescue you, because they are useless. For the sake of his great name the LORD will not reject his people, because the LORD was pleased to make you his own. As for me, far be it from me that I should sin against the LORD by failing to pray for you. And I will teach you the way that is good and right. But be sure to fear the LORD and serve him faithfully with all your heart; consider what great things he has done for you. Yet if you persist in doing evil, both you and your king will perish." (1 Sam. 12:20–25)

Samuel's point is clear. It is not a king that will save or destroy Israel, but the choices of the people. If they turn to God and if the king they choose does the same, God will bless them. And if they do not, he will not. The issue is not political leadership. The issue of blessing is the condition of the people being led.

God is pleading with the people of Israel, with or without a king, not to turn away from the blessing of living in his ways.

SAUL, 1051–1011 BC[1]

Saul is the first of the kings God did not want. Although the people have made a choice that is not God's desire, he will seek to bless them in their choices. Saul is the best man God can find for the job, and the people agree and appoint him king.

Saul is a Benjamite. His appearance is impressive; he is taller and more handsome than anyone else in Israel. With amazing detail, God leads Samuel to Saul and says, "About this time tomorrow I will send you a man from the land of Benjamin. Anoint him ruler over my people Israel; he will deliver them from the hand of the Philistines. I have looked on my people, for their cry has reached me" (1 Sam. 9:16). In spite of Saul's flaws, there is no doubt God is behind him. The people cried out for help, and God heard.

Samuel proceeds to anoint Saul with oil and pronounce him God's choice for king. But Saul does not have the authority of king until the people choose him. Samuel brings all the tribes together, presents Saul, and "the people shouted, 'Long live the king!'" (1 Sam. 10:24). There are dissenters who question Saul's leadership, but the people have made their choice.

Saul becomes king at the age of thirty, and he reigns for forty-two years (1 Sam. 13:1). He rules from his home in Gibeah, as the judges ruled from their homes in the past.

When Nahash the Ammonite tries to annex the area of Jabesh Gilead,[2] Saul sends out a call to arms and raises an army of 300,000 from the twelve tribes. "The terror of the Lord fell on the people, and they came out together as one" (1 Sam. 11:7). They soundly defeat the enemy. Saul's kingship is confirmed, and any civil dissent over his leadership is quelled.

Saul's army nearly mutinies in their next military engagement, which is against the Philistines. Saul has a standing army of three thousand men, two thousand under his leadership and one thousand under his son Jonathan. They are up against an enemy with three thousand chariots, six thousand charioteers, and soldiers too numerous to count. Frustrated by Samuel's late arrival to the battlefield and concerned for his army's courage, Saul offers the pre-battle sacrifice. Samuel, now functioning in a priestly role, arrives and is furious. Saul is calling on the name of the Lord while breaking his law. Only the priests are allowed to make a burnt offering; making offerings is not within the authority or function of the king.

"'You have done a foolish thing,' Samuel said. 'You have not kept the command the Lord your God gave you; if you had, he would have established your kingdom over Israel for all time. But now your kingdom will not endure; the Lord has sought out a man after his own heart and appointed him ruler of his people, because you have not kept the Lord's command'" (1 Sam. 13:13–14).

Saul has six hundred men left in his army, and none of them except Saul and Jonathan has a sword; the Philistines have a blacksmith monopoly in order to keep Israel militarily weak. In secret, Jonathan leads the initial attack with his armor-bearer, reasoning, "Nothing can hinder the Lord from saving, whether by many or by few" (1 Sam. 14:6). The success of these two men against twenty throws the Philistine camp into a panic sent by God, and the Philistines flee. The victory goes to Israel.

Saul drifts farther and farther from God during his reign. He does not obey God in the battle with the Amalekites. His men are made wealthy by keeping plunder and livestock, which God has specifically told them not to keep, and Saul does not execute the Amalekite king as instructed.

"Then the word of the Lord came to Samuel: 'I regret that I have made Saul king, because he has turned away from me and has not carried out my instructions.' Samuel was angry, and he cried out to the Lord all that night" (1 Sam. 15:10–11).

When Samuel arrives, Saul swears he has kept the word of the Lord. But there the livestock are, and there is King Agag, alive. When Saul begins to make excuses, Samuel says, "Enough!" and continues: "Let me tell you what the Lord said to me last night. . . . Although you were once small in your own eyes, did you not become the head of the tribes of Israel? The Lord anointed you king over Israel. And he sent you on a mission, saying, 'Go and completely destroy those wicked people, the Amalekites; wage war against them until you have wiped them out.' Why did you not obey the Lord? Why did you pounce on the plunder and do evil in the eyes of the Lord?" (1 Sam. 15:16–19).

Saul persists in his denial, saying they took the best in order to offer it to the Lord in thanksgiving for victory. Ouch!

Samuel declares these now famous words: "Does the Lord delight in burnt offerings and sacrifices as much as in obeying the Lord? To obey is better than sacrifice, and to heed is better than the fat of rams. For rebellion is like the sin of divination, and arrogance like the evil of idolatry. Because you have rejected the word of the Lord, he has rejected you as king" (1 Sam. 15:22–23).

Saul had already lost his dynasty; now he is losing God's blessing. Israel's first king continues to spiral downward. The Spirit of the Lord departs from him, making room for an evil spirit. Saul is tormented and probably depressive. David, who has been his armor-bearer, now also becomes his musical therapist. David is drawn into the limelight when he kills Goliath, and a long period of rivalry begins. Saul attempts to murder David, and three times David refuses to assassinate Saul even though he has the opportunity.

After Samuel's death, Saul seeks out a witch to call up Samuel's dead spirit. The Philistines are attacking, and Saul knows that God has turned away from him and no longer gives him direction. The dead Samuel rebukes Saul for calling up the dead, again breaking God's law, and tells Saul he will be defeated and his defeat will be the judgment of God. God is tearing the kingdom from Saul's hands, and it will be given to another. Saul and all but his youngest son will die in this war.

Saul—first king of Israel, defender of his people, attempted murderer, unrepentant lawbreaker, seeker of witches, and disappointment to God—commits suicide after being wounded in battle.

DAVID, 1011–971 BC

David! King David, beloved by God, Israel, and Jesus, is the second of the kings that God did not want. But if Israel was to have a king, then David was the best man God could recommend for the job.

David, the forgotten and possibly illegitimate son of Jesse, enters the service of Saul as a personal musician. He is also one of Saul's armor-bearers. David kills the Philistine giant with a slingshot and stone. He is a great military leader and delivers the Jews from the Philistines again and again. As David's fame increases, Saul's jealousy grows and he begins to plot to kill David. David flees Israel to save his life.

In fleeing Saul, David takes bread from the altar and the sword of Goliath from the priests of Nob. When Saul finds out, he kills the entire family of the priests for assisting David. David flees to Achish, king of Gath. But David's fame is so great as a warrior and king that his life is in danger, and in front of Achish he pretends to be insane to escape execution. While living in exile, David gathers a force of six hundred men. In this season, David nearly murders Nabal for insulting him and his men and is only spared this evil because Nabal's wife Abigail intervenes. To his credit he refuses many times to kill Saul when he has the opportunity.

When Saul and his sons are dead, David asks the Lord if it is time for him to return to Judah. The tribe of Judah makes David king, but the northern tribes appoint Ish-Bosheth, Saul's last son, as king with the encouragement of Abner, commander of Saul's army. A divided kingdom is again on the horizon. Ish-Bosheth rules in Mahanaim for two years, and David is king of Judah in Hebron. David understands that the northern tribes have the right to reject or choose his leadership.

The war between the house of Saul and the house of David lasts for more than seven years. Finally, Abner crosses over to make a treaty with David. Abner convinces the northern tribes to accept David as king. Joab, David's military commander, assassinates Abner without permission from David. The king mourns Abner and disclaims any responsibility for Abner's death. Amazingly, David keeps Joab on as military commander without consequence.

Ish-Bosheth is assassinated by Benjamites, and his head is taken to David as tribute and revenge on his enemy Saul. David is livid and executes the two assassins and makes a public spectacle of their bodies. David now becomes king of all of Israel. He is thirty years old.

David reconquers Jerusalem. He builds a palace in a walled fortress now called the city of David. He takes many concubines and wives to add to the three wives he already has. He begins to populate the earth with sons and daughters. God gives him tremendous victory over the

Philistines. Things are going so well that David decides to bring the ark of God to Jerusalem with great fanfare. However, disaster occurs when one of the men carrying the ark drops dead. David is angry and afraid of the Lord and leaves the ark where they stopped.

David goes home to study the law of Moses, and when he returns three months later, he makes sure the Levites are carrying the ark as prescribed by Moses. Like Saul, David has blurred the line between the palace and the priesthood.

Now that David is settled in his palace and has peace in the country, he turns his ambition toward building a house for God. Nathan the prophet tells King David to go ahead and build it, but that night God speaks to Nathan in his sleep. The message is that God will bless David greatly in establishing Israel and the kingdom, but he is not chosen to build the temple. His son will do that. David's humility is obvious in his prayer in response to the Lord.

David's military victories continue. He establishes the borders of Israel. He finds out that his great friend Jonathan had a son who survived, Saul's grandson, and to honor his friend he brings the crippled Mephibosheth into the palace and makes him part of his court.

David's family story is not glorious. His wife Michal, Saul's daughter, worships idols and despises David. David commits adultery with Bathsheba, who conceives. He then makes sure her husband, Uriah, is killed in battle, and David takes Bathsheba as his wife. Their child dies. Bathsheba gives David a second son, Solomon. David's son Amnon rapes his half-sister Tamar, Absalom's sister. David does nothing to deal with Amnon nor to care for Tamar, in spite of the law's requirement that Amnon marry Tamar. A bitterness brews in Absalom. Absalom begins to plot against Amnon and David. He murders his brother and leads a military coup against his father. Absalom even sleeps with his father's concubines in the sight of all of Israel, on the palace roof, as an insult to his father.

David flees, but he is spared complete defeat because Absalom listens to bad counsel. David regroups his military. Under Joab's leadership, they defeat the troops of Absalom, and Joab personally kills Absalom in spite of a direct order from David to capture him alive. Because of David's mourning for Absalom, Joab is angry with the king for dishonoring the troops that have saved his kingdom, and he rebukes the king. David is angry with Joab but again does nothing to him and, again, leaves him as head of his army.

As David attempts to reunite Israel, civil war breaks out with the Benjamites under the leadership of Sheba. Sheba's army is defeated, and he is beheaded as a peace offering from the city of Abel Beth Maakah.

As David's reign comes to a close, he is forced to deal with the Gibeonites, who had a treaty with Joshua to live in peace in Israel but had been attacked by Saul, breaking the treaty. God brings famine to Israel in order to draw attention to the injustice. The Gibeonites accept the death of seven of Saul's family in retribution, in spite of the law that says a son should not die for the sins of the father. Then, on top of the famine, David brings another judgment on Israel by disobeying the Lord in taking a census of the military.

David waits too long for succession, and another son, Adonijah, starts a second rebellion before David turns the kingdom over to Solomon.

David was a great poet, a worshiper of the Lord, a military giant, an adulterer and murderer, and a husband to seven hundred women. He was father to a rapist, a murderer, and treasonous and incestuous sons. David, the inconsistent follower of the law who loves God, dies. He ruled Israel for forty years.

SOLOMON, 971–931 BC

Solomon takes Israel to its highest development in all of Jewish history. Spared from fratricide by his mother Bathsheba's intervention with the aged David, Solomon is made king. He is the chosen of God to lead Israel into the next generation. He takes the throne in the midst of a coup led by his brother Adonijah.

David charges Solomon to lead from the decrees, commands, and requirements of the law of Moses. If he, Solomon, will be faithful to them, God will be faithful to Solomon and the continuation of his throne in Israel. David leaves Solomon with a list of blessings for those subjects who have been loyal to him and a long list of grievances to resolve, including Joab's betrayal. David still remembers the murders his military commander perpetrated without consequence, and now Joab has conspired with Adonijah.

Solomon's attempts to rehabilitate his brother Adonijah fail, and Adonijah is executed for treason. Joab is executed as well.

Solomon follows David's instructions, but not completely. There is a problem:

> The people, however, were still sacrificing at the high places, because a temple had not yet been built for the Name of the LORD. Solomon showed his love for the LORD by walking according to the instructions given him by his father David, except that he offered sacrifices and burned incense on the high places.
>
> The king went to Gibeon to offer sacrifices, for that was the most important high place, and Solomon offered a thousand burnt offerings on that altar. At Gibeon the LORD appeared to Solomon during the night in a dream, and God said, "Ask for whatever you want me to give you." (1 Kings 3:2–5)

Do you see this? Solomon is in the middle of offering one thousand sacrifices in Israel's high places when God speaks to him in a dream. Solomon has married Moabites, Ammonites, Edomites, Sidonians, Hittites, and Egyptians, and he follows all their gods! But God desires to bless Israel in spite of the idolatry of the king and the people.

In the dream, Solomon prays: "So give your servant a discerning heart to govern your people and to distinguish between right and wrong. For who is able to govern this great people of yours?" (1 Kings 3:7–9).

We often focus on the humility Solomon showed in his prayer, and it was a humble prayer. But he was being humble in the middle of his pagan idolatry, and he was being humble in his sleep. It is God who is faithful and pursues Solomon, not faithful Solomon who pursues God. There are no heroes here except God!

"Then Solomon awoke—and he realized it had been a dream. He returned to Jerusalem, stood before the ark of the Lord's covenant and sacrificed burnt offerings and fellowship offerings. Then he gave a feast for all his court" (1 Kings 3:15).

Is it possible that Solomon realized he was in the wrong place as he made his offerings?

As God promised, Solomon does indeed have "discernment in administering justice" (though, as we will see, he has wisdom in very little else). Because there is peace throughout most of his rule, Solomon is able to focus his attention on national development. Solomon does not only build the temple of the Lord, his own palace, and the wall around Jerusalem—themselves huge undertakings. He also creates a systematic infrastructure for governance and economics that is the greatest in the world at the time. The Queen of Sheba[3] comes to visit this famous kingdom and concludes: "The report I heard in my own country about your achievements and your wisdom is true. But I did not believe these things until I came and saw with my own eyes. Indeed, not even half was told me; in wisdom and wealth you have far exceeded the report I heard" (1 Kings 10:6–7).

The promise of God in the wilderness has been fulfilled. He has made Israel a great nation, one of the greatest of Solomon's time. But meanwhile God is repeating over and over again:

And if you walk in obedience to me and keep my decrees and commands as David your father did, I will give you a long life. (1 Kings 3:14)

But if you or your descendants turn away from me and do not observe the commands and decrees I have given you and go off to serve other gods and worship them, then I will cut off Israel from the land I have given them and will reject this temple I have consecrated for my Name. Israel will then become a byword and an object of ridicule among all peoples. This temple will become a heap of rubble. All who pass by will be appalled and will scoff and say, "Why has the LORD done such a thing to this land and to this temple?" (1 Kings 9:4–9)

It is *sustainable* development for generations that God desires for Israel. The system the Israelites have chosen will bless them for a time. But will Israel continue to flourish?

The LORD became angry with Solomon because his heart had turned away from the LORD, the God of Israel, who had appeared to him twice. Although he had forbidden Solomon to follow other gods, Solomon did not keep the LORD's command. So the LORD said to Solomon, "Since this is your attitude and you have not kept my covenant and my decrees, which I commanded you, I will most certainly tear the kingdom away from you and give it to one of your subordinates. Nevertheless, for the sake of David your father, I will not do it during your lifetime. (1 Kings 11:9–12)

God raises up an enemy for Israel in the Edomites and an enemy for the house of Solomon in Jeroboam. Jeroboam supervises construction of Solomon's terraces. God tells Jeroboam that he will divide the kingdom and give part of it to Jeroboam to lead after Solomon's death. When Solomon tries to kill Jeroboam, he flees to Egypt and exile until the king is dead.

Solomon, son of adulterers, husband of a thousand wives and concubines, builder of the temple, wisdom of Israel, worshiper of the idolatrous high places, worshiper of the gods of his wives, builder of new pagan shrines, dies. Solomon reigned in Israel for forty years.

THE KINGS IN ASCENT

What is God highlighting in this history? There is no end to the depth of what God can reveal from his word, but here are some of the things worth noting from the political leaders so far:

- God will honor his delegation of political authority to the people being governed regardless of their choices. But the consequences of those choices stand.
- Even if God disagrees with the choices a people make, he will still do his best to bless them within those choices. He seeks to mitigate the damages.
- When we add layers of authority to God's system of governance, we add complexity of change. Not only must the populace change, but the system must change as well.
- God will indicate the best political leader to choose, but "best" is very different from good.

- When the people cry out for God's help, he will work even through a bad leader.
- Unlike in the time of the judges, as we move into the time of the kings, we hear less and less often the words, "And the people cried out to the Lord." The people are looking more and more to government to solve the problem.
- The kings at their best always return to the law for their counsel and instruction.
- Undealt with insurrection will never go away; it will return with a vengeance at a future date. Our history holds some of the keys to the future of our political process.
- Political enemies are often from God. The question is not only "How do we deal with our enemy?" but also "What is God saying to us through our enemy?"
- It took three generations of relative peace to build up the nation to an observable quality of life as in Solomon's day.
- Any system may build up a nation in some category, but not all systems are sustainable.

At this point in Israel's history, we may think that God has been mistaken in his disapproval of a king for his model nation. Look at what the kings have accomplished. The Israelites are now the nation God promised them they would be in the wilderness. Aren't they?

The kings continue.

CHAPTER 19

THE KINGS IN DECLINE

The Kings of Divided Israel

The nation of Israel reached the zenith of its development politically and economically in Solomon's day. If Jesus had come at this point in history, we would have had a very clear idea of how to disciple a nation politically. We would focus our attention on a strong but benevolent sovereign leader who would develop the nation by giving direction and making the people do what is right. Political power would be a top-down institution, and discipleship would be a takeover strategy. But Jesus did not come in 931 BC, and Solomon is not the end of Israel's history. God has not finished making his point yet. We are not ready for that revelation yet. We have thirty-eight kings to go, nineteen in the northern kingdom and nineteen in the southern kingdom.

Israel wanted a king like those of all the nations around them. In spite of God's discouragement, Israel made the choice to move their system of governance from a federation of independent tribes to a sovereign monarchy. For three generations of political leaders, it looked as though God made a mistake, because the nation prospered with kingship. But God has not been in error. When political power is moved up, rapid development is achievable, but decline can come even faster.

Can we bear what God wants us to see in this history?

Rehoboam, Judah, 930–913 BC (17 years)

We are not told why Rehoboam is chosen from Solomon's sons to lead Israel, but "all Israel" went to Shechem "to make him king" (2 Chron. 10:1). Jeroboam is called back from exile in Egypt to take the people's labor disputes to the new king. True to what God told the people about life with a king, the Israelites are discontent with the burden of King Solomon's national building projects, and they want relief. Rehoboam disregards the counsel of the elders who served his father. Instead he follows the advice of his young advisors and responds that he will put an even heavier workload on the people. The very people who have just appointed him to lead them have no voice as far as he is concerned. The new king will tell *them* what to do. Or will he?

> When all Israel saw that the king refused to listen to them, they answered the king: "What share do we have in David, what part in Jesse's son? To your tents, Israel! Look after your own house, David!"
>
> So the Israelites went home. But as for the Israelites who were living in the towns of Judah, Rehoboam still ruled over them.
>
> King Rehoboam sent out Adoniram, who was in charge of forced labor, but all Israel stoned him to death. King Rehoboam, however, managed to get into his chariot and escape to Jerusalem. So Israel has been in rebellion against the house of David to this day.
>
> When all the Israelites heard that Jeroboam had returned, they sent and called him to the assembly and made him king over all Israel. Only the tribe of Judah remained loyal to the house of David. (1 Kings 12:16–20)

The people of Israel do not reach consensus, and the ten northern tribes refuse to be ruled by Rehoboam. Israel is now divided into two kingdoms, Israel in the north and Judah in the south. Israel will not be united again under its own authority until the twentieth century.

Solomon's son Rehoboam barely escapes being stoned to death in this civil dispute and returns to Jerusalem, retained as Judah's capital, to rule from there. He musters an army from Judah and Benjamin to fight Jeroboam and the northern tribes but has enough sense to listen when a prophet tells him that God will not bless him with victory because this division of the kingdom is from him.

Why would God split the very kingdom he has been promising to establish for a thousand years? What danger is he trying to avert? Would Israel have dissolved into total destruction even more rapidly if there had not been a division of power? We don't know, but God seems to use civil war to both warn the nation and retard their decline. God is giving Israel time.

There is an unexpected blessing in this civil war. We find out in 2 Chronicles 11 that because Jeroboam (the leader God raised up) builds two golden idols and appoints his own priests, the Levitical priests give up their own lands and homes and move to Judah in protest. And "those from every tribe of Israel who set their hearts on seeking the Lord, the God of Israel, followed the Levites to Jerusalem" (2 Chron. 11:16). This mass influx of God's faithful people strengthens the kingdom of Judah and the leadership of Rehoboam.

The support of these people who follow the ways of David influences Rehoboam for three years until he is "established" and "strong" (2 Chron. 12:1). Then the king and Judah turn away from the ways of God. In other words, the hearts of the people and the king were not changed, but they saw blessing because of the influence of the godly remnant from the north. It was a short-lived impact, however.

In Rehoboam's fifth year as king, because he and the people have been unfaithful to the Lord, God raises up an enemy in Shishak king of Egypt, who invades Judah. For the first time we read: "He carried off the treasures of the temple of the Lord and the treasures of the royal palace. He took everything, including all the gold shields Solomon had made" (1 Kings 14:26). Rehoboam replaces the shields with bronze.

This theme of ransacking and stripping the temple, Israel's symbol of the presence of God, will persist throughout their history, as will the ransacking of the palace. But we will let God develop that theme as we go.

In all of his unworthiness, Rehoboam and his leaders humble themselves and ask God for help. And God responds by limiting the damage Shishak does, and so Judah is "not totally destroyed" (2 Chron. 12:12).

Because of God's mercy, Rehoboam is strengthened again in his rule. But he does "evil because he had not set his heart on seeking the Lord" (2 Chron. 12:14). This is God's evaluation of Judah during the reign of Rehoboam: "Judah did evil in the eyes of the Lord. By the sins they committed they stirred up his jealous anger more than those who were before them had done . . . ; the people engaged in all the detestable practices of the nations the Lord had driven out before the Israelites" (1 Kings 14:22, 24).

The king and the people of Judah continue to turn away from God even with the presence of the righteous remnant of Jews. However, God continues to help them whenever they cry out to him.

Meanwhile, in the north, Jeroboam is creating a new religion for Israel with two golden calves.

JEROBOAM, ISRAEL, 930–909 BC (22 YEARS)

God raises up Jeroboam under Solomon's rule because the people have forsaken him and are worshiping the gods of the nations around them. The prophet Ahijah is sent with a message that God will tear ten tribes away from Solomon's heir and give them to Jeroboam. God makes Jeroboam the same conditional promise he has given every political leader since Moses: "If you do whatever I command you and walk in obedience to me and do what is right in my eyes by obeying my decrees and commands, as David my servant did, I will be with you. I will build you a dynasty as enduring as the one I built for David and will give Israel to you" (1 Kings 11:38).

Again, God has found the best man in Israel to lead his people and promised him blessing if he will follow God's ways. When Israel rebels against Rehoboam, they make Jeroboam king of Israel. When Rehoboam marshals his military against the revolt, God through the prophet Shemaiah tells them not to fight their brothers, and they obey! This division of the nation of Israel is from God.

Jeroboam is concerned that if the Jews of the north go to offer sacrifices at the temple in the south they will be lured away from him. So, after seeking advice, he builds two golden calves and calls the people to worship them. These idols will be their gods. Jeroboam builds shrines and high places and creates a priesthood for his new worship.

Those who are faithful to God leave Israel, the northern kingdom, and move to Jerusalem in Judah, the southern kingdom. These two golden calves and the institutional idolatry they represent are the "sins of Jeroboam" that will remain prominent in the development of Israel. Remember then this institutionalized idolatry as well as that of Solomon and his high places.

Prophets begin to speak out against the idolatry of Jeroboam and his gods and altars, and the king begins to persecute the prophets. In one encounter, Jeroboam's hand shrivels up as he points to a prophet in violence; his hand is restored when he asks the prophet to pray for him.

Ahijah, the prophet who once brought Jeroboam the news of his coming kingship, now delivers a different message from God:

> I raised you up from among the people and appointed you ruler over my people Israel. I tore the kingdom away from the house of David and gave it to you, but you have not been like my servant David, who kept my commands and followed me with all his heart, doing only what was right in my eyes. You have done more evil than all who lived before you. You have made for yourself other gods, idols made of metal; you have aroused my anger and turned your back on me. (1 Kings 14:7–9)

The best leader God could find for the northern kingdom has totally turned away from God. The clock is ticking on the destruction of the house of Jeroboam as "this was the sin of the house of Jeroboam that led to its downfall and to its destruction from the face of the earth" (1 Kings 13:34). In one generation, Israel has gone from enjoying greatness to sowing the seeds of their total destruction. How could this happen? The king has the power to take them there, and they willingly follow!

Jeroboam rules Israel for twenty-two years, and Nadab his son succeeds him.

ABIJAH, JUDAH, 913–910 BC (3 YEARS)

Back in Judah, after Rehoboam's death, Rehoboam's son Abijah takes the throne and commits all the sins of his father. Yet, for the sake of David, God seeks to do his best with this king. Finally, real civil war breaks out between the northern and southern kingdoms. Abijah goes to field with 400,000 troops and Jeroboam with 800,000.

On the battlefield, Abijah makes an amazingly godly speech, calling Israel and Jeroboam to account for their golden calf idolatry and lawless priesthood. The king then declares that Judah, on the other hand, fights on behalf of the Lord God and his Levitical priesthood and observes the requirements of God. Next comes the battle:

> Now Jeroboam had sent troops around to the rear, so that while he was in front of Judah the ambush was behind them. Judah turned and saw that they were being attacked at both front and rear. Then they cried out to the LORD. The priests blew their trumpets and the men of Judah raised the battle cry. At the sound of their battle cry, God routed Jeroboam and all Israel before Abijah and Judah. The Israelites fled before Judah, and God delivered them into their hands. Abijah and his troops inflicted heavy losses on them, so that there were five hundred thousand casualties among Israel's able men. The Israelites were subdued on that occasion, and the people of Judah were victorious because they relied on the LORD, the God of their ancestors. (2 Chron. 13:13–18)

Was Abijah's speech genuine? Did he have a moment of conscience? We don't know, but the people were trusting in God, and God delivered them in spite of their political leader.

Abijah dies and his son Asa takes the throne.

ASA, JUDAH, 910–869 BC (41 YEARS)

In Jeroboam's twentieth year, Asa becomes king in Judah. Asa does right in the eyes of the Lord, as David did. He expels the shrine prostitutes, gets rid of the idols his father had made, deposes his pagan grandmother who had been Queen Mother, and replaces the silver and gold articles Egypt had taken from the temple. He makes repairs in the temple and calls the people together to recommit themselves to God and his law. Judah has peace for years.

The Cushites[1] come to war with Judah. Asa can field an army of

580,000 armed men. But the Cushites come with 300,000 chariots and a vast army. Asa calls on the Lord, who helps the "powerless against the mighty" (2 Chron. 14:11). Judah devastates the Cushite army.

The prophet Azariah has a word for King Asa: "Listen to me, Asa and all Judah and Benjamin. The Lord is with you when you are with him. If you seek him, he will be found by you, but if you forsake him, he will forsake you. For a long time Israel was without the true God, without a priest to teach and without the law. But in their distress they turned to the Lord, the God of Israel, and sought him, and he was found by them" (2 Chron. 15:2–4). Will Asa continue to turn to the Lord?

In the latter years of his reign, facing civil war with the northern kingdom, Asa makes a treaty with Ben-Hadad, king of Aram, who rules in Damascus, giving him all the silver and gold that is left in the temple treasuries. In exchange, Ben-Hadad breaks his treaty with Israel and fights for Judah against the northern tribes. Hanani the seer comes to the king with a word: "Because you relied on the king of Aram and not on the Lord your God, the army of the king of Aram has escaped from your hand. Were not the Cushites and Libyans a mighty army with great numbers of chariots and horsemen? Yet when you relied on the Lord, he delivered them into your hand. For the eyes of the Lord range throughout the earth to strengthen those whose hearts are fully committed to him. You have done a foolish thing, and from now on you will be at war" (2 Chron. 16:7–9).

Asa is so angry that he puts the prophet in prison and begins to brutally oppress some of the people. He is afflicted with a terrible foot disease but does not seek God's help in this either and dies of his ailments.

Asa, whose "heart was fully committed to the Lord all his life" (1 Kings 15:14), does not remove the high places, dies mad at God, and ensures that Judah will be at war throughout the rest of its history.

His son Jehoshaphat succeeds him.

NADAB, ISRAEL, 909–908 BC (2 YEARS)

In the second year of Asa king of Judah, Nadab son of Jeroboam becomes king of Israel. "He did evil in the eyes of the Lord, following in the ways of his father and committing the same sin his father had caused Israel to commit" (1 Kings 15:26). He worships the golden calves. Note how the son continues the institutionalized idolatry created by the father. Jeroboam has instituted official pagan worship. This officially sanctioned worship is different from idolatry practiced independently by some of the citizens. Its impact will last for generations.

Baasha, from the tribe of Issachar, assassinates Nadab when the king and his army are besieging a Philistine town.

Nadab rules Israel for two years, then Baasha makes himself king and succeeds him. Blood is flowing; the red thread of violence continues.

BAASHA, ISRAEL, 908-886 BC (24 YEARS)

Baasha is raised up by God to deal with the evil the house of Jeroboam is bringing on Israel with the golden calves. As soon as Baasha becomes king, having already killed Nadab, he kills all of Jeroboam's family "because of the sins Jeroboam had committed and had caused Israel to commit, and because he aroused the anger of the Lord, the God of Israel" (1 Kings 15:30).

But Baasha himself "did evil in the eyes of the Lord, following the ways of Jeroboam and committing the same sin Jeroboam had caused Israel to commit" (1 Kings 15:34). To this God responds: "I lifted you up from the dust and appointed you ruler over my people Israel, but you followed the ways of Jeroboam and caused my people Israel to sin and to arouse my anger by their sins. So I am about to wipe out Baasha and his house, and I will make your house like that of Jeroboam son of Nebat" (1 Kings 16:2–3). So Baasha the avenger is no better. There is no righteous leadership in Israel.

Baasha attempts war with Judah but backs off when he loses his ally in Aram.

Baasha reigns in Israel for twenty-four years, and his son Elah succeeds him as king.

ELAH, ISRAEL, 886–885 BC (2 YEARS)

Elah becomes king of Israel during the twenty-sixth year of Asa king of Judah. While Elah is getting drunk in the home of his palace administrator, another of his officials, the commander of half his chariots, assassinates him. As soon this man, Zimri, is seated on the throne, he kills off the whole family of Baasha "because of all the sins Baasha and his son Elah had committed and had caused Israel to commit, so that they aroused the anger of the Lord, the God of Israel, by their worthless idols" (1 Kings 16:13).

Elah rules Israel for two years and is succeeded by Zimri.

ZIMRI, ISRAEL, 885 BC (7 DAYS)

As soon as the army, encamped near the Philistine town of Gibbethon, hears that Zimri has assassinated the king and proclaimed himself king, they proclaim their commander Omri king over Israel instead. Omri and the army lay siege to the capital city, Tirzah. When they take the city, Zimri retreats into the citadel of the royal palace and sets fire to the palace with himself inside.

"So he died, because of the sins he had committed, doing evil in the eyes of the Lord and following the ways of Jeroboam and committing the same sin Jeroboam had caused Israel to commit" (1 Kings 16:18–19).

Zimri is king in Israel for seven days and Omri takes his place. The political system of Israel is in free fall, and violence is rampant.

OMRI, ISRAEL, 885–874 BC (12 YEARS)

Omri's rule begins with civil war: "Then the people of Israel were split into two factions; half supported Tibni son of Ginath for king, and the other half supported Omri. But Omri's followers proved stronger than those of Tibni son of Ginath. So Tibni died and Omri became king" (1 Kings 16:21–22). The nation of Israel, split from Judah, is in danger of splitting again.

In the thirty-first year of Asa, Omri takes the throne. He buys the hill of Samaria and builds the city of Samaria, which will remain significant in Israel far into the future, even in the time of Jesus. God's evaluation of Omri: "But Omri did evil in the eyes of the Lord and sinned more than all those before him. He followed completely the ways of Jeroboam son of Nebat, committing the same sin Jeroboam had caused Israel to commit, so that they aroused the anger of the Lord, the God of Israel, by their worthless idols" (1 Kings 16:25–26).

Omri worships the two golden calves. He rules Israel for twelve years and is buried in Samaria. His son Ahab succeeds him.

AHAB, ISRAEL, 874–853 BC (22 YEARS)

As impossible as it may seem at this juncture in Israel's history, Ahab does more evil than all the kings that came before him. "He not only considered it trivial to commit the sins of Jeroboam son of Nebat, but he also married Jezebel daughter of Ethbaal king of the Sidonians, and began to serve Baal and worship him. He set up an altar for Baal in the temple of Baal that he built in Samaria. Ahab also made an Asherah pole and did more to arouse the anger of the Lord, the God of Israel, than did all the kings of Israel before him" (1 Kings 16:31–33).

Ahab worships the two golden calves and tops the evil of previous kings by adding more gods. God raises up many prophets in Ahab's day. The great prophet Elijah is a nemesis to Ahab's power. Elisha, Micaiah, and others are also busy making God's thoughts clear to all who will listen. The more dire the national condition, the harder God tries to call the people back to himself.

Ben-Hadad king of Aram pulls together thirty-two allied kings and attacks the city of Samaria. He wants all Ahab's wealth, wives, children, and everything else of value. Ahab consults the elders, and they all agree to resist the demands. Ben-Hadad swears he will destroy them.

> Meanwhile a prophet came to Ahab king of Israel and announced, "This is what the LORD says: 'Do you see this vast army? I will give it into your hand today, and then you will know that I am the LORD.'"
>
> "But who will do this?" asked Ahab.
>
> The prophet replied, "This is what the LORD says: 'The junior officers under the provincial commanders will do it.'"
>
> "And who will start the battle?" he asked.
>
> The prophet answered, "You will." (1 Kings 20:13–14)

And they do! The 232 young commanders summoned by Ahab lead seven thousand troops to defeat the armies of thirty-two (granted, they are drunk) kings. The Arameans flee, suffering heavy losses. God uses one of the worst kings to win a victory and to honor his own name.

Ben-Hadad's advisors tell him that his coalition was defeated because they fought in the hills. The Israelite gods, he is told, have power in the hills but not on the plains. So Ben-Hadad leads another army in attack the next spring.

Again the prophet comes to Ahab and says: "This is what the Lord says: 'Because the Arameans think the Lord is a god of the hills and not a god of the valleys, I will deliver this vast army into your hands, and you will know that I am the Lord'" (1 Kings 20:28). We are not told exactly how vast this army is, but Israel was "like two small flocks of goats, while the Arameans covered the countryside" (1 Kings 20:27). The Israelite army kills 100,000 in one day, and another 27,000 die when the walls of the city fall on them as they flee.

Twice God gives this awful king military victory on behalf of Israel and his name. God blesses the people and their leader as best he can if they will listen to him in even one area. Israel has deserted God. He has not deserted them.

But the king's obedience has been incomplete in this second victory. Even though God has told him to kill Ben-Hadad, Ahab spares him. He signs a treaty, letting the king of Aram live in return for the cities the Arameans have taken and the right to trade in the markets of Damascus. God sends another prophet to tell Ahab that it will be his life for the life of the king he has spared.

Meanwhile, during a time of peace, Ahab develops an urgent need for a vegetable garden. He wants to buy a vineyard close to his palace but is refused by the owner. Naboth will not sell the inheritance of his fathers, according to the law of Moses. Ahab accepts Naboth's refusal but sulks at home. His wife Jezebel, a Sidonian princess, berates Ahab over his concept of authority: "Is this how you act as king over Israel? Get up and eat! Cheer up. I'll get you the vineyard of Naboth the Jezreelite" (1 Kings 21:7). She conspires with leaders of Naboth's city in Ahab's name to have him executed on false charges. And Ahab gets his vegetable garden.

Then the word of the LORD came to Elijah the Tishbite: "Go down to meet Ahab king of Israel, who rules in Samaria. He is

now in Naboth's vineyard, where he has gone to take possession of it. Say to him, 'This is what the LORD says: Have you
not murdered a man and seized his property?' Then say to him,
'This is what the LORD says: In the place where dogs licked up
Naboth's blood, dogs will lick up your blood—yes, yours!'"

Ahab said to Elijah, "So you have found me, my enemy!"

"I have found you," he answered, "because you have sold
yourself to do evil in the eyes of the LORD." (1 Kings 21:17–20)

In great detail, the prophet pronounces disaster for Ahab's house.

When Ahab heard these words, he tore his clothes, put on sackcloth and fasted. He lay in sackcloth and went around meekly.

Then the word of the LORD came to Elijah the Tishbite:
"Have you noticed how Ahab has humbled himself before me?
Because he has humbled himself, I will not bring this disaster
in his day, but I will bring it on his house in the days of his son."
(1 Kings 21:27–29)

Ahab repents and cries out to God. And again God, who loves
mercy, hears him and responds. He will delay the judgment. God
requires so little to extend his mercy, and still his people reject him.

Three years after he spares Ben-Hadad king of Aram, Ahab dies in
battle with Ben-Hadad's army. His son Ahaziah succeeds him as king.

JEHOSHAPHAT, JUDAH, 872-848 BC (25 YEARS)

In the fourth year of Ahab, Jehoshaphat son of Asa becomes king in
Judah. "In everything he followed the ways of his father Asa and did
not stray from them; he did what was right in the eyes of the Lord" (1
Kings 22:43).

It is important to read both accounts of Jehoshaphat (1 Kings 22;
2 Chron. 17–20) to get a clear picture of his rule. He has a strange and
conflicting relationship with the tribes of the northern kingdom.

The Chronicles account tells us that in his early years Jehoshaphat
strengthened himself against Israel and sought God rather than following the north's paganism. He was devoted to the ways of God and
sent officials and priests throughout the southern kingdom to teach the

Book of the Law. Jehoshaphat rids Judah of the shrine prostitutes, but he does not remove the high places. The people continue to worship and make sacrifices there.

Jehoshaphat restores the judicial system from the law of Moses, and Judah becomes a powerful military force to which even the Philistines pay tribute.

He then makes peace with Ahab, the worst king in the history of Israel, and marries into his family. The two kings go to war with the king of Aram to retake Ramoth Gilead,[2] and Ahab is killed on the battlefield. The seer Jehu rebukes Jehoshaphat on God's behalf, asking, "Should you help the wicked?" (2 Chron. 19:2), referring to the way Jehoshaphat went to war with Ahab.

The Moabites and the Ammonites make war with Judah, and Jehoshaphat leads Judah in seeking God, turning to the Lord for help. All the men, women, and children gather before the Lord, and the Spirit of God comes on the prophets, proclaiming a victory for Judah, which the Lord delivers.

At one point Jehoshaphat makes an alliance with Ahaziah, son of Ahab, now king of Israel. Together they construct a fleet of ships for the purpose of going to Ophir to trade in gold. Again God speaks through the prophets to rebuke the king for aligning himself with wickedness, and the ships are all destroyed by fire before they ever set sail.

After Joram becomes king of Israel in the eighteenth year of Jehoshaphat's rule, Jehoshaphat again goes to war to assist his northern brothers in Israel. Joined by the king of Edom, they take their armies to deal with revolt in Moab. On the journey, they run out of water, and Jehoshaphat demands that they inquire of the prophets of the Lord for direction. Elisha is nearest, and the three kings go to inquire of him. Elisha makes it clear that, were it not for Jehoshaphat, he would have nothing to do with the other two kings. After seeking God, Elisha prophesies victory over the Moabites.

Jehoshaphat is thirty-five years old when he becomes king, and he rules Judah for twenty-five years. His son Jehoram succeeds him.

Ahaziah, Israel, 853–852 BC (2 years)

Ahaziah, son of Ahab, becomes king of Israel in the seventeenth year of Jehoshaphat. He does evil in the eyes of the Lord as his father and his mother, Jezebel, did. The king suffers a fall from the terrace of his palace rooms. He sends messengers to seek the god of Ekron about the outcome of his injuries. Meanwhile, the angel of the Lord sends Elisha to intercept King Ahaziah's messengers. Elisha tells them God has said the king will die of his injuries. And he does!

Ahaziah leads Israel for two years, and Joram, another son of Ahab, takes his place on the throne.

JORAM, ISRAEL, 852–841 BC (12 YEARS)

Because Ahaziah has no son, Joram becomes king after his brother. This son of Ahab and Jezebel "did evil in the eyes of the Lord, but not as his father and mother had done. He got rid of the sacred stone of Baal that his father had made. Nevertheless he clung to the sins of Jeroboam son of Nebat, which he had caused Israel to commit; he did not turn away from them" (2 Kings 3:2–3). Joram worships the two golden calves.

With Ahab dead, the Moabites rise up, and Judah and Edom join Israel in the fight. Because of the uprightness of Judah's king, Jehoshaphat, Elisha prophesies victory.

Later the city of Samaria is besieged by the king of Aram, Ben-Hadad. Elisha is trapped in the city along with King Joram. The conditions are so extreme that people are eating human flesh to survive. Israel is reduced to cannibalism, and we hear echoes of the blood violence before the flood. Joram seeks out Elisha. God speaks through Elisha, and the Arameans flee the siege in utter confusion during the night, leaving behind all their supplies.

Again God blesses the unrighteous when they cry out to him.

JEHORAM, JUDAH, 848–841 BC (8 YEARS)

Jehoram, the son of Jehoshaphat, is thirty-two years old when he becomes king of Judah. He marries Ahab's daughter and walks in the ways of the kings of Israel, just as the house of Ahab did. Once he strengthens his position on the throne, Jehoram puts all his brothers to death and some of the princes of Israel as well. His father's marriage into the house of Ahab brought the evils of the northern kingdom into the Jerusalem. The violence is flowing in the southern kingdom as in the northern kingdom.

Jehoram does evil in the eyes of the Lord. "Nevertheless, for the sake of his servant David, the Lord was not willing to destroy Judah" (2 Kings 8:19).

During Jehoram's reign, persisting conflicts begin when Edom rebels, setting up its own king, and Libnah revolts against Judah, too, "because Jehoram had forsaken the Lord" (2 Chron. 21:10).

Elijah sends Jehoram a letter decrying his turning Judah to wickedness and the murder of his own brothers. He prophesies that the king's own family will be destroyed and that the king himself will die slowly of a disease causing his bowels to fall out.

The Philistines and Arabs plunder Judah, and the king dies as Elijah said. Jehoram is not honored in death as his predecessors were, having "passed away, to no one's regret" (2 Chron. 21:20). Ahaziah, Jehoram's youngest and only surviving son, becomes king.

AHAZIAH, JUDAH, 841 BC (1 YEAR)

Ahaziah is Jehoram's son and a grandson of King Ahab. His mother is a granddaughter of King Omri of Israel. Ahaziah is deeply enmeshed in his violent, dysfunctional family. He is twenty-two years old when he becomes king, and he does evil in the eyes of the Lord as Ahab did.

When Ahaziah takes the throne, Joram is king in Israel. Under Ahaziah, Judah joins forces again with Israel to fight the Arameans in Ramoth Gilead in spite of all God's warnings about the alliance.

During this time, God raises up a leader, a military commander named Jehu, son of Jehoshaphat (former king of Judah). Elisha calls on a young member of the "company of prophets" and commissions him to take a flask of oil to Ramoth Gilead (presumably where the war is going on) and anoint Jehu privately with the words: "This is what the Lord says: I anoint you king over Israel." Then with great wisdom Elisha says to the prophet, "Then open the door and run; don't delay!" (2 Kings 9:3). What political drama! And God is engaged in all of it.

Sure enough, the prophet anoints Jehu and runs. Jehu's fellow commanders want to know what the "maniac" has said (2 Kings 9:11), and when Jehu fesses up, they immediately pledge their allegiance to him and proclaim him king. A military coup commences.

Wounded in battle at Ramoth Gilead, King Joram has retired to Jezreel to heal. King Ahaziah has come down to visit him. Jehu takes his troops to Jezreel, joined by the soldiers of Joram who are loyal to him as he encounters them. The approaching troops are spotted from Jezreel's watchtower.

> "Hitch up my chariot," Joram ordered. And when it was hitched up, Joram king of Israel and Ahaziah king of Judah rode out, each in his own chariot, to meet Jehu. They met him at the plot of ground that had belonged to Naboth the Jezreelite. When Joram saw Jehu he asked, "Have you come in peace, Jehu?"
>
> "How can there be peace," Jehu replied, "as long as all the idolatry and witchcraft of your mother Jezebel abound?"
>
> Joram turned about and fled, calling out to Ahaziah, "Treachery, Ahaziah!" (2 Kings 9:21–23)

Jehu shoots King Joram in his chariot, and his body is dumped on the field of Naboth the Jezreelite. This is the land that Jezebel stole for Ahab's vegetable garden by having Naboth murdered. Jehu orders, "Pick him up and throw him on the field that belonged to Naboth the Jezreelite. Remember how you and I were riding together in chariots behind Ahab his father when the LORD spoke this prophecy against him: 'Yesterday I saw the blood of Naboth and the blood of his sons, declares the LORD, and I will surely make you pay for it on this plot of ground, declares the LORD.' Now then, pick him up and throw him on that plot, in accordance with the word of the LORD" (2 Kings 9:25–26).

Jehu's troops then mortally wound King Ahaziah, who flees in his chariot to Megiddo and dies there. The kings of Judah and Israel are murdered at the same time!

JEHU, ISRAEL, 841–814 BC (28 YEARS)

Having assassinated the kings, Jehu continues God's judgment of the house of Ahab. He directs the killing of Jezebel, fulfilling the word of the Lord through Elijah. Then Jehu sends word to the elders of Samaria to fight him or join him, and in response they execute all seventy sons of the house of Ahab, bringing him their heads at Jezreel. Before leaving Jezreel, Jehu orders the execution of Ahab's entire family and entourage of leaders, close friends, and priests in that place.

Jehu then sets out for Samaria. On the way there, he encounters the remaining family of Ahaziah king of Judah. He kills all of them. Once again, God is using the most extreme of measures to retard the red thread of violence. When he gets to Samaria, Jehu finishes what has been started: "When Jehu came to Samaria, he killed all who were left there of Ahab's family; he destroyed them, according to the word of the Lord spoken to Elijah" (2 Kings 10:17).

Jehu then calls a solemn assembly of all the followers of Baal throughout Israel. Not one Baal worshiper stays away from what Jehu promises will be a great sacrifice in honor of Baal. Once Baal's servants have filled the temple wall to wall, and have worshiped and sacrificed to their god, Jehu charges the eighty officers and guards stationed at the doors to kill them all. Jehu's men then destroy the temple of Baal and turn the site into a latrine.

"The Lord said to Jehu, 'Because you have done well in accomplishing what is right in my eyes and have done to the house of Ahab all I had in mind to do, your descendants will sit on the throne of Israel to the fourth generation.' Yet Jehu was not careful to keep the law of the Lord, the God of Israel, with all his heart" (2 Kings 10:30–31). Instead, Jehu worships the golden calves of Jeroboam! Twice we are told, "He did not turn away from the sins of Jeroboam son of Nebat, which he had caused Israel to commit—the worship of the golden calves at Bethel and Dan" (2 Kings 10:29).

Now we read these somber words: "In those days the Lord began to reduce the size of Israel" (2 Kings 10:32). They begin to lose the promised land.

There is less and less God can do and fewer people he can use to turn the tide of Israel's and Judah's self-destruction. As in the days of Noah, the condition of the people and their leaders is nearing the point of no remedy. Like the nations God destroyed in the land when Israel came, the tribes of Israel have become a virulent melanoma endangering all of life. Their reign of violence has reached its limits. The only way out of this pre-flood insanity seems to be the most drastic purging of both nations.

Jehu reigns over Israel in Samaria for twenty-eight years. His son Jehoahaz succeeds him as king.

QUEEN ATHALIAH, JUDAH, 841–835 BC (7 YEARS)

At the death of Ahaziah, as though things couldn't get worse, Judah gets his mother, Athaliah, granddaughter of Israel's King Omri, as queen. In her bid to take power, she begins to assassinate what remains of the royal family. Who is left? In another round of palace intrigue, Ahaziah's sister, Jehosheba, daughter of King Jehoram of Judah, steals away one child of King Ahaziah from among those about to be murdered. She rescues a newborn named Joash and hides this one living child of King Ahaziah from the queen. For six years while Athaliah rules, Jehosheba hides her brother's son and his nurse in the temple of the Lord with the help of her husband, the priest Jehoiada.

In collaboration with the military leadership, the Levites, and the heads of the families of Judah, Jehoiada plots to overthrow the queen and put Joash, great-grandson of Jehoshaphat, on the throne. When Joash is seven years old, Jehoiada and the military place him on a throne in front of the temple and declare him king. The people of Judah are ecstatic. As in the days of Samuel, there is no better hope for Judah's leadership than a child.

Athaliah hears the crowds and comes out to the temple. Seeing the king, she cries, "Treason! Treason!" The military leaders bring her out of the temple and execute her. Jehoiada then leads the people in making a covenant between the Lord, the king, and the people that they will be "the Lord's people" (2 Kings 11:17). They proceed as a crowd from there to tear down the temple of Baal and kill the priest of Baal before Baal's own altars.

JOASH, JUDAH, 835–796 BC (40 YEARS)

Joash is seven years old when he becomes king of Judah, and he reigns for forty years in Jerusalem. Joash "did what was right in the eyes of the Lord" (24:2) with the help and counsel of the priest Jehoiada—but only as long as the priest Jehoiada lived.

Joash repairs the temple of the Lord with offerings from the people. But he does not remove the high places, and the people continue to worship there.

The account in 2 Chronicles 24 tells us that after the priest Jehoiada's death, the king and his officials abandon worship in the temple and return to the worship of Asherah poles and other idols. The priest Zechariah, Jehoiada's son, speaks a word of God's judgment publicly, and King Joash has him stoned to death, in spite of Jehoiada's goodness to him as a young king.

The king of Aram, Hazael, attacks Jerusalem, and despite having a smaller army, the Arameans defeat Judah and wound King Joash. The king's officials conspire and assassinate him in retribution for his killing of Zechariah. Joash reigns over Judah for forty years, and Amaziah his son succeeds him as king.

JEHOAHAZ, ISRAEL, 814–798 BC (17 YEARS)

Jehoahaz succeeds his father, Jehu, in Israel. He does not follow the Lord but continues in the sins of Jeroboam, "which he had caused Israel to commit" (2 Kings 13:2).

The Lord repeatedly brings the kings of Aram against Israel as an enemy. "Then Jehoahaz sought the Lord's favor, and the Lord listened to him, for he saw how severely the king of Aram was oppressing Israel" (2 Kings 13:4). As in the days of the judges, when Jehoahaz and the people cry out to him, God raises up help and a deliverer for the nation. Israel defeats the stronger Aramean army, but the cost is great. Jehoahaz is left with fifty horsemen, ten chariots, and an army of ten thousand foot soldiers.

With Aram defeated, the people are once again able to live in their own homes, but neither they nor the king turn away from the worship of the golden calves or their sacred Asherah pole.

Jehoahaz dies, and his son Jehoash succeeds him as king.

JEHOASH, ISRAEL, 798–782 BC (16 YEARS)

In the thirty-seventh year of the reign of Joash king of Judah, Jehoash becomes king of Israel. He does evil in the eyes of the Lord and continues in the sins of Jeroboam, the worship of the golden calves.

During this time Judah is at war with the Edomites. King Amaziah has succeeded his father in Judah. He hires 100,000 troops from King Jehoash of Israel. But then, on the advice of a prophet that God will not bless the alliance with wickedness, Amaziah sends the Israelite troops home. King Jehoash is angry, and goaded by Amaziah, he wages war against Judah. Civil war results, and Israel tears down a section of the wall of Jerusalem, taking all the silver and gold from the temple and the palace.

Jehoash dies and his son Jeroboam takes the throne.

AMAZIAH, JUDAH, 796–767 BC (29 YEARS)

Amaziah, son of King Joash, succeeds his father in the southern kingdom. He does right in the eyes of the Lord, but not wholeheartedly like his forefather David.

Amaziah executes the officials who murdered his father, but he spares their sons according to the law of Moses. He fights and defeats the attacking Edomites, following the word of the Lord to not use the hired troops of Israel, as God would not bless them.

Following the great victory that God gives him, Amaziah brings back the gods of the Edomites and sets them up as his own gods, worshiping them and making sacrifices to them. He rejects the rebuke of the Lord's prophet and continues in his idolatry. Amaziah provokes King Jehoash, and Israel attacks and defeats Judah. Amaziah is assassinated by his own people.

Azariah his son (also called Uzziah) is chosen by the people to be king.

JEROBOAM II, ISRAEL, 793–753 BC (41 YEARS)

"In the fifteenth year of Amaziah son of Joash king of Judah, Jeroboam son of Jehoash king of Israel became king in Samaria" (2 Kings 14:23). He does evil in the eyes of the Lord and continues in the sins of the first King Jeroboam, worshiping the golden calves.

In accordance with the word of the Lord through a prophet, Jeroboam II restores some boundaries of Israel. He also recovers for Israel Damascus and Hamath, which had belonged to Judah.

Even though Jeroboam II disregards God, the Lord shows Israel mercy: "The Lord had seen how bitterly everyone in Israel, whether slave or free, was suffering; there was no one to help them. And since the Lord had not said he would blot out the name of Israel from under heaven, he saved them by the hand of Jeroboam son of Jehoash" (2 Kings 14:26–27). Amazing grace of God.

Zechariah, son of Jeroboam II, becomes king in Israel after his father.

AZARIAH (UZZIAH), JUDAH, 792–740 BC (52 YEARS)

"In the twenty-seventh year of Jeroboam king of Israel, Azariah son of Amaziah king of Judah began to reign" (2 Kings 15:1). King Azariah is sixteen when all the people of Judah choose him to take the throne after his father. He does what is right in the eyes of the Lord as his father did.

Azariah seeks God, and the prophet Zechariah instructs him in the fear of the Lord. However, he does not take away the high places, and the people continue to worship and make sacrifices there.

As long as Azariah seeks God, the Lord gives him success in all that he does. He defeats the Philistines, Arabs, and Meunites. The Ammonites pay him tribute. He fortifies the wall of Jerusalem with towers. He has a passion for agriculture. He digs many cisterns and develops the land and livestock. He has a trained military with newly invented weapons.

But as he gains power and fame, Azariah becomes proud. Like Saul before him, he begins to cross the boundaries between the role of the king and the role of the priesthood. He enters the temple to burn incense before the Lord. The priests confront him with the fact that Moses gave this role to the priesthood and the descendants of Aaron. They order him to leave the sanctuary. The king begins to rage against the priests, and he is struck with leprosy.

Azariah has leprosy the rest of his life and runs the affairs of Judah through his son Jotham. Azariah is king fifty-two years. At his death, Jotham becomes king in Judah.

ZECHARIAH, ISRAEL, 753 BC (6 MONTHS)

"In the thirty-eighth year of Azariah king of Judah, Zechariah son of Jeroboam became king of Israel in Samaria, and he reigned six months"

(2 Kings 15:8). Zechariah does evil in the eyes of the Lord and does not turn away from the sins of Jeroboam. He and the people continue to worship the golden calves. Shallum, son of Jabesh, assassinates him publicly and succeeds him as king. "So the word of the Lord spoken to Jehu was fulfilled: 'Your descendants will sit on the throne of Israel to the fourth generation'" (2 Kings 15:12).

The violence continues to escalate, and the pace quickens.

SHALLUM, ISRAEL, 752 BC (1 MONTH)

Shallum takes the throne in Israel after assassinating Zechariah and rules one month before being assassinated by Menahem son of Gadi, who takes the throne.

MENAHEM, ISRAEL, 752–742 BC (10 YEARS)

Menahem does evil in the eyes of the Lord. He does not stop the worship of the golden calves of Jeroboam. He sacks Tiphsah when the city refuses to open its gates, attacking everyone in the vicinity and ripping open all the pregnant women. Assyria[3] invades, and King Menahem pays tribute to keep his power in Israel, taxing the people to pay off Assyria's king.

After Menahem's death, his son Pekahiah is king.

PEKAHIAH, ISRAEL, 742–740 BC (2 YEARS)

As king, Pekahiah continues to do evil in the eyes of the Lord as his father Menahem did. He continues to lead Israel in the worship of Jeroboam's two golden calves. His military captain, Pekah, along with fifty Gileadites, attacks and assassinates him in the palace after only two years.

Pekah succeeds him as king.

PEKAH, ISRAEL, 752–732 BC (20 YEARS)

"In the fifty-second year of Azariah king of Judah, Pekah son of Remaliah became king of Israel in Samaria, and he reigned twenty years" (2 Kings 15:27).

Like the king he assassinated, Pekah also does evil in the eyes of the Lord by continuing the worship of Jeroboam's calves and leading the people of Israel to do the same. During the reign of Ahaz king of Judah, God uses Pekah to bring judgment on Judah for forsaking the Lord. He invades, inflicts heavy casualties, and plunders the southern kingdom. While Pekah is king of Israel, the king of Assyria invades the northern territories and takes the people captive to Assyria.

King Pekah is assassinated by Hoshea, who becomes king.

JOTHAM, JUDAH, 750–735 BC (16 YEARS)

In the southern kingdom, Jotham becomes king after the death of his father, Azariah (also known as Uzziah). He does right in the eyes of the Lord as his father did, but he does better in that he does not enter the priestly part of the temple the way Azariah did. However, the high places are not removed, and the people continue their corrupt practices.

Jotham rebuilds the upper gate of the temple, fortifies the wall, and strengthens Judah's border defenses. He goes to war with and defeats the Ammonites, conquering their territory and collecting tribute. "Jotham grew powerful because he walked steadfastly before the Lord his God" (2 Chron. 27:6).

But in Jotham's day, God begins to raise up the Arameans and Israel against Judah. Jotham's son Ahaz becomes king at his death.

AHAZ, JUDAH, 732–715 BC (16 YEARS)

King Ahaz, son of Jotham, rules Judah for sixteen years. He does not do what is right in the eyes of the Lord as David did, but walks in the ways of the kings of Israel.

Ahaz follows the "detestable practices" of the nations God drove out of the land, including human sacrifice. He sacrifices his own son in fire. Ahaz casts idols of the Baals for Judah to worship, and he *increases* the high places throughout Israel.

God hands Judah over to Aram, and many of the people of Judah are carried off as prisoners. Trouble arises from the Edomites and Philistines. Even Israel is used by God to judge Judah. Ahaz makes an agreement with the king of Assyria to rescue Judah. He gives him gold and silver from the palace and the temple as a tribute. It's not clear that this tribute buys Judah help rather than harm. The Assyrians lay siege to and capture the Aramean city of Damascus, taking prisoners and killing the king of Aram.

Ahaz goes to Damascus to meet with the king of Assyria. He sees an altar in Damascus that impresses him so much that he sends a drawing of it to a priest in Jerusalem so the priest can build a duplicate inside the temple in Jerusalem. This altar will now be used for sacrifices, and God's bronze altar will be used when the king inquires of the Lord. Ahaz also makes other changes to the Lord's temple "in deference to the king of Assyria" (2 Kings 16:18).

In his times of trouble, Ahaz becomes even more unfaithful to God. The king begins to worship the gods of Damascus. He closes the doors of the Lord's temple and builds up altars to other gods on every street corner in Jerusalem.

Ahaz "promoted wickedness in Judah," and the nation was "humbled" because of him (2 Chron. 28:19). The gods and idols he promotes and worships are "his downfall and the downfall of all Israel" (2 Chron. 28:23).

When Ahaz dies, his son Hezekiah becomes king in Judah.

HOSHEA, ISRAEL, 732–722 BC (9 YEARS)

"In the twelfth year of Ahaz king of Judah, Hoshea son of Elah became king of Israel in Samaria, and he reigned nine years" (2 Kings 17:1). Hoshea becomes king after assassinating Pekah in one of the many coups that followed the end of the house of Jehu.

Hoshea is the last king of Israel. He does evil in the eyes of the Lord, but not like Israel's kings before him. He stops paying tribute to Assyria and seeks help from the Egyptians. The Assyrians invade and take him prisoner, and the Assyrian military lays siege to Samaria for three years, finally taking the city and deporting the people to Assyria.

Now we read these sobering summarizing words about the kings of Israel:

All this took place because the Israelites had sinned against the LORD their God, who had brought them up out of Egypt from under the power of Pharaoh king of Egypt. They worshiped other gods and followed the practices of the nations the LORD had driven out before them, as well as the practices that the kings of Israel had introduced. The Israelites secretly did things against the LORD their God that were not right. From watchtower to fortified city they built themselves high places in all their towns. They set up sacred stones and Asherah poles on every high hill and under every spreading tree. At every high place they burned incense, as the nations whom the LORD had driven out before them had done. They did wicked things that aroused the LORD's anger. They worshiped idols, though the LORD had said, "You shall not do this." The LORD warned Israel and Judah through all his prophets and seers: "Turn from your evil ways. Observe my commands and decrees, in accordance with the entire Law that I commanded your ancestors to obey and that I delivered to you through my servants the prophets."

But they would not listen and were as stiff-necked as their ancestors, who did not trust in the LORD their God. They rejected his decrees and the covenant he had made with their ancestors and the statutes he had warned them to keep. They followed worthless idols and themselves became worthless. They imitated the nations around them although the LORD had ordered them, "Do not do as they do."

They forsook all the commands of the LORD their God and made for themselves two idols cast in the shape of calves, and an Asherah pole. They bowed down to all the starry hosts, and they worshiped Baal. They sacrificed their sons and daughters in the fire. They practiced divination and sought omens and sold themselves to do evil in the eyes of the LORD, arousing his anger.

So the LORD was very angry with Israel and removed them from his presence. Only the tribe of Judah was left, and even Judah did not keep the commands of the LORD their God. They followed the practices Israel had introduced. Therefore the LORD rejected all the people of Israel; he afflicted them and gave them into the hands of plunderers, until he thrust them from his presence.

The text pretty much speaks for itself:

> When he tore Israel away from the house of David, they made
> Jeroboam son of Nebat their king. Jeroboam enticed Israel
> away from following the LORD and caused them to commit a
> great sin. The Israelites persisted in all the sins of Jeroboam and
> did not turn away from them until the LORD removed them
> from his presence, as he had warned through all his servants
> the prophets. So the people of Israel were taken from their
> homeland into exile in Assyria, and they are still there.
>
> The king of Assyria brought people from Babylon, Kuthah,
> Avva, Hamath and Sepharvaim and settled them in the towns
> of Samaria to replace the Israelites. (2 Kings 17:7–24)[4]

God has consistently reached out to his people, and they have consistently pulled away. But he is not finished.

HEZEKIAH, JUDAH, 715-686 BC (29 YEARS)

Back in Judah, Hezekiah, the son of Ahaz, is taking the throne. He does what is right in the eyes of the Lord so that there is no one like him among all the kings of Judah, before or after. He removes the high places, smashes the sacred stones, cuts down the Asherah poles, and smashes the bronze snake of Moses. He keeps the commands of Moses and is successful in everything he undertakes. King Hezekiah cuts off the influence of Assyria and defeats the Philistines, all the way to Gaza.

In the fourth year of his reign, the northern kingdom falls; Samaria is attacked by Assyria and the people of Israel are taken captive. Ten years later, Assyria again attacks Judah and the Assyrians capture the fortified cities. Hezekiah offers to pay tribute and gives them all the silver from the palace and temple and the gold from the temple doors and doorposts.

In response, the Assyrians challenge the people of Judah to rebel against Hezekiah, saying he has torn down their real gods and now they are powerless. Hezekiah tells the people to be silent and to trust God. Then he tears his clothes, puts on sackcloth and ashes, and goes to the house of the Lord. The king sends a message to the prophet Isaiah, son of Amoz. The prophet encourages Hezekiah, telling him that the Lord will fight those who fight against him. Hezekiah receives the word of the prophet and takes it to the house of the Lord to pray. God answers: he will spare the city for David.

The next morning, eighty-five thousand Assyrian soldiers are mysteriously dead in their camp and the remaining troops withdraw to Nineveh.

Hezekiah is ill, and the prophet says he will not recover. The king implores the Lord to remember all his faithfulness and weeps bitterly. God sends the prophet back with the message that God will give the king fifteen more years, and Hezekiah is healed.

Babylon sends envoys to Judah, and King Hezekiah shows them all his treasures. The prophet Isaiah comes to him with the message that God says that was mistake. He prophesies that the Babylonians will come and take it all back to Babylon, along with some of Hezekiah's family. But, the prophet says, this will not happen while Hezekiah lives. The king calls this troubling message "good," satisfied that they will have peace and security in his own lifetime.

Hezekiah rules for twenty-nine years, and his son Manasseh takes the throne.

MANASSEH, JUDAH, 697–642 BC (55 YEARS)

Manasseh, Hezekiah's son, succeeds him as king at the age of twelve. He does evil in the eyes of the Lord and follows the detestable practices of all the nations God had driven out. He rebuilds the high places, makes new altars to Baal, and makes an Asherah pole, undoing the work of his father. He bows down to the stars and builds two pagan altars in the temple. He sacrifices his own son, practices witchcraft and divination, and consults mediums and spiritists. He leads Judah "so that they did more evil than the nations the Lord had destroyed before the Israelites" (2 Chron. 33:9). "Moreover, Manasseh also shed so much innocent blood that he filled Jerusalem from end to end" (2 Kings 21:16).

At this time God says: "I am going to bring such disaster on Jerusalem and Judah that the ears of everyone who hears of it will tingle. I will stretch out over Jerusalem the measuring line used against Samaria and the plumb line used against the house of Ahab. I will wipe out Jerusalem" (2 Kings 21:12–13).

God sends the Assyrians against Judah, and they take King Manasseh back to Babylon as prisoner. While there, Manasseh humbles himself before God and realizes how wrong he has been. Amazingly, God hears his cry for help and makes a way for him to return to Jerusalem! "Then Manasseh knew that the Lord is God" (2 Chron. 33:13).

Manasseh begins a campaign to rebuild the outer wall of Jerusalem, remove the pagan altars and images from the temple, and rid Judah of foreign gods. But the people continue to worship at the high places.

After reigning over Judah for fifty-five years, Manasseh dies, and his son Amon replaces him.

AMON, JUDAH, 642–640 BC (2 YEARS)

Amon continues to do evil in the eyes of the Lord as his father Manasseh did, worshiping the idols his father had made. "But unlike his father Manasseh, he did not humble himself before the Lord; Amon increased his guilt" (2 Chron. 33:23).

After only two years, Amon's own officials assassinate him in the palace. The people revolt and kill all the assassins. They put Josiah, Amon's son, on the throne.

JOSIAH, JUDAH, 640–609 BC (31 YEARS)

Once again the best that God can do for leadership is a child. Amon's son Josiah takes the throne of Judah at age eight. "He did what was right in the eyes of the Lord and followed completely the ways of his father David, not turning aside to the right or to the left (2 Kings 22:2).

At age sixteen, Josiah begins to seek God earnestly. At age twenty, the king begins to purge Judah of the high places built by Solomon, the Asherah poles, and the altars and carved and cast images used for pagan worship. By the age of twenty-six, Josiah has turned his attention to the restoration of the temple. During this process, the priests find the Book of the Law and read it to the king. Stricken, Josiah takes action to seek God's direction in light of what is written in the book:

When the king heard the words of the Book of the Law, he tore his robes. He gave these orders to Hilkiah the priest, Ahikam son of Shaphan, Akbor son of Micaiah, Shaphan the secretary and Asaiah the king's attendant: "Go and inquire of the LORD for me and for the people and for all Judah about what is written in this book that has been found. Great is the LORD's anger that burns against us because those who have gone before us have not obeyed the words of this book; they have not acted in accordance with all that is written there concerning us." (2 Kings 22:11–13)

The king's representatives consult the prophetess Huldah:

She said to them, "This is what the LORD, the God of Israel, says: Tell the man who sent you to me, 'This is what the LORD says: I am going to bring disaster on this place and its people, according to everything written in the book the king of Judah has read. Because they have forsaken me and burned incense to other gods and aroused my anger by all the idols their hands have made, my anger will burn against this place and will not be quenched.' Tell the king of Judah, who sent you to inquire of the LORD, 'This is what the LORD, the God of Israel, says concerning the words you heard: Because your heart was responsive and you humbled yourself before the LORD when you heard what I have spoken against this place and its people—that they would become a curse and be laid waste—and because you tore your robes and wept in my presence, I also have heard you, declares the LORD. Therefore I will gather you to your ancestors, and you will be buried in peace. Your eyes will not see all the disaster I am going to bring on this place.'" (2 Kings 22:15–20)

In response, Josiah gathers all the people of Jerusalem, great and small, along with the elders of Judah. The king reads to them the entire law and leads them in making a covenant with the Lord to follow his commandments. The king then directs a thorough destruction of pagan worship throughout Judah, beginning with cleansing the temple itself of pagan artifacts, pagan priests, and male prostitutes. King Josiah destroys and defiles all the pagan high places, including those where the people had sacrificed their children. He continues this destruction even into Samaria, tearing down the high places that Jeroboam had built. In the end, "Josiah removed all the detestable idols from all the territory belonging to the Israelites" (2 Chron. 34:33). Then King Josiah returns to Jerusalem, and he leads the country in celebrating Passover for the first time since the days of the prophet Samuel.

We are told that never before or after was there a king like Josiah who turned so completely to God and the law of Moses. But we are also told:

> Nevertheless, the LORD did not turn away from the heat of his fierce anger, which burned against Judah because of all that Manasseh had done to arouse his anger. So the LORD said, "I will remove Judah also from my presence as I removed Israel, and I will reject Jerusalem, the city I chose, and this temple, about which I said, 'My Name shall be there.'" (2 Kings 23:26–27)

Egypt moves its army to the Euphrates River to assist Assyria in battle, and King Josiah goes out to confront Pharaoh Necho. But Necho, king of Egypt, sends messengers to turn Josiah away, telling him he has no fight with him. "Josiah, however, would not turn away from him, but disguised himself to engage him in battle. He would not listen to what Necho had said at God's command but went to fight him on the plain of Megiddo" (2 Chron. 35:22).

Josiah is wounded in this battle and dies in Jerusalem as a result. His son Jehoahaz is chosen by the people to rule in his place.

JEHOAHAZ, JUDAH, 609 BC (3 MONTHS)

Josiah's son Jehoahaz, who is twenty-three when he begins to reign, does evil in the eyes of the Lord just as his ancestors did. Pharaoh Necho takes Jehoahaz captive to Egypt and makes his brother Eliakim king in his stead. The Pharaoh changes Eliakim's name to Jehoiakim.

Egypt levies taxes on Judah and takes silver and gold from the people of the land to pay it. There is not enough left in the temple and the palace.

JEHOIAKIM, JUDAH, 609–598 BC (11 YEARS)

Jehoiakim is twenty-five when he takes the throne, and he continues to do evil in the eyes of the Lord as his ancestors did. During his time, Nebuchadnezzar king of Babylon invades the land, makes Jehoiakim his vassal, and takes the wealth from the palace and the temple. Jehoiakim rebels against Nebuchadnezzar after three years, and God sends enemies against him to destroy Judah.

"The Lord sent Babylonian, Aramean, Moabite and Ammonite raiders against him to destroy Judah, in accordance with the word of the Lord proclaimed by his servants the prophets. Surely these things happened to Judah according to the Lord's command, in order to remove them from his presence because of the sins of Manasseh and all he had done, including the shedding of innocent blood. For he had filled Jerusalem with innocent blood, and the Lord was not willing to forgive" (2 Kings 24:2–4).

Babylon takes control of the land from the Wadi of Egypt all the way to the Euphrates River. This description resembles the original boundaries of the garden of Eden and the original promise of land to Abraham.

When Jehoiakim dies, his eighteen-year-old son Jehoiachin replaces him as king.

JEHOIACHIN, JUDAH, 598–597 BC
(3 MONTHS, 10 DAYS)

Jehoiachin also does evil in the eyes of the Lord. Soon after he is crowned, Babylon lays siege to Jerusalem and captures the city. Nebuchadnezzar takes the king, his family, and his officials prisoner and sacks the palace and the temple.

> He carried all Jerusalem into exile: all the officers and fighting men, and all the skilled workers and artisans—a total of ten thousand. Only the poorest people of the land were left. Nebuchadnezzar took Jehoiachin captive to Babylon. He also took from Jerusalem to Babylon the king's mother, his wives, his officials and the prominent people of the land. The king

of Babylon also deported to Babylon the entire force of seven thousand fighting men, strong and fit for war, and a thousand skilled workers and artisans—a total of ten thousand. Only the poorest people of the land were left. (2 Kings 24:14–16)

Not only has Judah lost its land, but now it loses all its talent and leadership. The land is left to those who have been most oppressed by the wickedness of Judah: the poor!

ZEDEKIAH (MATTANIAH), JUDAH, 597–586 BC (11 YEARS)

Jehoiachin's uncle Mattaniah is appointed by Babylon to run Jerusalem under Nebuchadnezzar's authority, and his name is changed by Nebuchadnezzar to Zedekiah. He also does evil in the eyes of the Lord. He refuses to humble himself at the word of the Lord brought by the prophet Jeremiah. He is stiff-necked, and the leaders of the priests and the people themselves become even more unfaithful to the Lord and increase their detestable practices and defiling of the temple.

Zedekiah rebels against Babylon, and the Babylonians launch a siege against Jerusalem that lasts several months. Those left in the city, along with the king and the soldiers, break through the walls and flee toward the Arabah. Many are captured, including the king and his family. All of Zedekiah's sons are slaughtered before him, and he himself is blinded, bound, and taken to Babylon.

The Babylonian military breaks down all the walls of the city and burns the temple of the Lord, the king's house, and every important building in the city. Finally most of the people are taken to Babylon, along with the rest of the gold, silver, and bronze left from the house of the Lord. Only the poorest of the poor are left to work the vineyards and fields.

We are told why all this came about:

The LORD, the God of their ancestors, sent word to them through his messengers again and again, because he had pity on his people and on his dwelling place. But they mocked God's messengers, despised his words and scoffed at his prophets until the wrath of the LORD was aroused against his people and *there was no remedy*. He brought up against them the king of the Babylonians, who killed their young men with the sword in the sanctuary, and did not spare young men or young women, the elderly or the infirm. God gave them all into the hands of Nebuchadnezzar. He carried to Babylon all the articles from the temple of God, both large and small, and the treasures of the LORD's temple and the treasures of the king and his officials. They set fire to God's temple and broke down the wall of Jerusalem; they burned all the palaces and destroyed everything of value there. (2 Chron. 36:15–19)

"There was no remedy." As in the days of Adam, Cain, Noah, the sons of Jacob, and the Shechemites, both Israel and Judah reach the point of no return in their violence and destructiveness. In his mercy, God sends Israel and Judah into exile. Even while doing so, God promises them a time of return to their land and to him. God is always faithful to himself, his ways, and his people.

Within the next hundred years or so, the rulers of these countries of exile will be sending the people of Israel back to their land, rebuilding the temple, and paying to rebuild the wall of Jerusalem. But the nation will not be restored to the glory days of Solomon. It will suffer occupation and exile by the Persians, Greeks, Egyptians, and Syrians, and the rule of the Hasmonean Dynasty. It will be known as Palestine for a millennium.

What is God showing us in this long and difficult history? What is he highlighting for our instruction? Is there anything in this history to instruct us in political justice and to teach us God's ways for our nations in the twenty-first century? We must measure our thinking about political power and authority—what it can and cannot accomplish and where it resides—against what God is telling us about political justice in this history of the Jews. But that history is incomplete unless we bring the message of the prophets alongside.

CHAPTER 20

THE PROPHETS

As the previous chapters revealed, the kings ultimately failed in their leadership of God's people, and the conditional blessing of God was dashed. It is the prophets God sends to the Jews who remind them of what God said in the five books of Moses, review what Israel and Judah specifically have been doing within their kingdoms, and what the consequences are of moving away from God's design to their own idea of justice.

First let's review some of the values God has emphasized for us throughout the Scriptures.

KEY FEATURES OF POLITICAL JUSTICE

Political justice means moving political power down. God wanted a grass-roots political process that would be the responsibility of the people and empower individuals as much as possible. In the Mosaic model, except in the case of a war, the court system and executive power was delegated down to populations of ten and the tribal elders. But Israel wanted a king with sovereign power over them. True, the first three kings seemed to improve and develop Israel at an amazing pace, but it only took one king, Rehoboam, to destroy it all. While grassroots authority is fraught with difficulty, moving political authority up creates more problems long-term than it solves.

God is willing and able to use anyone, and every leader is a mixed package. God used good kings to bring difficulty upon Israel, bad kings to bring blessing, and vice versa. Some good kings got sick and died young, and some bad kings were healed and lived long. Great political leaders sometimes produced awful children, and a few bad leaders produced children who were great political leaders. *Chosen* apparently did not mean *all good*, as all of the chosen leaders had significant issues. The economy did not seem to be a good indication of the direction of the country, as sometimes there was a boom when evil was at the top and a bust when a more upright leader was in the palace. There were times when the plans of the wicked succeeded and the plans of the upright failed. The enemies of the nation, whether there was a good king or a bad king, always came from God. God responded to the outcry of the people. But God responded to political leaders when they cried out to him as well, no matter who they were. The leaders of Israel came from the same cultural environment as the people, and they deteriorated as the society did. The people consistently returned to their ways no matter what happened in the palace. God's emphasis is not on the perfection of the leader. A good leader does not assure good times, and a bad leader is not hopeless.

The faithful individual is not forsaken in the political scramble. Some of Scripture's great stories of blessing recount the experiences of faithful individuals during dire times of political chaos. Ruth, Esther, Ezra, Nehemiah, Daniel, Joseph, and of course, later, Jesus and the apostles all lived and worked and glorified God during severe political turmoil and even in exile. God was at work when good people were in power, and God was at work when terrible people were in power. God used some of Israel's greatest political crises for the blessing of the nation.

God's intervention means momentary respite. No time of blessing or difficulty in Israel was permanent. But all times worked for the purposes of God. Times of blessing revealed what God wanted for the people and the community, and times of difficulty revealed the difficult choices the people and the community had to make in order to sustain blessing. Is it possible that today we focus too much on the circumstances and how to change them, and too little on what God is doing in political circumstances and how we can serve him in them?

God is absolutely consistent. From the first chapter of Genesis, God is completely consistent in his dealings with his human creatures. He tells us what his dreams are for us. He tells us what authority and power he has given us and the limits he has placed on both. He tells us what we must do if we want blessing and what will happen if we make different choices. But he also makes it clear that we are free to make those choices. God is totally transparent with us. There is no hidden agenda, no manipulation, and no tyrannical use of control.

THE PROPHETS

The prophets are used in the times of the judges and the kings as a kind of disaster-warning system for cultural drift. They are God's megaphone of warning and come as a last effort to get the nation to look at where it is heading and what the consequences will be in the fairly near future. They weave the laws of Moses with current events within the countries and project what is coming.

And what is the message of the prophets? What do they add to the revelation God has already given us? They continue the themes we have already looked at in Mosaic law. As each prophet holds the nations accountable for their actions and the consequences, they are working with what God has already said through Moses and applying it to current events. They reveal why the people are in difficulty, what got them there, and what they must do to turn the tide of their nation's future. When the prophets are active, they make God's desperate appeal to the people, to listen to what he has already told them.

If we ask the prophets what the nation's people are doing that is destroying them, we get a very interesting addition to our biblical template. All the prophets highlight five specific sins:

- Political injustice
- Economic injustice
- Adultery and the destruction of the family
- Loss of the value of our words
- Idolatry among the people of God and his clergy

Hosea, Jeremiah, and Malachi each list these sins in a single passage:

There is only cursing, lying and murder, stealing and adultery; they break all bounds, and bloodshed follows bloodshed. (Hos. 4:2)

Will you steal and murder, commit adultery and perjury, burn incense to Baal and follow other gods you have not known, and then come and stand before me in this house, which bears my Name, and say, "We are safe"—safe to do all these detestable things? (Jer. 7:9–10)

"So I will come to put you on trial. I will be quick to testify against sorcerers, adulterers and perjurers, against those who defraud laborers of their wages, who oppress the widows and the fatherless, and deprive the foreigners among you of justice, but do not fear me," says the LORD Almighty. (Mal. 3:5)

What do these five sins look like in daily life? Does God have a definition of political justice, economic justice, family wholeness, and truth in our speech? When God condemns idolatry in the Jews, what is he talking about? Let's see how the prophets describe the sins that bring such tragedy to Israel, and to our own nations today.

POLITICAL INJUSTICE

Political injustice is violent death that is tolerated, if not condoned, in society. The "red thread of violence" continues as the number-one priority for the prophets to warn against as they tell the Jewish people why they will lose the land that God has given them. Having delivered them from violence and tyranny in Egypt, having used them to conquer the seven nations in Canaan so consumed with violence that they must be eliminated, God now must bring that same judgment against the nation of Israel, who, rather than eliminate, absorbed the same practices. *Chosen nation* does not mean exemption from accountability and responsibility to God and his decrees. Israel, which has God's law, fails at political justice just as the Canaanites failed without it. Having been slaves for over four hundred years, they have no more respect for human life than Cain did for Abel.

It is so important as you read God's heart in these passages from the prophets that you remember it is the Jews to whom God is speaking, not the pagans. Remember, God is speaking to his people! Let him speak to you.

Here are a few key verses:

When you spread out your hands in prayer, I hide my eyes from you; even when you offer many prayers, I am not listening. Your hands are full of blood! (Isa. 1:15)

Everyone lies in wait to shed blood; they hunt each other with nets. Both hands are skilled in doing evil; the ruler demands gifts, the judge accepts bribes, the powerful dictate what they desire—they all conspire together. (Mic. 7:2–3)

They have filled this place with the blood of the innocent. They have built the high places of Baal to burn their children in the fire as offerings to Baal. (Jer. 19:4–5)

In you are people who accept bribes to shed blood. (Ezek. 22:12)

On the very day they sacrificed their children to their idols, they entered my sanctuary and desecrated it. That is what they did in my house. (Ezek. 23:39)

Why do you make me look at injustice? Why do you tolerate wrongdoing? Destruction and violence are before me; there is strife, and conflict abounds. Therefore the law is paralyzed, and justice never prevails. (Hab. 1:3–4)

The people of God tolerate violence in their communities and in their places of worship. Political justice, in contrast, is intolerance of violence anywhere.

Political injustice is oppression of the poor, the alien, widows, and orphans. Scripture speaks in the defense of justice for the outcast of society. God measures our society's commitment to justice by how we treat the weakest and most helpless in our communities. Remember, God is speaking to his people! Let him speak to you.

Here are just a few passages:

> Woe to those who make unjust laws, to those who issue oppressive decrees, to deprive the poor of their rights and withhold justice from the oppressed of my people, making widows their prey and robbing the fatherless. (Isa. 10:1–2)

> Among my people are the wicked who lie in wait like men who snare birds and like those who set traps to catch people. Like cages full of birds, their houses are full of deceit; they have become rich and powerful and have grown fat and sleek. Their evil deeds have no limit; they do not seek justice. They do not promote the case of the fatherless; they do not defend the just cause of the poor. (Jer. 5:26–28)

> The people of the land practice extortion and commit robbery; they oppress the poor and needy and mistreat the foreigner, denying them justice. (Ezek. 22:29)

> This is what the LORD Almighty said: "Administer true justice; show mercy and compassion to one another. Do not oppress the widow or the fatherless, the foreigner or the poor. Do not plot evil against each other." (Zech. 7:9–10)

Every nation in the world can be measured judicially by the quality of justice demanded for the weakest in that society. It is important that we hold our presidents and other powerful people accountable to the courts, but it is equally important, if not more, that we defend the rights of the disenfranchised in our daily lives.

And who is responsible for political justice within our societies? The prophets tell us it is the rulers, the prophets, the priests, and the people. In other words, everyone.

Rulers

Hear this, you leaders of Jacob, you rulers of Israel, who despise justice and distort all that is right; who build Zion with bloodshed, and Jerusalem with wickedness. (Mic. 3:9–10)

Her officials within her are roaring lions, her rulers are evening wolves, who leave nothing for the morning. (Zeph. 3:3)

Her officials within her are like wolves tearing their prey; they shed blood and kill people to make unjust gain. (Ezek. 22:27)

Prophets

Hear this, you leaders of Jacob, you rulers of Israel, who despise justice and distort all that is right; who build Zion with bloodshed, and Jerusalem with wickedness. Her leaders judge for a bribe, her priests teach for a price, and her prophets tell fortunes for money. Yet they look for the LORD's support and say, "Is not the LORD among us? No disaster will come upon us." (Mic. 3:9–11)

The People

So justice is driven back, and righteousness stands at a distance; truth has stumbled in the streets, honesty cannot enter. Truth is nowhere to be found, and whoever shuns evil becomes a prey. The LORD looked and was displeased that there was no justice. He saw that there was no one, he was appalled that there was no one to intervene. (Isa. 59:14–16)

Go up and down the streets of Jerusalem, look around and consider, search through her squares. If you can find but one person who deals honestly and seeks the truth, I will forgive this city. (Jer. 5:1)

ECONOMIC INJUSTICE

There is always a connection between political injustice and economic injustice. In a world where sin is real and freedom is valued, there must be some limits to corruption and greed. And it is the responsibility of government to set at least minimal boundaries. In any poor neighborhood in the world, you will find a small store that gears its products to the poorest of the poor. The quantities and products carried in these stores are geared to the lowest economic stratum. If you do the math, much of the time the poorest of the land are paying more for their food than those who are better off. Also prevalent in the poorest communities of the world are lending schemes that charge exorbitant interest. Here is what the prophets highlight.

Just Weights and Measures

The material world is real and measurable, and time and matter have a value. Further, those measurements and values can be established. In a just economy, the product actually is what was advertised, and the rights of consumers are respected.

> Your silver has become dross; your choice wine is diluted with water. Your rulers are rebels, partners with thieves; they all love bribes and chase after gifts. (Isa. 1:22–23)

> The merchant uses dishonest scales and loves to defraud. Ephraim boasts, "I am very rich; I have become wealthy. With all my wealth they will not find in me any iniquity or sin." (Hos. 12:7–8)

> Am I still to forget your ill-gotten treasures, you wicked house, and the short ephah, which is accursed? Shall I acquit someone with dishonest scales, with a bag of false weights? (Mic. 6:10–12)

> Stop dispossessing my people, declares the Sovereign LORD. You are to use accurate scales, an accurate ephah and an accurate bath. The ephah and the bath are to be the same size, the bath containing a tenth of a homer and the ephah a tenth of a homer; the homer is to be the standard measure for both. The shekel is to consist of twenty gerahs. Twenty shekels plus twenty-five shekels plus fifteen shekels equal one mina. (Ezek. 45:9–12)

Hear this, you who trample the needy and do away with the poor of the land, saying, "When will the New Moon be over that we may sell grain, and the Sabbath be ended that we may market wheat?"—skimping the measure, boosting the price and cheating with dishonest scales, buying the poor with silver and the needy for a pair of sandals, selling even the sweepings with the wheat. (Amos 8:4–6)

The Poor

As for political justice, the emphasis of economic justice in Scripture is the poorest of the poor. God directs our attention not to the top economic strata or a nation's GNP but to what achieving that GNP is doing to the bottom economic stratum. It is not a question of whether executives are paid more but whether the workers are being paid enough to live. It is not a question of whether there is unemployment but whether we could have increased employment.

You levy a straw tax on the poor and impose a tax on their grain. Therefore, though you have built stone mansions, you will not live in them; though you have planted lush vineyards, you will not drink their wine. For I know how many are your offenses and how great your sins. (Amos 5:11–12)

This is what the LORD says: Do what is just and right. Rescue from the hand of the oppressor the one who has been robbed. (Jer. 22:3)

Private Property

The way the prophets insist on economic justice assumes the importance of the material world and the value of an individual's life, time, and work, reminding Israel of the destructiveness of stealing. Securing the rights to own is essential to political justice.

There is only cursing, lying and murder, stealing and adultery; they break all bounds, and bloodshed follows bloodshed. (Hos. 4:2)

> Moreover, say to the royal house of Judah, "Hear the word of the LORD. This is what the LORD says to you, house of David: 'Administer justice every morning; rescue from the hand of the oppressor the one who has been robbed, or my wrath will break out and burn like fire because of the evil you have done—burn with no one to quench it.'" (Jer. 21:11–12)

> The people of the land practice extortion and commit robbery; they oppress the poor and needy and mistreat the foreigner, denying them justice. (Ezek. 22:29)

> This is the curse that is going out over the whole land; for according to what it says on one side [of the scroll], every thief will be banished. (Zech. 5:3–4)

Rights of the Worker

Can a person's time working be worth less than what it takes to clothe, feed, and house himself? In other words, if a person works six days a week, eight to twelve hours a day, should she not be able to live? And by "live," the Bible means a person should be able to eat, sleep, and be sheltered and clothed. And if we believe in family, if two people work, should they not be able to care for their offspring, meaning they can eat, sleep, and be sheltered and clothed? Can the value a worker adds to an enterprise be less than what is necessary to live on? If a worker's added value is not repaid with a livable wage, is this not slavery? When we build our quality of life on another's lack of quality of life, is this not exactly what the Egyptians did with Israel? And didn't God deliver Israel? It is impossible to have political justice without securing some level of the rights of the worker as well as the owner.

> "Why have we fasted," they say, "and you have not seen it? Why have we humbled ourselves, and you have not noticed?" Yet on the day of your fasting, you do as you please and exploit all your workers. (Isa. 58:3)

> So all the officials and people who entered into this covenant agreed that they would free their male and female slaves and

no longer hold them in bondage. They agreed, and set them free. But afterward they changed their minds and took back the slaves they had freed and enslaved them again. (Jer. 34:10–11)

"So I will come to put you on trial. I will be quick to testify against . . . those who defraud laborers of their wages . . . but do not fear me," says the LORD Almighty. (Mal. 3:5)

Land

The prophets show that the future of a nation and people will be determined in part by the culture's views of the value of land, land ownership, and land distribution. In Israel an "inheritance" was land, and economic justice encompassed the use of land, even for foreigners. There is no political justice without some sort of protection of land ownership.

Woe to you who add house to house and join field to field till no space is left and you live alone in the land. The LORD Almighty has declared in my hearing: "Surely the great houses will become desolate, the fine mansions left without occupants." (Isa. 5:8–9)

They covet fields and seize them, and houses, and take them. They defraud people of their homes, they rob them of their inheritance. (Mic. 2:2)

"You are to distribute this land among yourselves according to the tribes of Israel. You are to allot it as an inheritance for yourselves and for the foreigners residing among you and who have children. You are to consider them as native-born Israelites; along with you they are to be allotted an inheritance among the tribes of Israel. In whatever tribe a foreigner resides, there you are to give them their inheritance," declares the Sovereign LORD. (Ezek. 47:21–23)

Profit and Greed

There are no limits to profit in Scripture, and the law does not put a quantitative measurement on greed. However, greed and unjust or dishonest gain are prominent subjects in Scripture. What do the prophets say about these sins? We've already heard their condemnation of greed and unjust gain through the use of dishonest weights and measurements and the abuse of land and of the poor and the worker. In addition, the prophets speak specifically against abusive interest, often called usury. This is money lent at exorbitant interest rates, meaning rates higher than the norm for that time in the nation. Abusive interest is interest that the borrower clearly will never be able to repay. The prophets also condemn unjust pledges. These are collateral taken that, not returned, will destroy the health, welfare, or future of the owner. And, of course, a bribe is simply an added cost that has nothing to do with the value of the service and goes directly to the one serving.

> But your eyes and your heart are set only on dishonest gain, on shedding innocent blood and on oppression and extortion. (Jer. 22:17)

> There is a conspiracy of her princes within her like a roaring lion tearing its prey; they devour people, take treasures and precious things and make many widows within her. (Ezek. 22:25)

> In you are people who accept bribes to shed blood; you take interest and make a profit from the poor. You extort unjust gain from your neighbors. And you have forgotten me, declares the Sovereign LORD. (Ezek. 22:12)

> This is what the LORD says: "For three sins of Israel, even for four, I will not relent. They sell the innocent for silver, and the needy for a pair of sandals. They trample on the heads of the poor as on the dust of the ground and deny justice to the oppressed. . . . They lie down beside every altar on garments taken in pledge. In the house of their god they drink wine taken as fines. (Amos 2:7–8)

> Suppose there is a righteous man who does what is just and right. He does not eat at the mountain shrines or look to the

idols of Israel. He does not defile his neighbor's wife or have sexual relations with a woman during her period. He does not oppress anyone, but returns what he took in pledge for a loan. He does not commit robbery but gives his food to the hungry and provides clothing for the naked. He does not lend to them at interest or take a profit from them. He withholds his hand from doing wrong and judges fairly between two parties. (Ezek. 18:5–8)

Notice how much Scripture has to say about this ideal righteous man's economic life. Not only is he righteous in his worship, sexuality, and impartial judgment, but he is righteous economically. In other words, the ideal righteous person "does what is right and just" in the economic realm, this space where our values, decisions, and actions affect others in the human community, influencing both their quality of life and even their ability to live at all. Consistently, the prophets name economic justice as a mark of righteousness and condemn economic injustice for the sin it is.

DESTRUCTION OF THE FAMILY

Political injustice is exacerbated by the dissolution of the core family. Adultery—sex between a married person and someone who is not that person's wife or husband—breaks five of the Ten Commandments in the prescriptive law and contributes greatly to the breaking of a sixth. Adultery dishonors two sets of parents, steals from a spouse, reduces our vows to false testimony, and covets what is not ours. Throughout history, including Israel's, the fruit of jealousy, lying, and betrayal in the family has contributed to the level of violence in our societies. Surely this obsession with sex is some sort of idolatry? The lusts for power, fortune, and sex do more to oppress and destroy political freedom than all other factors put together.

The land is full of adulterers; because of the curse the land lies parched and the pastures in the wilderness are withered. (Jer. 23:10)

One man commits a detestable offense with his neighbor's wife, another shamefully defiles his daughter-in-law, and another violates his sister, his own father's daughter. (Ezek. 22:11)

They are all adulterers, burning like an oven whose fire the baker need not stir from the kneading of the dough till it rises. (Hos. 7:4)

Father and son use the same girl and so profane my holy name. (Amos 2:7)

Another thing you do: You flood the LORD's altar with tears. You weep and wail because he no longer looks with favor on your offerings or accepts them with pleasure from your hands. You ask, "Why?" It is because the LORD is the witness between you and the wife of your youth. You have been unfaithful to her, though she is your partner, the wife of your marriage covenant. (Mal. 2:13–14)

Even when their drinks are gone, they continue their prostitution; their rulers dearly love shameful ways. (Hos. 4:18)

They cast lots for my people and traded boys for prostitutes; they sold girls for wine to drink. (Joel 3:3)

Can we say it is so different in our day with the global need to campaign against sex trafficking, especially of children?

THE DEVALUATION OF OUR WORDS

Political justice is lost when the value of our words can no longer be trusted. Because God is, and is who he says he is, because we are made in his image, and because the material world is real and functions by law, we can know the truth. If truth can be known, then lying is definable. If God's words have power and if humankind is made in the image of God, then our words have power and we are responsible for them.

Beginning with Abraham's lie to Abimelek, Isaac's copycat lie, and ultimately Jacob's deception of his father, telling the truth was a problem for Israel. As we have followed the history of Israel through the Law and the Prophets, the people cultivated a culture of lies while being the very people to whom God had given the truth. And if you take the word of the prophets, it would seem no one lied in Israel more than some of the prophets:

> The elders and dignitaries are the head, the prophets who teach lies are the tail. Those who guide this people mislead them, and those who are guided are led astray. (Isa. 9:15–16)

> If a prophet or a priest or anyone else claims, "This is a message from the LORD," I will punish them and their household. This is what each of you keeps saying to your friends and other Israelites: "What is the LORD's answer?" or "What has the LORD spoken?" But you must not mention "a message from the LORD" again, because each one's word becomes their own message. So you distort the words of the living God, the LORD Almighty, our God. (Jer. 23:34–36)

> You [prophets] have profaned me among my people for a few handfuls of barley and scraps of bread. By lying to my people, who listen to lies, you have killed those who should not have died and have spared those who should not live. (Ezek. 13:19)

> If a liar and deceiver comes and says, "I will prophesy for you plenty of wine and beer," that would be just the prophet for this people! (Mic. 2:11)

And the problem is not only with the prophets. Any of us can devalue our words.

If our words have no value, there is no true worship.

> The LORD says: "These people come near to me with their mouth and honor me with their lips, but their hearts are far from me." (Isa. 29:13)

My people come to you, as they usually do, and sit before you to hear your words, but they do not put them into practice. Their mouths speak of love, but their hearts are greedy for unjust gain. (Ezek. 33:31)

If our words have no value, there is no justice.

. . . those who with a word make someone out to be guilty, who ensnare the defender in court and with false testimony deprive the innocent of justice. (Isa. 29:21)

If our words have no value, there is no love or intimacy.

"They make ready their tongue like a bow, to shoot lies; it is not by truth that they triumph in the land. They go from one sin to another; they do not acknowledge me," declares the LORD. "Beware of your friends; do not trust anyone in your clan. For every one of them is a deceiver, and every friend a slanderer. Friend deceives friend, and no one speaks the truth. They have taught their tongues to lie; they weary themselves with sinning. . . . Their tongue is a deadly arrow; it speaks deceitfully. With their mouths they all speak cordially to their neighbors, but in their hearts they set traps for them. (Jer. 9:3–5, 8)

If our words have no value, there are no promises, contracts, treaties, or covenants.

They make many promises, take false oaths and make agreements; therefore lawsuits spring up like poisonous weeds in a plowed field. (Hos. 10:4)

The highways are deserted, no travelers are on the roads. The treaty is broken, its witnesses are despised, no one is respected. (Isa. 33:8)

As surely as I live, declares the Sovereign LORD, he shall die in Babylon, in the land of the king who put him on the throne, whose oath he despised and whose treaty he broke. Pharaoh with his mighty army and great horde will be of no help to him in war, when ramps are built and siege works erected to destroy many lives. He despised the oath by breaking the covenant. Because he had given his hand in pledge and yet did all these things, he shall not escape. Therefore this is what the Sovereign Lord says: As surely as I live, I will repay him for despising my oath and breaking my covenant. (Ezek. 17:16–19)

[On breaking the covenant] You have wearied the Lord with your words. "How have we wearied him?" you ask. By saying, "All who do evil are good in the eyes of the Lord, and he is pleased with them" or "Where is the God of justice?" (Mal. 2:17)

How can you say, "We are wise, for we have the law of the Lord," when actually the lying pen of the scribes has handled it falsely? (Jer. 8:8)

"For the lips of a priest ought to preserve knowledge, because he is the messenger of the Lord Almighty and people seek instruction from his mouth. But you have turned from the way and by your teaching have caused many to stumble; you have violated the covenant with Levi," says the Lord Almighty. "So I have caused you to be despised and humiliated before all the people, because you have not followed my ways but have shown partiality in matters of the law." (Mal. 2:7–9)

If our words have no value, there is no correction.

When I say to a wicked person, "You will surely die," and you do not warn them or speak out to dissuade them from their evil ways in order to save their life, that wicked person will die for their sin, and I will hold you accountable for their blood. But if you do warn the wicked person and they do not turn from their wickedness or from their evil ways, they will die for their sin; but you will have saved yourself.

Again, when a righteous person turns from their righteousness and does evil, and I put a stumbling block before them, they will die. Since you did not warn them, they will die for their sin. The righteous things that person did will not be remembered, and I will hold you accountable for their blood. But if you do warn the righteous person not to sin and they do not sin, they will surely live because they took warning, and you will have saved yourself. (Ezek. 3:18–21)

"These are the things you are to do: Speak the truth to each other, and render true and sound judgment in your courts; do not plot evil against each other, and do not love to swear falsely. I hate all this," declares the LORD. (Zech. 8:16–17)

If our words have no value, there is no meaning; conspiracies without basis abound.

"Do not call conspiracy everything this people calls a conspiracy; do not fear what they fear, and do not dread it." (Isa. 8:12)

When we lose the value of words and the reality of their meaning, we not only are open to deception and fear, but we lose the blessings of contracts, promises, vows, commitments, covenants, and honesty.

IDOLATRY AMONG GOD'S PEOPLE

Political injustice is maintained and perpetrated when those who seek God do not serve God. As we come to the close of the Old Testament with all its violence, it is hard to bear the suffering of God in this scene, even to the limited extent we can imagine it:

"The multitude of your sacrifices—what are they to me?" says the LORD. "I have more than enough of burnt offerings, of rams and the fat of fattened animals; I have no pleasure in the blood of bulls and lambs and goats. When you come to appear before me, who has asked this of you, this trampling of my courts? Stop bringing meaningless offerings! Your incense is detestable to me. New Moons, Sabbaths and convocations—I cannot bear your worthless assemblies. Your New Moon feasts and your appointed festivals I hate with all my being. They have become a burden to me; I am weary of bearing them. When you spread out your hands in prayer, I hide my eyes from you; even when you offer many prayers, I am not listening. Your hands are full of blood! Wash and make yourselves clean. Take your evil deeds out of my sight; stop doing wrong. Learn to do right; seek justice. Defend the oppressed. Take up the cause of the fatherless; plead the case of the widow." (Isa. 1:11–17)

What a tragedy! Think of all that is lost. Lost between God and his chosen people. Lost to a world filled with darkness. Those who were to be the light of the nations are no better and sometimes worse:

This is what the Sovereign Lord says: This is Jerusalem, which I have set in the center of the nations, with countries all around her. Yet in her wickedness she has rebelled against my laws and decrees more than the nations and countries around her. She has rejected my laws and has not followed my decrees.

Therefore this is what the Sovereign Lord says: You have been more unruly than the nations around you and have not followed my decrees or kept my laws. You have not even conformed to the standards of the nations around you. (Ezek. 5:5–7)

In this, we are no different from the people of Israel. When the thinking and practice of God's people are indistinguishable from or, God forbid, more evil than those of our surrounding cultures, there is no light. There is no distinction between the values of those who declare God and those who do not. There is no choice. The lights have gone out.

Her prophets are unprincipled; they are treacherous people. Her priests profane the sanctuary and do violence to the law. (Zeph. 3:4)

And when the lights go out, the human race returns to baseness, and the red thread of violence flows even in the temple.

They turned their backs to me and not their faces; though I taught them again and again, they would not listen or respond to discipline. They set up their vile images in the house that bears my Name and defiled it. They built high places for Baal in the Valley of Ben Hinnom to sacrifice their sons and daughters to Molek, though I never commanded—nor did it enter my mind—that they should do such a detestable thing and so make Judah sin. (Jer. 32:33–35)

And you took your sons and daughters whom you bore to me and sacrificed them as food to the idols. Was your prostitution not enough? You slaughtered my children and sacrificed them to the idols. (Ezek. 16:20–21)

It is a hard thing to put ourselves as Christians today in the same shoes as these Jews of old. But when we look at the darkness around us, can we say that we have a significant impact on our societies and communities, even when we are the majority group in many nations? God says that it is the absence of light that creates the vacuum of darkness. Could it be that we are blind to our own loss of biblical thinking? Do we Christians suffer idolatry within our beliefs? Are we focused on the deficiencies of those who do not know God (the world) while missing what God is saying is strategic, the deficiencies in his people?

COME, LORD JESUS

And thus ends the overview of political justice in the Old Testament. Sin pollution permeates everyone and everything. Even with the clearly defined law of Moses and the repeated messages of the prophets—even possessing the thinking of God—the people of Israel, and by extension we ourselves, are not "good." Will we believe what God is telling us about ourselves?

From the very start of his ministry, Jesus makes it clear that he has not come to replace Moses or the prophets but to complete them. This is a great enigma for the modern church, as we have spent so much of our history discussing how we are no longer under the law but under the

Spirit. This statement is true, but what does it mean? We are not under the law, but what are we to do with it?

We don't fling the law aside and commit ourselves solely to the New Testament revelation. Isolated from the Old Testament, we are more easily led into mysticism and a complete estrangement from the world we live in and are called to engage. But neither should we return to the arduous life of the Orthodox Jew with its detailed observances of minutiae, a life in which we are "saved" by militant adherence to the law.

Not being under the law does not mean that now we give up on earthly justice and the political process. Jesus chooses to come as a king. But what kind of king is he? How does he exert his authority? How does he rule? Certainly not the way most of the Jews wanted him to. He was a great disappointment to them as a king. And they rejected him.

And yet, everywhere the message of Jesus prospered, in time so did political justice. Better political justice, though never perfect, followed the spread of biblical thought. There were Christian atrocities, true, but there was more positive influence on the value of the individual and basic human rights.

Let's take a look at political justice through the life and teaching of Jesus and his apostles and consider their impact on the thinking of the world over the last two millennia. Will we be disappointed? Or will see the King as he is in all his glory?

PART IV

JESUS AND POLITICAL JUSTICE

If Our Lord insisted upon obedience He would become a task-master, and He would cease to have any authority. He never insists on obedience, but when we do see Him we obey Him instantly, He is easily Lord, and we live in adoration of Him from morning till night. The revelation of my growth in grace is the way in which I look upon obedience. We have to rescue the word "obedience" from the mire. Obedience is only possible between equals; it is the relationship between father and son, not between master and servant. "I and My Father are one." "Though He were a Son, yet learned He obedience by the things which He suffered." The Son's obedience was as Redeemer, *because He was Son*, not in order to be Son.

—Oswald Chambers, *My Utmost for His Highest* (July 19)

CHAPTER 21

JESUS REVEALS THE LAW IN HIS LIFE

Now we come to the tipping point in history: the mark between BC and AD (or BCE and CE as it is sometimes called today). This is an event so monumental that all of Christianity and the rest of the world will mark their calendar from here. God has been laying the foundation for this time for multiple millennia. Moses, the prophets, and all of the history of Israel serve to inform us about the meaning of Jesus's message. Some things have changed and changed forever. But God, his values, and his desire for the human race have not. He will not call another Abraham or Moses, nor will he use again a single nation as the template for nations. Now the exponential multiplication of individuals and nations who reveal the glory of God begins.

But from the beginning, Jesus's life and message reveal the values and ways of God that have been since the beginning of time.

JESUS'S CONCEPTION

From the very start of Scripture, God weaves the theme of the One coming to restore us to him. Confirming the forward movement of time, God is saying from the beginning that we are here (present), but One is coming (future), and when he comes, things will change (past). Jesus was conceived in time. He was born and learned to eat and walk, read and write. He grew in height and strength and comprehension of the world around him, just as we do. He was a human being, born of the Father and filled with the Spirit of God.

There is no more dramatic example of the material world, created by God, merging with the unseen world, created by God, than this impregnation of a woman by the Spirit of God. From the moment of conception, the divide created in the minds of human beings by sin, as recorded in Genesis 3, begins to be broken down. God, the Ruler of all, seen and unseen, earthly and heavenly, is returning for the first time since creation, this time in the form of a man. Christ is bridging the gap for us with the Father.

The angels are very busy, visiting Mary, speaking to Joseph, preparing Elizabeth. God continues his amazing affirmation of the authority of the individual by working through one willing young woman to continue his eternal purposes as he did through Adam, Noah, Abraham, and Moses. One individual is again called of God to serve the human community.

The importance of family is affirmed as God prepares Joseph to stay with Mary, providing a husband and father. He also prepares for Mary a safe haven from the ignorance of the community by speaking to her cousin Elizabeth, who takes Mary in and protects her during her pregnancy.

JESUS'S BIRTH

The birth is announced by the angels to individual shepherds, and the material world declares Jesus's arrival with a special star. Foreign dignitaries know a king has been born. They prepare gifts and make a very long journey to witness the foretold king. The political leader of the day, Herod, is unsettled by the news the visiting Magi bring of a new king, and he prepares to deal with a potential loss of his authority.

Jesus is born into a family and into the protection of that family's authority. Mary and Joseph flee the danger of Herod to protect the child, disregarding the mandate from the government that all the boys in his age group be killed. The Magi also disregard Herod's mandate that they return to tell him where the child is. They leave the country without passing on any information to the ruler.

The institution of the priesthood is silent at this point, but two individuals, an old priest and a praying widow, know that the One who was promised has come.

Authorities and institutions are being both affirmed and questioned before Jesus is even three.

JESUS'S UPBRINGING

Jesus embraces his heavenly Father's earthly world, learning to eat and walk. He affirms the importance of words and relationships by learning to talk. He builds relationships within his family and his community. He attends synagogue and learns the Torah. He learns his father Joseph's skill and begins to work and support his family and serve his community. Jesus validates all these aspects of human life as valuable parts of his Father's creation. He is living the values of the law.

JESUS ACCEPTS THE LAW BUT NOT THE TRADITIONS

From his conception forward, Jesus challenges traditional interpretations of the law held by the Jews. He recognizes the authority of the law but sees his position in relation to the law differently than have all Jews before him. What does that look like?

When Jesus is twelve years old, he accompanies his parents to Jerusalem for the Festival of the Passover. At the end of the festival, having journeyed a day or two toward home, Mary and Joseph realize that Jesus is not in their traveling company. They retrace their steps.

> After three days they found him in the temple courts, sitting among the teachers, listening to them and asking them questions. Everyone who heard him was amazed at his understanding and his answers. When his parents saw him, they were astonished. His mother said to him, "Son, why have you treated us like this? Your father and I have been anxiously searching for you."

"Why were you searching for me?" he asked. "Didn't you
know I had to be in my Father's house?" But they did not
understand what he was saying to them.

Then he went down to Nazareth with them and was obedi-
ent to them. But his mother treasured all these things in her
heart. (Luke 2:46–51)

A twelve-year-old is questioning and offering answers to the teachers in the temple! A twelve-year-old is assuming his parents understand
that he has a higher authority than theirs. He is not disrespecting or
dishonoring his parents or the priesthood. He understands that God
has created these authorities as well. But he sees himself in a different
position to these authorities than Jewish tradition would have taught.
Rather than seeing tradition as the law, he sees God as the authority over
the law. And He sees authority within himself as an individual directly
linked with his Father in heaven as well: "I had to be about my Father's
business" (Luke 2:49). He respects the authority of the priesthood and
he respects the authority of his parents, but he sees his heavenly father
as the one who shows him how, as an individual, to live out that tension
of respect for various authorities. Jesus is obeying his Father's intent in
every way, but he is not necessarily following Jewish tradition on how to
do that. This is the first time Jesus speaks in public for himself and the
first time he speaks of God as his Father.

All authority has boundaries in his Father's kingdom, and Jesus
obeys the appropriate authority at the appropriate time, but the boundaries are not always rightly represented in the traditions of the Jews.
There is unavoidable tension here, created by God. And Jesus is raising
that tension the first time he speaks of his heavenly Father and his purpose, at twelve!

We know that Jesus challenges the authority of demons and of
Satan in the wilderness. He also begins to preach and teach publicly
in his own authority. He challenges the Jewish elite regarding who can
forgive sin and whether or not the law allows healing on the Sabbath.
Jesus applauds a Roman centurion's definition of faith—learned from a
pagan Roman culture as a kingdom definition, one in which authority
is "given" and if you have it, you command it. The centurion understands that Jesus has new authority, not previously recognized, while

the Jews around him still question in whose authority he does these things. He is not following their traditions.

While Jewish tradition said that Jews could not even have Samaritan dust on their sandals, Jesus takes all twelve disciples straight into Samaria to minister. Jesus even talks with and accepts a drink from a Samaritan, and not just a Samaritan but a Samaritan woman. He eats with tax collectors and sinners. He and his followers do not always wash their hands before eating, challenging the Jewish laws of cleanliness. Jesus challenges the Jewish teachings on fasting and whether a person passing through a field can pick grain to eat. He challenges the Jewish elite regarding who can forgive sin and whether or not the law allows healing on the Sabbath. Over and over, Jesus corrects the Pharisees in their traditional understanding of faith, defined by strict adherence to their interpretation of the law. For example, in one Pharisee's home, he commends the faith of a prostitute who washes his feet with her tears, saying that hers is the kind of faith the Father looks for.

At each point, Jesus is stepping on the toes of traditional Jewish understandings of authority and their customs of how to obey the laws of God. "When Jesus had finished saying these things, the crowds were amazed at his teaching, because he taught as one who had authority, and not as their teachers of the law" (Matt. 7:28–29).

When the mother of two of Jesus's disciples comes to request seats of honor for her sons beside Jesus's future throne, Jesus challenges his disciples' understanding of authority and leadership. His disciples view authority as power over others, rather than as service to others. Jesus's view of authority is not the traditional view of the Jews.

When Jesus sees moneylenders doing business in the temple, he takes it upon himself, a layman, to throw them all out. It is an amazing scene. Jesus has no institutional authority in the priesthood to take this action. His authority for this shocking action comes from his Father, for whom the house was built, and it is carried out by him as his Son, the individual.

When Jesus enters Jerusalem on a donkey, the people see and respond to the authority they see in Jesus himself. They understand he is a king. But he is not a king in any sense that the Jewish establishment will recognize. Many ask the obvious question, "Where does your authority come from?"

THE AUTHORITY OF JESUS QUESTIONED

When the Sanhedrin questions Jesus after his arrest, they ask him if he is the Christ, the coming king of the Jews, and Jesus refuses to tell them.

> Jesus entered the temple courts, and, while he was teaching, the chief priests and the elders of the people came to him. "By what authority are you doing these things?" they asked. "And who gave you this authority?"
>
> Jesus replied, "I will also ask you one question. If you answer me, I will tell you by what authority I am doing these things. John's baptism—where did it come from? Was it from heaven, or of human origin?"
>
> They discussed it among themselves and said, "If we say, 'From heaven,' he will ask, 'Then why didn't you believe him?' But if we say, 'Of human origin'—we are afraid of the people, for they all hold that John was a prophet."
>
> So they answered Jesus, "We don't know."
>
> Then he said, "Neither will I tell you by what authority I am doing these things." (Matt. 21:23–27)

> Not until halfway through the festival did Jesus go up to the temple courts and begin to teach. The Jews there were amazed and asked, "How did this man get such learning without having been taught?"
>
> Jesus answered, "My teaching is not my own. It comes from the one who sent me. Anyone who chooses to do the will of God will find out whether my teaching comes from God or whether I speak on my own." (John 7:15–17)

Jesus challenges the authority of death on the cross as he did with Lazarus in the tomb. He does not challenge the fact of death. His Father has declared that the death penalty is required because of sin. And we will die. Jesus challenges the authority of death to hold on to us. He then challenges the barrier created by sin between the earthly and the heavenly.

After his resurrection from the dead, Jesus meets two men on the road to Emmaus:

He asked them, "What are you discussing together as you walk along?"

They stood still, their faces downcast. One of them, named Cleopas, asked him, "Are you the only one visiting Jerusalem who does not know the things that have happened there in these days?"

"What things?" he asked.

"About Jesus of Nazareth," they replied. "He was a prophet, powerful in word and deed before God and all the people. The chief priests and our rulers handed him over to be sentenced to death, and they crucified him; but we had hoped that he was the one who was going to redeem Israel. And what is more, it is the third day since all this took place. In addition, some of our women amazed us. They went to the tomb early this morning but didn't find his body. They came and told us that they had seen a vision of angels, who said he was alive. Then some of our companions went to the tomb and found it just as the women had said, but they did not see Jesus."

He said to them, "How foolish you are, and how slow to believe all that the prophets have spoken! Did not the Messiah have to suffer these things and then enter his glory?" And beginning with Moses and all the Prophets, he explained to them what was said in all the Scriptures concerning himself.

As they approached the village to which they were going, Jesus continued on as if he were going farther. But they urged him strongly, "Stay with us, for it is nearly evening; the day is almost over." So he went in to stay with them.

When he was at the table with them, he took bread, gave thanks, broke it and began to give it to them. Then their eyes were opened and they recognized him, and he disappeared from their sight. They asked each other, "Were not our hearts burning within us while he talked with us on the road and opened the Scriptures to us?" (Luke 24:17–32)

Jesus restores access between the seen and the unseen world. He breaks the barrier created by sin between the heavenly and the earthly. Anyone who believes in him can go through as well. He re-creates access to the throne room of the Father for all of us. We can again bring the wisdom and insight of God into our daily lives and activities, as our brother Adam did before the fall. We have access to the thinking of Christ.

Jesus takes the teaching of Moses and the prophets, and in his authority as Son and Heir to the kingdom, he reinterprets those same values for his times. The values applied are exactly the same as God gave Moses, but the applications are completely new and dynamic. These two men, who were already familiar with the Law and the Prophets and the teaching of Jesus, now see the Scriptures with new eyes; they see the Word of God with new insight. They are seeing what Jesus demonstrated with the woman caught committing adultery.

THE WOMAN CAUGHT IN ADULTERY

Adultery has apparently been legal in Israel since the time of David. God gave the people of Israel the authority to change the civil laws that he gave them through Moses, and they did change the laws. However, they had no authority to change moral law. That is the domain of God and God alone. The community may make something legal, but that doesn't mean that God will bless it. The Pharisees are trying to get Jesus to implement an application of civil law that is no longer legal. Adultery is not illegal in the Roman Empire. These Pharisees have no interest in authentic obedience to God in this situation. As the passage says, they are trying to trap Jesus so that they can legally charge him with something and get rid of him. In this case, stoning the woman without authority under Roman law would constitute a charge of murder.

> At dawn he appeared again in the temple courts, where all the people gathered around him, and he sat down to teach them. The teachers of the law and the Pharisees brought in a woman caught in adultery. They made her stand before the group and said to Jesus, "Teacher, this woman was caught in the act of adultery. In the Law Moses commanded us to stone such women. Now what do you say?" They were using this question as a trap, in order to have a basis for accusing him.
> But Jesus bent down and started to write on the ground with

his finger. When they kept on questioning him, he straightened up and said to them, "Let any one of you who is without sin be the first to throw a stone at her." Again he stooped down and wrote on the ground.

At this, those who heard began to go away one at a time, the older ones first, until only Jesus was left, with the woman still standing there. Jesus straightened up and asked her, "Woman, where are they? Has no one condemned you?"

"No one, sir," she said.

"Then neither do I condemn you," Jesus declared. "Go now and leave your life of sin." (John 8:2–11)

In this scene, adultery is no longer illegal, perhaps because there are so few who are not adulterous. Who would execute the law? However, adultery is still a sin and destroys the lives of adulterers and the community. Jesus exhorts the woman to use her own authority over her life to stop this destructive behavior for her own sake and for the sake of the community around her.

Twice Jesus bends down to write in the dirt. Whatever he may be writing—and there are many ideas about that—Jesus is giving his Father time to speak to him. In his authority as Son and Heir of the kingdom, Jesus is asking the Father to interpret his law for the people for their time. The interpretation and application of his Father's values will be dynamic. Jesus is seeking the Father for a way to hold his values in tension. Individual responsibility and authority, community responsibility and authority, moral justice, civil justice, and the authority of the existing government—all these values are included in Jesus's response. Jesus acts in this situation as a man, in relationship with the Father and with the help of the Holy Spirit. He is modeling for us our individual authority restored in Christ. We have access to God and the mind of Christ as heirs and children of God.

Far from lowering the standards of the kingdom, Jesus is raising them: "You have heard that it was said, 'You shall not commit adultery.' But I tell you that anyone who looks at a woman lustfully has already committed adultery with her in his heart" (Matt. 5:27–28). But while Jesus takes the values of the law deeper, he is not seeking a return to the application of Mosaic law through civil law. Why not? It didn't work.

Jesus is not saying that there is no authority in the law. He is dem-onstrating the return of authority to himself as Head of all authority. He is now the one who interprets how the laws should be applied. The guardians are replaced; the angels step aside. The Christ is come, and he is now in his rightful place as Son of Man. He is making way for the veil to be torn and for all of us who choose his way to return to our place in the kingdom as heirs and children of God.

When Jesus next speaks to the crowd in the Gospel of John after the scene with the woman caught in adultery, he says: "I am the light of the world. Whoever follows me will never walk in darkness, but will have the light of life" (John 8:12).

When we face decisions and issues in our nations and governments, in our work and in our personal life, we are not alone. We are not the heirs of Moses coming to reinstitute the law in our understanding. We are the heirs of Christ, here to seek the Father with the help of the Holy Spirit for what Jesus would have us do now! What is the best justice now? What would be the best civil law now? What can we persuade our community of now, and what is the best way to do that? How can we bless our nation now?

CHAPTER 22

JESUS REVEALS THE VALUES OF THE LAW IN HIS TEACHING

The Gospels begin with the exhortation in Matthew that Jesus has not come to abolish the Law or the Prophets but to take them to their fulfillment. Spiritual maturity in the kingdom of God is revealed in the ability to marry the Old and the New revelations.

Nowhere are the weavings of God's values and truths more intricate and subtle than in the teaching of Jesus. Whether Jesus is teaching the Jews or speaking in parables to the mixed public, everything he says contains layer after layer of Moses's law and the messages of the prophets.

If we start at the beginning of Matthew and work our way through the book, what does Jesus emphasize in his teaching?

THE SHEDDING OF INNOCENT BLOOD

In chapter 5 of Matthew, Jesus works his way through several points of the law of Moses and builds on them. As in the law, his first concern is violence. Jesus exhorts his followers to not only abstain from violence but also refuse anger in their hearts. For the believer, contemplating murder is the same as murder. Jesus exhorts his disciples to settle grievances quickly, before court is even necessary. We are to be pursuers of peace, not only abstainers from violence.

In this address his second concern is divorce. Jesus, like Moses and the prophets, highlights the destructiveness of divorce. Still confirmed by crime statistics today, nothing escalates violence more than lust, adultery, and divorce. They lead to violent crime and disruption, not only of the family, but also of the community.

Nothing has changed in Jesus's message about the importance of our words. Continuing in Matthew 5, like Moses and the prophets, he challenges us to make our *yes* mean *yes* and our *no* mean *no*! Nothing will destroy a community, escalate grievances, and create social chaos faster than a culture of deception. There is no peace where there is no trust, and there is no trust where there is no truth in our words.

Jesus continues on the subject of violence by exhorting his disciples to not seek revenge but to walk away from a disagreement if necessary. We as a people are to not worry about retribution but seek to love, not only our neighbor but also our enemy.

What does this mean? Do we eliminate the judicial system in our communities and let everyone act with impunity? Of course not. Jesus and the apostles continue to support the necessity of law and governance, because not everyone will follow Jesus. But as believers working for political justice in our communities, we must accept that Jesus calls us to live a higher standard than our courts are able to uphold in our communities. We do not seek judicial perfection but the best system of deterrents to violence we can legislate and enforce. We ourselves stand before the court of Christ and agree with a much higher standard of self-governance.

Yes, everything is fallen! We can expect the continuation of community disruption and even war. But in the end everything will be judged by God's perfect standard. Meanwhile, we do our best to bless a fallen world. No one can legislate sin out of existence. It is difficult enough to get those who claim to love Jesus to follow him in their daily lives. Jesus will sit on the bench in the court of final and perfect justice.

Unjust Communities and Authorities

Jesus continues the emphasis, as in the Law and the Prophets, on evaluating whole community systems, not only individuals. As the prophets call out warnings to Judah, Israel, and nations throughout the region, warning them of the coming consequences of their choices and actions, Jesus speaks to unrepentant cities in Matthew 11 and laments over Jerusalem in Matthew 23. The concern of the king is not only that individuals live life abundantly but also that individuals come together to build communities that promote peace and abundant life. We must disciple not only people, but also communities, through the systems and institutions that create the environment in which people live. God is revealed in how we live together.

Even as we work toward better justice, God works in the midst of human imperfection. In Matthew 22 Jesus says to pay your taxes, even though the government is Roman. We still need government. God can use even Rome. You may even find an example of true faith in an officer of the Roman army. Jesus and Peter pay the temple tax in Matthew 17, even though the priesthood has lost its way. God is still using the institution regardless of imperfection. We live out God's design and seek for our community the highest level of justice and the best institutions they will accept.

In Matthew 5 we are to be "salt and light," for our cultures and institutions as well as for lost individuals. As those called to public service in civil institutions of government, our concern is for the community and, wherever possible, the individual.

The Power of One

The parables of Jesus can be used to understand many things about the kingdom. The parable of the Good Samaritan, for instance, can be used to understand how God views the good acts of the lost and the inappropriate acts of the righteous. It can be used to understand one of the ways to use our money and time. It can be used to tell us of the condition of safety on the roads in the day. For our purposes here we are using it to look at the emphasis on the importance of the individual.

Jesus continues in his teaching and parables to emphasize the king-dom of God in the individual created in the image of God. Whether it is salt in food, light in darkness, leaven in dough, or faith the size of a mustard seed, the power of a small thing to impact the greater environ-ment is seen again and again in Jesus's message. Jesus illustrates the value and significance of the individual with the parables of the lost coin, the lost lamb, the returned prodigal son, and the importance of the widow's mite in the offering. He draws our attention to individuals taking action in their circumstances as illustrations of the kingdom of God. The Good Samaritan stops to help an injured man on the road. The widow wears down the unwilling judge by pressing her case before him until he finally relents.

In his parables, Jesus emphasizes the importance of our choices and, all too often, the disaster we bring on ourselves with our poor choices. In Matthew 25 he tells the story of ten virgins waiting for the groom to arrive at the wedding, five of whom do not prepare by making sure they have enough oil for their lamps. The five unprepared virgins are out in the city looking for an oil vendor when the other five enter the wedding feast and the doors are closed. In the parable in Matthew 18, Jesus tells us about a servant forgiven a great debt who fails to extend his debtors the same grace. The cancellation of this unforgiving man's own debt is rescinded. In another of Jesus's parables, a boss goes away on a trip and leaves different amounts of money with several of his workers to invest and multiply what they have been given. There is great disap-pointment when one does nothing but bury his allotment of money and return it. The important thing was not the amount the workers were given, but what each of them has chosen to do with it. The "worthless servant" is cast out while the others are honored in Matthew 25 and Luke 19. Throughout his teaching, Jesus made invitations. As his Father is recorded as doing all through Scripture, Jesus speaks and lives the truth, sharing his wisdom and yet recognizing the God-given authority of each individual to decide. He tells us, as he told the people then,

> Therefore everyone who hears these words of mine and puts
> them into practice is like a wise man who built his house on the
> rock. The rain came down, the streams rose, and the winds blew

and beat against that house; yet it did not fall, because it had its foundation on the rock. But everyone who hears these words of mine and does not put them into practice is like a foolish man who built his house on sand. The rain came down, the streams rose, and the winds blew and beat against that house, and it fell with a great crash. (Matt. 7:24–27)

Listen to Jesus! Are we hearing God's words and putting them into practice? Jesus really wants us to get this. On another occasion, he tells us about two sons who are asked to do something for their father. Initially, one refuses and one agrees. But the one who refuses turns around and obeys, and the one who said he would do it never does (Matt. 21:28–32). Jesus's hearers, then and now, have no problem picking out which son did what the father wanted. Maybe we have made poor decisions in the past but are ready now to give up the ground we've staked out in error. Or maybe we've made a strong statement of commitment to God but are wavering now. We just don't follow through. What will we choose going forward?

Jesus teaches that the astute see the potential and take action as shown in three parables in Matthew 13: the man who found a treasure hidden in a field and sold everything he had to buy the field, the man who found a pearl of great value and sold everything to buy it, and the fishermen who kept only the best of the fish in the net. Luke recounts a parable Jesus told of a dishonest manager. He is fired because he has been wasteful in the management of his boss's assets. Of course, Jesus is not commending theft. He is commending this man's ability to see potential within his own circumstances and take action. "The people of this world are more shrewd in dealing with their own kind than are the people of the light" (Luke 16:8).

The parable in which Jesus asks why a person would choose to waste the light by hiding it is repeated four times. The kingdom of God is built by those who, in their circumstances, see what God would have them do and seize the opportunity. You may or may not have "a position of influence," but regardless of your position, you have influence. The kingdom of God is in you . . . not your position!

TRADITIONS

Jesus continues challenging traditional views in his teaching and parables. He is questioned about why his disciples do not always fast when
appropriate, why his disciples do not always wash their hands before
eating, why he heals on the Sabbath, and why he picks grain to eat on
the Sabbath. The whole of Jesus's Sermon on the Mount in Matthew
exhorts his listeners to look closely at what they think Moses means
in the law. And Jesus turns the people's traditional concept of leadership upside down when he tells them that greatness and authority in
the kingdom is akin to the lowly position of the child and the servant.
In each one of these examples Jesus is supporting the values of the law
but questioning Jewish traditional interpretation of what it meant and
how it was to be lived out in daily life. They have the right source in the
Scriptures. They have the wrong understanding of its meaning.

Jesus tells the people that they must learn to marry the Old, the
message of Moses and the prophets, and the New, the message of Christ,
to understand the kingdom of God:

> "Have you understood all these things?" Jesus asked.
> "Yes," they replied.
> He said to them, "Therefore every teacher of the law who
> has become a disciple in the kingdom of heaven is like the
> owner of a house who brings out of his storeroom new trea-
> sures as well as old." (Matt. 13:51–52)

In order to build the kingdom, we must be people who can interpret
this present time and know how to apply the values of the Old and New
in relevant situations today. No precedent, legal or religious, is sacred.
What matters to God is whether his values and truths are applied.

THE MATERIAL WORLD IS REAL AND GOOD

When Jesus teaches in public, he uses common-sense wisdom that
draws on what his listeners already know in their daily lives. From this
cause-and-effect world that they know, he builds a foundation for the
kingdom that goes beyond their experience and comprehension. In

other words, the material world the Father made is built on the same values and truths as the world beyond. Counter to some worldviews, the world is not divided between conflicting realities, seen and unseen. The world, seen and unseen, is created and ruled over by one God. The idea that the seen and unseen worlds are split is a delusion of sin. Moses gave us the values of the seen world. Now Jesus comes to reveal to us the unseen world, where the values and the principles are the same. Jesus comes to restore our authority as individuals created in God's image in both worlds. They are both the kingdom of God.

Jesus blesses the ordinary when he likens God to a good shepherd who seeks out one lost sheep, a widow who diligently searches her house for a lost coin, and a father who finds a lost son. And in a host of other parables, Jesus uses a variety of familiar things to picture the kingdom of God. The people of the kingdom of God are like salt, and salt that isn't salty is of no use. The kingdom of God is like yeast or like a mustard seed, which though small, multiplies exponentially. The kingdom of God is like a field in which a man has planted good grain, but an enemy has planted weeds among the wheat. (Does this remind you of our fallen world?) The man knows that if he worries too much about the weeds and tries to eliminate them all, he will disturb and perhaps destroy the grain, so he leaves them and focuses on the health of the grain.

The people of the kingdom of God are like the wise builder who considers the foundation before building; the building will not fall down and his work will not be wasted. People of the kingdom are like fishermen who go out and bring in a net full of fish. They keep the fish that have profit and throw the rest back in. The kingdom of God is like a man who finds a treasure in a field and like a merchant who finds a fine pearl; each sells everything he has to make a better purchase, choosing to value the treasure or the pearl above everything he owns. Such is the kingdom of God! (Did you notice that this one pair of parables includes principles of private property, business, the right of land ownership, and the authority of the individual?)

Throughout the Gospels, earthy examples permeate the teaching of Jesus, who likens himself to a vine, his Father to a gardener, and us to branches. Jesus urges his listeners to be as discerning of people as they are with fruit trees; a bad tree will bear bad fruit, a good tree, good fruit. And he pointedly warns those judging others that a fig tree that bears no fruit will be cut down, and if it isn't, it is only because of the gardener's mercy.

Jesus's teachings consistently emphasize the wisdom of God's creation, and the Son of God draws freely on the natural world—its goodness, dangers, and laws—to build his explanation of the kingdom.

What does this say about political justice in our communities? A great deal! This world and these times matter. The temporal and the eternal are connected and share the same values and truths. As Jesus himself, and all of Scripture, teaches us, any just system of law will build on the reality of time, space, evidence, and testimony. There can be no biblical concept of justice in a system without this foundation, because if the material world is not real, then there is no objective truth and therefore no justice. Findings are arbitrary and reveal only who is in power. Justice requires a good and real creation, the very world we have.

Thanks be to God, the Creator, Redeemer, and Sustainer of the seen and unseen! As Jesus shows so plainly, the Father has given us a buildable foundation for justice.

RIGHTS AND RESPONSIBILITIES

Jesus includes the themes of authority and responsibility, and the limits to both, in the parables about kings and landowners. In Matthew 20, we have the interesting story of the landowner who hires day workers in the market, negotiating and agreeing with them on the value of their day's work. Later in the day, the landowner hires more workers and pays them the same amount even though they have worked a shorter day. When the morning crew complains, the landowner responds that he has not cheated them. It is his land and his money; he has the authority to pay more if he likes—though not less than he has promised. Do you see the weaving of values? The values include the owner's rights to the use of his own money. The workers that came earlier have the right to be paid what they agreed to.

Matthew 21 has a second parable about a landowner who has purchased and developed a vineyard and then rented it out. At harvest he sends workers to collect the rent. The renters kill two consecutive representatives, and finally the owner sends his own son, thinking they will give more respect to his authority. These wicked individuals have the power to reject the son's authority, but now the owner of the vineyard has the authority to come, and will come in time, to collect what is his own. Not surprisingly, this parable is repeated in three of the four Gospels. It lays the foundation for the most basic questions of the kingdom. The landowner has the right to his land and the rent that those using the land have agreed to pay.

Two parables take up the subject of kings inviting subjects to a banquet he has prepared. In the parable in Matthew 22, the subjects, for their various reasons, reject the invitation. Which is their right! Some become violent and, like the tenants in the parable of the landowner, kill the messenger. The king sends his army to deal with the murderers. Which is his right! The king invites the street people, beggars, and the poor to his banquet and provides appropriate clothing for them to attend. Which is his right! However, one poor man comes to the banquet without the appropriate clothes the king has provided, which is his choice, and the king throws him out of his home, which is his right! The king has the right to his own home and the right to create his own guest list. The guest has the right to wear what he wants. The king then has the right to throw him out. These are the same rights given to any person and his home in the law. But notice the king does not have the right to kill the offending man, as when Saul tried to murder David.

We can go through each and every parable that Jesus uses and draw out exactly the same values, rights and responsibilities that God gave through Moses and the law.

A MOST UNJUST TRIAL

Jesus supports the law; this much is clear. But he challenges the traditions that the Jews have laid over the law. In their minds, he is breaking the law, and this blasphemy gives them cause to pursue his execution. In reality, though they don't recognize it, Jesus is revealing a much higher understanding of the law.

The Jewish leadership and the Romans pursue an unjust trial even when measured by their own cultures' definitions of justice. They pay lying witnesses, fabricate evidence, and make public admission that there is no crime, and certainly not one punishable by death. But they execute Jesus anyway. In every way, the justice Jesus receives violates the values of God's system of justice and that of the Roman Empire.

His death brings confusion and chaos to his followers. They have no idea what to do except wait. Perhaps this all comes to nothing, they think. All our Jewish history, all the work of Moses and the prophets, all the hope we have placed in this man . . . all for nothing? The revelation, however, is not finished. There is still a great mystery prepared from before the foundations of the earth that has not been revealed. There is more to come.

In the same chapter, Jesus appears to the disciples:

> Then he opened their minds so they could understand the Scriptures. He told them, "This is what is written: The Messiah will suffer and rise from the dead on the third day, and repentance for the forgiveness of sins will be preached in his name to all nations, beginning at Jerusalem. You are witnesses of these things. I am going to send you what my Father has promised; but stay in the city until you have been clothed with power from on high." (Luke 24:45–49)

The minds of Jesus's disciples are being opened. They are seeing the Scriptures in new ways. But still Jesus is not finished. There is more to be revealed.

> Again Jesus said, "Peace be with you! As the Father has sent me, I am sending you." And with that he breathed on them and said, "Receive the Holy Spirit." (John 20:21–22)

And there is more:

> Then Jesus came to them and said, "All authority in heaven and on earth has been given to me. Therefore go and make disciples of all nations, baptizing them in the name of the Father and of the Son and of the Holy Spirit, and teaching them to obey everything I have commanded you. And surely I am with you always, to the very end of the age" (Matt. 28:18–20).

On one occasion, while he was eating with them, he gave them this command: "Do not leave Jerusalem, but wait for the gift my Father promised, which you have heard me speak about. For John baptized with water, but in a few days you will be baptized with the Holy Spirit."

Then they gathered around him and asked him, "Lord, are you at this time going to restore the kingdom to Israel?"

He said to them: "It is not for you to know the times or dates the Father has set by his own authority. But you will receive power when the Holy Spirit comes on you; and you will be my witnesses in Jerusalem, and in all Judea and Samaria, and to the ends of the earth." (Acts 1:4–8)

Jesus leaves his disciples with vague instructions and the admonition to wait. There was more to come, more power, more authority, and more understanding.

Jesus gives his apostles a final global mandate and is taken up into heaven as they watch. They must wait. There is more.

And so the disciples wait!

CHAPTER 23

THE GREAT MYSTERY REVEALED

If, at the core, the question of political justice is one of authority and power, and God's original design was disrupted by the fall in Genesis 3, then what changed in authority and power after Jesus ascended and the Holy Spirit fell on the disciples gathered in Jerusalem? We know what we lost through sin. The human race, intended to rule with God, was put under the supervision of guardians (angels), separated from God because of sin but not abandoned. The proper order—justice— of the kingdom of God was damaged, as humankind could no longer commune directly with God. We had dominion of the earth, but we had no idea what to do with our dominion. Our identity as heirs of the kingdom was intact, but our relationship with the king was severed. The seen and the unseen world became irreconcilable to us. What did we gain in Christ? Do the apostles answer this question?

On the day of Pentecost, the disciples have no idea how to answer that question. They are confused by what is taking place. But something has shifted, and it is dramatically demonstrated from the very first hours. We see it in the disciples, laymen flooding the streets preaching the gospel. We see it in these same laymen crossing the cultural barriers of religion and speaking out a truth that is for all nations and all languages. We see it as mere mortals began to perform deliverances and healings. The people think the disciples are angels or gods. Power and authority have shifted, but how, to whom, and for what? It will take the apostles decades to understand the answer to these questions. It is a message that comes to them, not in words, but in demonstrations. This is revelation from God that they receive and understand as they step out in obedience to do what God tells them to do.

Let's try to capture the revelation as they articulate it in their letters, letting it build into our minds and hearts as it did for those first disciples.

WHY ARE YOU WAITING?

As Jesus ascends, the disciples stand there watching, and two angels appear and ask them a question: "They were looking intently up into the sky as he was going, when suddenly two men dressed in white stood beside them. 'Men of Galilee,' they said, 'why do you stand here looking into the sky? This same Jesus, who has been taken from you into heaven, will come back in the same way you have seen him go into heaven'" (Acts 1:10–11). Two angels come to tell them they have work to do! No more waiting on someone else to change the world. No more waiting for someone else to receive the word of the Lord. Now they are restored to their ability to seek God's mind and take action, and so are we today.

Led by a fisherman, about 120 of them meet and pray. Peter proposes that they appoint a replacement for Judas who had been witness to the whole three years of Jesus's ministry. The group chooses two men they believe qualify. They pray, ask God for his direction, and cast lots between the two, taking Matthias. Where did all that come from? There is no biblical record of laymen participating in choosing priests. There is no history of priests choosing priests. Jesus didn't cast lots when he chose the disciples. This is all new. They are creating with God.

Almost immediately, they run afoul of existing authority. These laymen are preaching. The Jewish establishment is enraged. This is not the tradition of our people! This is not our interpretation of the law! The ringleaders are called before the Sanhedrin: "Then they called them in again and commanded them not to speak or teach at all in the name of

Jesus. But Peter and John replied, 'Which is right in God's eyes: to listen to you, or to him? You be the judges! As for us, we cannot help speaking about what we have seen and heard'" (Acts 4:18–20). These men are questioning the authority of the Sanhedrin on this point. God has spoken to them to preach! Mere laymen are preaching and interpreting the Scriptures? Under whose authority?

In the next chapter, the apostles are brought back before the Sanhedrin for continuing to preach in the name of Jesus. And the apostles reply: "We must obey God rather than human beings!" (Acts 5:29). They are not following Jewish tradition. They are questioning the authority of the traditional Jewish understanding of how God works. This is a complete realignment of where Jews place authority. The disciples no longer see themselves as under the authority of Jewish tradition. They are under Christ. Now the angels are sent to help them by releasing them from jail. The apostles are the messengers, and the angels are the helpers.

God begins to prepare Peter for another shocker. Peter is going to break tradition again, this time by going to a Gentile home. As Peter is praying, he has a vision of a mixture of clean and unclean animals. "Get up, Peter. Kill and eat." This doesn't just break tradition; this breaks the law of Moses as they have understood it. Peter responds: "Surely not!" God says: "Do not call anything impure that God has made clean" (Acts 10:10–15). This mystifying message takes three repetitions to sink in. The Jewish community has called eating these kinds of animals "unclean" for over a millennium. And tradition has told them that they were not to eat with the Gentiles, the unclean. This is what they have been taught the law means. Now God is saying something new to Peter.

God is not under the law. He is over the law. The law is not God. God is the maker and the interpreter of the law. We do not tell God what the law means and hold him accountable. God tells us what the law means and holds us accountable. Now we are no longer under the law or the traditional Jewish understanding of the law. Peter, along with us, is under Jesus! Our position of authority has been restored in the kingdom of God. We are, again, second in command. We are directly under God, and he relates directly with us. God speaks to us! We are no longer under guardians as children. In Christ, we are restored to our place of authority as children and heirs. Peter can hardly contain the radicalness of this revelation, but he obeys and goes to the Gentile home. Notice that because Cornelius is not yet "clothed in the Holy Spirit," angels go to speak to Cornelius, but God is speaking directly to Peter by the Holy Spirit. And this is only the beginning.

THE GENTILE FIRESTORM

The issue of circumcision, the oldest symbol of obedience to God within Jewish culture, heightens the issue of Jewish tradition and authority. As the message of the kingdom spreads throughout the Gentile tribes and nations, Gentile circumcision becomes a pivotal question regarding the relationship between the law and the new faith.

> Certain people came down from Judea to Antioch and were teaching the believers: "Unless you are circumcised, according to the custom taught by Moses, you cannot be saved." This brought Paul and Barnabas into sharp dispute and debate with them. So Paul and Barnabas were appointed, along with some other believers, to go up to Jerusalem to see the apostles and elders about this question. . . .
>
> After much discussion, Peter got up and addressed them: "Brothers, you know that some time ago God made a choice among you that the Gentiles might hear from my lips the message of the gospel and believe. God, who knows the heart, showed that he accepted them by giving the Holy Spirit to them, just as he did to us. He did not discriminate between us and them, for he purified their hearts by faith. Now then, why do you try to test God by putting on the necks of Gentiles a yoke that neither we nor our ancestors have been able to bear? No! We believe it is through the grace of our Lord Jesus that we are saved, just as they are." (Acts 15:1–2, 7–11)

The relationship of the law to the new faith was not only the first debate in the first century of the church. This is a pivotal question that continues to elicit "sharp dispute and debate" in the Christian community discussing the discipling of the nations and transformation today. What do we do with the law? As we focus on nation building and transformation, the question becomes even more acute. What is our political agenda? Is it to go back to the letter of the law of Moses? To form all governments around the system and application of Mosaic law? Do we use the law to enforce morality? If that is the case, do we just take over, seize power, and make societies obey? Or do we let societies run their destructive course while seeking to bring individuals to Christ?

The law and the prophets are from God. In them God reveals his thinking and his eternal values and truths. Jesus and the apostles make that clear. However, we are not to give any historical application of the law the same weight. God, who gave the symbol of circumcision to Israel, can create a new symbol of righteousness today. We do not throw the law out. But with the help of the Holy Spirit, we reinterpret the law's values and principles for current affairs. We marry the Old and the New and find a new dynamic application:

> Do not think that I have come to abolish the Law or the Prophets; I have not come to abolish them but to fulfill them. For truly I tell you, until heaven and earth disappear, not the smallest letter, not the least stroke of a pen, will by any means disappear from the Law until everything is accomplished. Therefore anyone who sets aside one of the least of these commands and teaches others accordingly will be called least in the kingdom of heaven, but whoever practices and teaches these commands will be called great in the kingdom of heaven. For I tell you that unless your righteousness surpasses that of the Pharisees and the teachers of the law, you will certainly not enter the kingdom of heaven. (Matt. 5:17–20)

The "righteousness of the Pharisees" was to do their best to obey the law while still not having a relationship with God himself. And no one worked harder at it than they did. But now we have the law and Jesus. No longer under guardians, we can go directly to the throne room of God and say, "Father, what would you have me do here?"

What does that look like? Like Jesus, we have access to the Father. We have the mind of Christ 24/7. Jesus has already shown us the way with the woman caught in adultery in John 8. The Pharisees were right. She had broken the law of Moses. They were right that the penalty under

Moses for this sin was death. But they completely ignored the change in that law hundreds of years earlier and the rights God gives people in the Mosaic law to make such changes. The Pharisees were saying that the civil law and the moral law of God cannot be divided. But God did divide them! God gives us a template of justice, but then he also gives us a choice in how we will be governed.

Jesus bends down to do what in the sand? To seek his Father as he did in every situation. "Father, what do I do here and now?" The answer was clear and simple. Uphold the legislative rights of the Jews and the Romans to make adultery legal, and for the sake of this poor woman, uphold my moral law by telling her to stop sinning. It is destroying her. Make sure she understands that she has a choice.

There was nothing in the Jewish framework to explain the kind of authority Jesus was demonstrating. The traditions of the law built a very safe, black-and-white world. You could always know what was right for you and for others to do. Jesus's authority made the Jewish establishment angry and afraid. It disturbed their carefully built fences.

As the gospel of the kingdom begins to take root across Gentile cultures, the controversy intensifies as the "great mystery" becomes clearer. It is not only the traditions of the Jewish people that will be challenged by this message. The traditions and authority of all nations and cultures will be challenged.

As Paul and the other apostles deal with the growth of the new faith in the Gentile nations, their letters reveal the developing theme of "the great mystery revealed." The mystery begins to take form in action as specific issues of culture and tradition are dealt with in the new churches.

THE GREAT MYSTERY

Taking the apostolic letters in the approximate order they were written, we can follow the development of the apostles' thinking about the meaning of what Jesus said during his three years of ministry. An understanding is there in the beginning, but it is less articulate. But by the time we get to Hebrews, the understanding of what Christ did on the cross is exploding. Let's watch the progression through the apostles' letters.

James (ca. late AD 40s to early AD 50s)

Traditionally attributed to James, the eldest of Jesus's brothers, the book of James has sometimes been criticized as being too works-oriented. But listen to the apostle's exhortation to early believers:

> Let perseverance finish its work so that you may be mature and complete, not lacking anything. If any of you lacks wisdom, you should ask God, who gives generously to all without finding fault, and it will be given to you. But when you ask, you must believe and not doubt, because the one who doubts is like a wave of the sea, blown and tossed by the wind. That person should not expect to receive anything from the Lord. Such a person is double-minded and unstable in all they do. (James 1:4–8)

> Do not merely listen to the word, and so deceive yourselves. Do what it says. Anyone who listens to the word but does not do what it says is like someone who looks at his face in a mirror and, after looking at himself, goes away and immediately forgets what he looks like. But whoever looks intently into the perfect law that gives freedom, and continues in it—not forgetting what they have heard, but doing it—they will be blessed in what they do. (James 1:22–25)

> Was not our father Abraham considered righteous for what he did when he offered his son Isaac on the altar? You see that his faith and his actions were working together, and his faith was made complete by what he did. And the scripture was fulfilled that says, "Abraham believed God, and it was credited to him as righteousness," and he was called God's friend. (James 2:21–23)

> Who is wise and understanding among you? Let them show it by their good life, by deeds done in the humility that comes from wisdom. But if you harbor bitter envy and selfish ambition in your hearts, do not boast about it or deny the truth. Such "wisdom" does not come down from heaven but is earthly, unspiritual, demonic. For where you have envy and selfish ambition, there you find disorder and every evil practice. But the wisdom

that comes from heaven is first of all pure; then peace-loving, considerate, submissive, full of mercy and good fruit, impartial and sincere. Peacemakers who sow in peace reap a harvest of righteousness. (James 3:13–18)

James is talking about a dynamic relationship with God on a daily basis, a relationship in which we seek wisdom for whatever is needed and God gives it to us. Abraham demonstrated this kind of faith before the law of Moses existed. And now, with the law and with the Holy Spirit, because of Christ, we too are to intentionally follow this radical life of seeking and obeying.

Galatians (ca. AD 49+)

In his letter to the Galatians, Paul worries that they are moving away from a gospel dependent on Christ and the revelation of the Spirit to a gospel built on the traditions of others—namely, at this point, Jewish traditions. Paul makes it clear that no one was more zealous for the Jewish traditions than he was. He confronts Peter and others for forcing the Gentiles to follow Jewish customs. He makes it clear that the law never led to receiving the Spirit and teaches that the law, on its own, reveals how condemned we are.

"Before the coming of this faith, we were held in custody under the law, locked up until the faith that was to come would be revealed. So the law was our guardian until Christ came that we might be justified by faith. Now that this faith has come, we are no longer under a guardian" (Gal. 3:23–25). *We are no longer under guardians.*

We are no longer under the law. We are over it! We live by applying the law as guided by the Spirit. We marry the Old and the New and seek new applications to our times.

1 Corinthians (ca. AD 55)

These themes begin to take shape in Paul's first letter to the Corinthians. He points out from the very first chapter that they, the believers in the Corinth church, lack no spiritual gift. They are complete in Christ. Christ will be revealed to them as they wait on God. They do not need to seek the "wisdom of Paul" or the "wisdom of Apollos." They have access to the wisdom of Christ. They are not under Paul. They are under Christ.

The message of the cross is the "power of God," meaning we are no longer dependent on the thinking and traditions of the world, whether that is Jewish thinking or Gentile thinking. We now have a direct link with Jesus, "who has become for us wisdom from God" (1 Cor. 1:30). It is this revelational relationship with God through Christ and the Holy Spirit that becomes our wisdom. We are restored to our position as co-rulers. We uphold the law, but the Spirit gives us the application for our times.

Paul challenges the Corinthians that this is a message for the "mature." This is a message of the "secret wisdom" of God held back from all, even the Jews, until now. We do not seek to follow the traditions of men because now, through Christ, we have access to the thinking of God. We make judgments in all matters by seeking "the mind of Christ," to which we have access through the Holy Spirit. "All things are yours . . . all are yours, and you are of Christ, and Christ is of God" (1 Cor. 3:21–23). We marry God's revelation in the Old Testament with his revelation in the New, as Jesus did.

2 Corinthians (ca. AD 55)

In his second letter to the Corinthian church, Paul clarifies that this "new covenant" Christ has made with us is "not of the letter but of the Spirit; for the letter kills, but the Spirit gives life" (2 Cor. 3:6). The Jews had the "letter" in the form of the law, but their "minds were made dull" because the veil of separation from God remained. But now that veil has been removed in Christ (2 Cor. 3:14). We, in Christ, now have the Spirit in order to interpret the law for our circumstances, as did Jesus with the Samaritan woman at the well and Peter with the revelation of going to the Gentile home.

Romans (ca. AD 57)

The confusion continues in Rome's church. Paul tells the church that no one was ever declared righteous by obeying the law. Abraham's righteousness, which preceded the law, was through faith in God, and by this same faith we are justified in Christ. However, "Do we, then, nullify the law by this faith? Not at all! Rather, we uphold the law" (Rom. 3:31). Paul is repeating what James has already said.

The law is the thinking of God revealed through the Jews. But we are not under a Jewish interpretation of the law. We are under the Spirit's revelation of the law for our times and our cultures. We are not under tradition but under God in dynamic, situational application of the values of the law to real-time circumstances. For example, in Jesus's response to the woman caught in adultery, adultery was still a sin, but the death penalty was no longer relevant in Rome. We are under Christ and seek him for revelation of an application of the values and truths of God for today, as Jesus did with God the Father.

"For those who are led by the Spirit of God are the children of God. The Spirit you received does not make you slaves, so that you live in fear again; rather, the Spirit you received brought about your adoption to sonship. And by him we cry, '*Abba*, Father'" (Rom. 8:14–15).

Paul tells us, "Do not conform to the pattern of this world, but be transformed by the renewing of your mind. Then you will be able to test and approve what God's will is—his good, pleasing and perfect will" (Rom. 12:2). We create with God, as Jesus did!

Colossians (ca. AD 60)

In Paul's pivotal epistle to the Colossian church, he is clearer than ever in his exhortation:

> For this reason, since the day we heard about you, we have not stopped praying for you. We continually ask God to fill you with the knowledge of his will through all the wisdom and understanding that the Spirit gives, so that you may live a life worthy of the Lord and please him in every way: bearing fruit in every good work, growing in the knowledge of God, being strengthened with all power according to his glorious might so that you may have great endurance and patience, and giving joyful thanks to the Father, who has qualified you to share in the inheritance of his holy people in the kingdom of light. (Col. 1:9–12)

Paul goes on to declare the supremacy of Christ over all creation, including our own thinking about how we are to live and serve: "For in him all things were created: things in heaven and on earth, visible and invisible, whether thrones or powers or rulers or authorities; all things have been created through him and for him" (Col. 1:16). Therefore, we are not under these thrones, powers, rulers, and authorities. We are over them in Christ! We are not to accept their thinking. We are to seek to be witnesses to God's thinking.

This is "the mystery that has been kept hidden for ages and generations, but is now disclosed to the Lord's people" (Col. 1:26). We are now restored to our position of co-rulership with Christ. We are no longer under the world's systems, traditions, or thinking. We are the creators of the kingdom as we obey the wisdom of the Spirit of God in all that we do. We are to imitate Christ in seeking God for wisdom in *all* that we do.

"See to it that no one takes you captive through hollow and deceptive philosophy, which depends on human tradition and the elemental spiritual forces of this world rather than on Christ. . . . Do not let anyone judge you by what you eat or drink, or with regard to a religious festival, a New Moon celebration or a Sabbath day. These are a shadow of the things that were to come; the reality, however, is found in Christ" (Col. 2:8, 16–17).

Ephesians (ca. AD 60)
To the church in Ephesus, Paul writes:

With all wisdom and understanding, he made known to us the mystery of his will according to his good pleasure, which he purposed in Christ, to be put into effect when the times reach their fulfillment—to bring unity to all things in heaven and on earth under Christ. . . . When you believed, you were marked in him with a seal, the promised Holy Spirit, who is a deposit guaranteeing our inheritance until the redemption of those who are God's possession—to the praise of his glory. . . .

I keep asking that the God of our Lord Jesus Christ, the glorious Father, may give you the Spirit of wisdom and revelation, so that you may know him better. I pray that the eyes of your heart may be enlightened in order that you may know the hope to which he has called you, the riches of his glorious inheritance in his holy people, and his incomparably great power for us who believe. That power is the same as the mighty strength he exerted when he raised Christ from the dead and seated him at his right hand in the heavenly realms, far above all rule and authority, power and dominion, and every name that is invoked, not only in the present age but also in the one to come. And God placed all things under his feet and appointed him to be head over everything for the church, which is his body, the fullness of him who fills everything in every way. (Eph. 1:8–10, 13–14, 17–23)

The "great mystery" is that everything is now under Christ, and that in Christ, we are restored. Our authority in God is restored in Christ. For those who believe, the proper order of creation is restored. God is over all, and in Christ we are second in authority. Order will be reestablished over all that has been made when Christ returns. But it is now reestablished in those of us who believe. We are under no authority but God's, and we have access to the wisdom and revelation of God in every circumstance of every day of our lives. The kingdom of God is within us. The Spirit of God lives in us. We are already living eternal life:

And God raised us up with Christ and seated us with him in the heavenly realms in Christ Jesus, in order that in the coming ages he might show the incomparable riches of his grace, expressed in his kindness to us in Christ Jesus. For it is by grace you have been saved, through faith—and this is not from yourselves, it is the gift of God—not by works, so that no one can boast. For we are God's handiwork, created in Christ Jesus to do good works, which God prepared in advance for us to do. (Eph. 2:6–10)

We are witness to the superiority of God's ways:

Surely you have heard about the administration of God's grace that was given to me for you, that is, the mystery made known to me by revelation, as I have already written briefly. In reading this, then, you will be able to understand my insight into the mystery of Christ, which was not made known to people in other generations as it has now been revealed by the Spirit to

God's holy apostles and prophets. This mystery is that through the gospel the Gentiles are heirs together with Israel, members together of one body, and sharers together in the promise in Christ Jesus. (Eph. 3:2–6)

This authority is not restored only to the Jews but equally to the Gentiles who are branches grafted into the tree in Christ. "So I tell you this, and insist on it in the Lord, that you must no longer live as the Gentiles do, in the futility of their thinking" (Eph. 4:17).

Not only Jewish tradition and definitions of authority are to be questioned but the thinking and traditions of every culture. "That, however, is not the way of life you learned when you heard about Christ and were taught in him in accordance with the truth that is in Jesus. You were taught, with regard to your former way of life, to put off your old self, which is being corrupted by its deceitful desires; to be made new in the attitude of your minds; and to put on the new self, created to be like God in true righteousness and holiness" (Eph. 4:20–24).

Philippians (early AD 60s)

Paul goes so far in this reevaluation of our cultural roots and traditions as to use the illustration of changed citizenship and loyalties. We no longer think as our cultures think:

Join together in following my example, brothers and sisters, and just as you have us as a model, keep your eyes on those who live as we do. For, as I have often told you before and now tell you again even with tears, many live as enemies of the cross of Christ. Their destiny is destruction, their god is their stomach, and their glory is in their shame. Their mind is set on earthly things. But our citizenship is in heaven. And we eagerly await a Savior from there, the Lord Jesus Christ, who, by the power that enables him to bring everything under his control, will transform our lowly bodies so that they will be like his glorious body. (Phil. 3:17–21)

1 Peter (early AD 60s)

Many misunderstand the exhortation in 1 Peter, perhaps because it has so often been used to condone control and misuse of authority. We misuse the word *submit* to mean "obey," and we define *obedience* as "compliance with the will of another." Peter writes:

> Submit yourselves for the Lord's sake to every human authority: whether to the emperor, as the supreme authority, or to governors, who are sent by him to punish those who do wrong and to commend those who do right. For it is God's will that by doing good you should silence the ignorant talk of foolish people. Live as free people, but do not use your freedom as a cover-up for evil; live as God's slaves. Show proper respect to everyone, love the family of believers, fear God, honor the emperor. (1 Pet. 2:13–17)

What does Peter mean? He is advocating what Jesus and the apostles *lived*. We are to give rightful authority to the institutions God has created, whether we agree with them or not. But when any authority crosses the boundaries designated by God, we must resist it. Paul himself disobeyed government and church officials when they told him to stop preaching. Saul was the king. But he had no authority as king to murder David. Pilate was the emperor's representative. He had the authority to govern and, under Roman law, to execute Christ—authority that Jesus acknowledged his Father gave Pilate. The Pharisees were right; the woman had committed adultery and adultery is a sin in God's kingdom. But adultery was no longer illegal in Rome. They had no right to stone her. We give authority where authority is appropriately due in the kingdom of God. This is proper order—justice.

Hebrews (ca. AD 70)

By the AD 70s it seems the message of the great mystery had gained such clarity that the author of Hebrews, whoever the writer was, wanted to capture it all again in a single letter. It is so difficult to summarize this letter, as every sentence is so important.

At length, over several chapters, the writer clarifies how God spoke in the past through Moses, the prophets, and angels, and how God is speaking to us now, through his Son.

In the past God spoke to our ancestors through the prophets at many times and in various ways, but in these last days he has spoken to us by his Son, whom he appointed heir of all things, and through whom also he made the universe. The Son is the radiance of God's glory and the exact representation of his being, sustaining all things by his powerful word. After he had provided purification for sins, he sat down at the right hand of the Majesty in heaven. So he became as much superior to the angels as the name he has inherited is superior to theirs. (Heb. 1:1–4)

Jesus has not come to get rid of the law but to take his rightful place over the law. He is the interpreter of the law. He upholds the law and the prophets, but he is the authority over their application. By the Spirit, we who belong to him are heirs to that authority. We are not subject to the law but subject to Christ and his interpretation of the law.

The writer of Hebrews emphasizes that the Son of God is, in all things, superior to angels. And if the message given by angels in the form of the law was binding, how much more binding is the message of Christ? Our position in God has been restored. As amazing as it seems, God has given men and women, created in his image and subject to his leadership, authority over the world to come. The writer ponders this blinding truth:

It is not to angels that he has subjected the world to come, about which we are speaking. But there is a place where someone has testified: "What is mankind that you are mindful of them, a son of man that you care for him? You made them a little lower than the angels; you crowned them with glory and honor and put everything under their feet."

In putting everything under them, God left nothing that is not subject to them. Yet at present we do not see everything subject to them. But we do see Jesus, who was made lower than the angels for a little while, now crowned with glory and honor because he suffered death, so that by the grace of God he might taste death for everyone.

In bringing many sons and daughters to glory, it was fitting that God, for whom and through whom everything exists, should make the pioneer of their salvation perfect through what he suffered. Both the one who makes people holy and those who are made holy are of the same family. So Jesus is not ashamed to call them brothers and sisters. He says, "I will declare your name to my brothers and sisters; in the assembly I will sing your praises." And again, "I will put my trust in him." And again he says, "Here am I, and the children God has given me."

Since the children have flesh and blood, he too shared in their humanity so that by his death he might break the power of him who holds the power of death—that is, the devil—and free those who all their lives were held in slavery by their fear of death. For surely it is not angels he helps, but Abraham's descendants. For this reason he had to be made like them, fully human in every way, in order that he might become a merciful and faithful high priest in service to God, and that he might make atonement for the sins of the people. Because he himself suffered when he was tempted, he is able to help those who are being tempted. (Heb. 2:5–18)

We are to let the builder of all creation lead us in the building of the kingdom on earth. This is not the work of angels but of human beings filled with the Holy Spirit. We are already his co-heirs and regents of his ways.

Therefore, holy brothers and sisters, who share in the heavenly calling, fix your thoughts on Jesus, whom we acknowledge as our apostle and high priest. He was faithful to the one who appointed him, just as Moses was faithful in all God's house. Jesus has been found worthy of greater honor than Moses, just as the builder of a house has greater honor than the house itself. For every house is built by someone, but God is the builder of everything. "Moses was faithful as a servant in all God's house," bearing witness to what would be spoken by God in the future. But Christ is faithful as the Son over God's house. And we are his house, if indeed we hold firmly to our confidence and the hope in which we glory. (Heb. 3:1–6)

We are the builders of everything new in Christ. We are co-creators of the kingdom of God. We have some authority restored to us now; we will have all authority restored when He returns. We use what we have now in service to our communities and in preparation for the greater task at hand. We are here to live the kingdom in our own choices over our own lives and seek to bless the nations in any way we can by seeking those same values and ideals. We have already changed our citizenship. We are here as ambassadors.

The writer of Hebrews goes on to warn the church of his concern that the body of Christ is remaining immature, feeding on milk rather than moving on to the meatier matters of the kingdom. He exhorts them to grow in understanding:

We have much to say about this, but it is hard to make it clear to you because you no longer try to understand. In fact, though by this time you ought to be teachers, you need someone to teach you the elementary truths of God's word all over again. You need milk, not solid food! Anyone who lives on milk, being still an infant, is not acquainted with the teaching about righteousness. But solid food is for the mature, who by constant use have trained themselves to distinguish good from evil. (Heb. 5:11–14)

What is the milk? What are the elementary truths of God's Word? Writing to Corinthian believers, Paul chastises them for remaining as infants and accepting only the milk of the gospel. Indeed, Paul says they are still "worldly" in that they spend their time talking about which apostle they follow rather than following Christ:

Brothers and sisters, I could not address you as people who live by the Spirit but as people who are still worldly—mere infants in Christ. I gave you milk, not solid food, for you were not yet ready for it. Indeed, you are still not ready. You are still worldly. For since there is jealousy and quarreling among you, are you not worldly? Are you not acting like mere humans? For when one says, "I follow Paul," and another, "I follow Apollos," are you not mere human beings? (1 Cor. 3:1–4)

Could the infants stuck on milk rather than meat live as "mere humans" rather than living as heirs and co-rulers with Christ?

The writer of Hebrews lists some of the elementary teachings, the milk: "Therefore let us move beyond the elementary teachings about Christ and be taken forward to maturity, not laying again the foundation of repentance from acts that lead to death, and of faith in God, instruction about cleansing rites, the laying on of hands, the resurrection of the dead, and eternal judgment. And God permitting, we will do so" (Heb. 6:1–3).

God's purpose is for all of us to mature in Christ and move on from the foundations of repentance from sin, saving faith, the cleansing laws, the authority of laying on of hands, the state of the dead, and heaven and hell. These are all milk! They are baby food.

By chapter 8, Hebrews has picked up momentum. There is a new covenant between Jesus and those who follow him. Now he will instruct their minds and their hearts in what to do with the law and how to be like him in all circumstances. We are with him in the Holy of Holies to inquire of God, wherever we are. "This is the covenant I will establish with the people of Israel after that time, declares the Lord. I will put my laws in their minds and write them on their hearts. I will be their God, and they will be my people" (Heb. 8:10; Jer. 31). Even the Holy Spirit testifies to this: "The Holy Spirit also testifies to us about this. First he says: 'This is the covenant I will make with them after that time, says the Lord. I will put my laws in their hearts, and I will write them on their minds'" (Heb. 10:15–16).

The writer of Hebrews continues to expound the revelation. "The law is only a shadow of the good things that are coming—not the realities themselves" (Heb. 10:1). He contrasts the repetitive sacrifices and offerings of the past with "the sacrifice of the body of Jesus Christ once for all" (Heb. 10:10). The priests making sacrifices and offerings according to the law never finished their work, but the priest of the new covenant has accomplished his:

But when this priest had offered for all time one sacrifice for sins, he sat down at the right hand of God, and since that time he waits for his enemies to be made his footstool. For by one sacrifice he has made perfect forever those who are being made holy. . . .

Therefore, brothers and sisters, since we have confidence to enter the Most Holy Place by the blood of Jesus, by a new and living way opened for us through the curtain, that is, his body, and since we have a great priest over the house of God, let us draw near to God with a sincere heart and with the full assurance that faith brings, having our hearts sprinkled to cleanse us from a guilty conscience and having our bodies washed with pure water. (Heb. 10: 12–14, 19–22)

We have access to the mind of Christ on anything, anytime, anywhere, forever!

1 John (between AD 85 and 95)

John begins to bring closure: "As for you, the anointing you received from him remains in you, and you do not need anyone to teach you. But as his anointing teaches you about all things and as that anointing is real, not counterfeit—just as it has taught you, remain in him" (1 John 2:27).

So what does this "great mystery" have to do with political justice? Everything! Our job is to use our circumstances and influence to model and legislate "proper order." Proper order, or justice, by God's definition is making sure the right people and institutions have the right to make the choices God has left for them to make . . . even if they are going to make the wrong choices. Political justice is about rights, responsibilities, and boundaries secured by God for individuals, communities, governments, religions, and families.

Political justice is about defining the freedoms that God has given, including the limits to those freedoms so that all may be free.

Let's see what the application of this great mystery began to look like for the apostles as they walked it out in their lives and message.

CHAPTER 24

THE APOSTOLIC MESSAGE

I n each of the twenty-one apostolic letters, Jesus's apostles weave Old
Testament themes into their teaching just as Jesus did in the Gospels. The values of the New Testament message are the same as those
we have seen in Moses and the Prophets. Only the circumstances and
applications have changed. As with Jesus and the woman caught in
adultery, the disciples are taking God's thinking in the Old and working with the Holy Spirit for a dynamic application in the New. What do
the apostles emphasize when they address the issues of authority and
power?

BEINGS OF AUTHORITY AND POWER

Throughout the letters, God and his two created beings of authority,
humans and angels, continue in their kingdom capacities. Glorious
servant angels continue with their amazing powers to serve Christ in
a lost world. Fallen angels continue to try to co-opt human authority
for themselves by deception and control. Human beings who are still
separated from God continue to be vulnerable to lies and confusion.
What is different now is that those who are redeemed in Christ have
access to the mind of Christ and his wisdom for all of life. They can
know what Jesus would do in any situation simply by asking him: not

317

for a stagnant, single answer to always be applied in every situation, but a dynamic strategy from the Holy Spirit for where they are at this moment, in this situation, at this time. If they do not ask God for his thinking, they will be vulnerable again to the elementary thinking of the world. Repeating the error of Adam and Eve in not consulting God, they subject themselves to thinking and traditions that are not of God and act as puppets rather than heirs of the kingdom.

But anyone who refuses such bandwagon thinking and takes the time to seek God anywhere, about anything, at any time will become like yeast or a mustard seed, something small and often hidden that has a sure and transformative effect on its environment. Now, in Christ, we have a choice. The veil is torn; we have access to the throne.

INSTITUTIONS OF AUTHORITY

All of the human institutions ordained by God in the Old Testament are present throughout the apostolic letters—the individual, family, civil government, and church—each with the authority and limits already laid out in the law of Moses.

In chapter 23 we discussed at length the apostles' revelation of the authority of the individual in Christ, restoring God's human creation to our original position and purpose.

The apostles spend time defining and reaffirming each of God's domains. Like Jesus before them, the apostles challenge Jewish and Gentile traditions and values but never leave us in a void. They are careful to restate God's values.

Family

In sixteen different passages, the designation of family as a husband and wife and their children is reaffirmed, and sexual immorality (sex outside of monogamous, heterosexual marriage) is condemned as sin, whether legal or not.[1] Believers are encouraged to abstain from all sex outside of this definition of marriage, recognizing it as defiling the church. Paul affirms that a husband and wife have exchanged authority with one another over each of their bodies, becoming one in Christ. They have exchanged with each other some of their individual rights over themselves. In three of the letters the principle that a husband leaves the authority of his parents in order to be united with his wife is affirmed. The wife should submit to the husband, not as a slave to a master but as the church does to Christ, as friend and heir of the kingdom. Husbands should love their wives as their own bodies, and children should obey their parents. Parents should not be overbearing but teach their children as Christ teaches us, with wisdom and gentleness. The apostles affirm the financial and legal responsibility of parents for their children and assume the financial responsibility for mothers who are widows and left without support.

The apostles' first emphasis is not on how the lost live. The priority for the apostles is that we as believers live as God has called us to live. For the apostles that meant, in part, that believers are called to reflect God's values in marriage and family. Those who are married are to honor their vows, and all are to abstain from sexual immorality because it destroys our families, our neighbors, and ourselves. We are to love and honor one another, using Christ's relationship with the church as an example. We are to lead our children in God's ways as Christ has led us. It does not matter what society has made legal or illegal. We live this way because we are in agreement with God. We work for better laws in order to bless our communities, *if they will agree*. But for us, it makes no difference. In our sphere of authority over self, we have already bowed to the will of God voluntarily.

As believers, we distinguish between moral and civil law and between the legal rights of the community and our own moral obligations to God. Our concern for affecting the legislation of our civil laws is concern for our neighbor and the good of our community. We have already agreed with God in our own moral choices.

"Marriage should be honored by all, and the marriage bed kept pure, for God will judge the adulterer and all the sexually immoral" (Heb. 13:4).

"Then he told me, 'Do not seal up the words of the prophecy of this scroll, because the time is near. Let the one who does wrong continue to do wrong; let the vile person continue to be vile; let the one who does right continue to do right; and let the holy person continue to be holy'" (Rev. 22:10–11).

Civil Government

In eight of the letters, the apostles seek to clarify the believer's relationship to the nation's civil government. In each of those letters, the role of civil law is confirmed and affirmed as God's plan. None is clearer than Romans 13:

> Let everyone be subject to the governing authorities, for there is no authority except that which God has established. The authorities that exist have been established by God. Consequently, whoever rebels against the authority is rebelling against what God has instituted, and those who do so will bring judgment on themselves. For rulers hold no terror for those who do right, but for those who do wrong. Do you want to be free from fear of the one in authority? Then do what is right and you will be commended. For the one in authority is God's servant for your good. But if you do wrong, be afraid, for rulers do not bear the sword for no reason. They are God's servants, agents of wrath to bring punishment on the wrongdoer. Therefore, it is necessary to submit to the authorities, not only because of possible punishment but also as a matter of conscience.
>
> This is also why you pay taxes, for the authorities are God's servants, who give their full time to governing. Give to everyone what you owe them: If you owe taxes, pay taxes; if revenue, then revenue; if respect, then respect; if honor, then honor. (Rom. 13:1–7)

Believers are encouraged to pray for political leaders and to submit to them, which means to recognize the authority they have and the boundaries of that authority. The apostles also demonstrate not submitting when authority is being abused, as when Paul flees persecution in Damascus and again when he appeals to his rights as a Roman citizen.

Believers are encouraged not to clog the courts with cases between believers (1 Cor. 6:1–11). Where one believer has wronged another, why go to court? Aren't the people of God able to provide unbiased judgment, and aren't the believers able to submit to those who are one in Christ? Wouldn't that be a revolution?

Believers are to respect and honor our civil government and its leaders. We pay our taxes and pray for our leaders. We uphold the law because without civil laws, imperfect as they are, we would live in violent chaos. At the same time we work to have the best possible governance we can get so that our neighbors can live at peace.

Church

All the apostles write extensively regarding the institution of the church. Defining and clarifying the authority of the apostles themselves is a major theme as are instructions for elders, deacons, and pastors. Instructions about meeting together are repeated several times. Believers may meet in temples with priests or in houses with pastors, but when they meet, the community of believers has a purpose and the apostles outline that purpose. Consistently, the epistles offer encouragement for unity and discouragement of divisions. The theme of false prophets and apostles, who do not have authority in Christ and therefore in the church, is a major component of almost every letter.

What is lacking is instructive too. The apostles do not advocate stopping other forms of worship, neither within the Christian community nor outside it. Instead they emphasize keeping our own faith pure. Religious freedom is upheld.

SINS THAT WILL DESTROY A NATION

Just as the books of the Old Testament prophets do, the epistles emphasize for the new communities of believers five areas of sin. The prophets spoke to whole nations, whereas the New Testament writings are directed at the body of Christ as a whole and at individual believers specifically. But the prophets and the apostles emphasize exactly the same issues. We looked at the importance of family and civil governance above. These are two of the five areas that the prophets and writers of the epistles warn believers to be careful in. Now we turn our attention to three other spheres of life in which sin has the power to destroy a nation.

Economic Injustice

Believers are encouraged to be people who work hard, who are not greedy but generous, and who do not show partiality to rich or poor.

They are told to no longer steal or covet, to be neither oppressive masters nor slovenly servants, and to keep themselves free from the love of money. They are to make sure that they settle every debt, and they are encouraged to consider the needs of the poor and to visit those in need. In other words, they are to live by the values of the law of Moses.

The apostles teach that work is created by God and that it is the essential way in which God blesses us physically. Our time is God-given and has value. We are to use it purposefully in our vocation, whatever our work is. We are encouraged to accept the assignment of God in our life. What we do—what our job is—is not nearly as important as how we do it and that we do it to the glory of God and for the good of our neighbor. No work is without kingdom value. We support our families and ourselves and give generously to those in need within and outside the church. We provide for those God has made us responsible for.

As believers we are to prioritize the needs of the poorest of the poor in our communities. The apostles teach that the welfare of prisoners, widows, orphans, and foreigners are all pressing concerns for the church and are worthy of our time, finances, and social action. To devalue any human being in any way—male or female, Greek or Jew, servant or master—is to deny the God who created us all. We do not ask, "Do these people deserve to be treated this way?" We assume no human being created in the image of God should ever be treated this way. And we act accordingly.

The Devaluation of Our Words

As followers of Christ, we speak truth with graciousness. Our words have value. We guard our tongues to make sure that what comes out is what Jesus would say and is in the Spirit he would say it. We despise and abstain from crude, foolish, ignorant, obscene, babbling, empty, and corrupting talk. We seek to give a sound defense without quarrelsomeness. We must not lie, but tame our tongues and exemplify sound speech. Our *yes* should be *yes* and our *no, no.*

In our words and contracts, our standard goes beyond expediency under the law. We do not prioritize "compliance" with the law. We ensure that our words are clear, and we remain committed to them regardless of legal threat.

Idolatry of the Believer

The greatest concern of the apostles by far is the corruption of the thinking and faith of believers. Over sixty-five passages in the letters take up this subject—more than twice as many as address any other single topic. What was the influence that so concerned these early leaders?

James writes very early on of worldliness entering the life of believers. This comes in a form of wisdom that is not from heaven but from earth. It is unspiritual and demonic. Paul calls these "elemental spirits," which have the appearance of the wisdom of God but are the wisdom of the world, deceitful ideas. John, in two of his letters, takes up the warning, encouraging the believers to test the spirits of what they are being taught. He warns that deceivers will come into the churches, drawing believers away from God's Word to lawlessness, or to thinking that has no revelational basis in Scripture.

It seems clear to the apostles that the greatest distortions of God's message and the greatest threats to our witness to the world will come from within the church. False prophets to the church and false teachings within the church are a major concern for every apostle. These "super apostles" in the early church drew believers to themselves and to what they had to say rather than to Christ and his progressive revelation for each of us. They began to remove from believers the responsibility for working though their faith in their daily lives, providing instead prescriptive answers and pushing strategies that would keep believers safe from having to ask God what to do.

The true apostles created in believers a dependency on Christ. Listening to them, the believer knew to say, "Jesus is greater than Moses or Paul or Apollos, and I have Jesus! Yes, none other than Jesus, the High Priest forever, not as appointed by earthly institutions, even those created and approved by God himself. Jesus, who sits at the right hand of the Father in the throne room of God, invites me into his chamber to consult on all controversies and issues, to test the spirits, and to leave with instructions for being salt and light in my setting. Jesus, who models and teaches about all authority, calls me to be his ambassador wherever I am. I can kneel, scribble in the dust, and wait for God's response wherever I am, whatever the issue, just as Jesus did."

WHAT DID JUSTICE LOOK LIKE?

In the apostolic letters, the instructions for living are incredibly simple and pragmatic. They focus on the individual believer and the body of Christ and how we are to live and conduct ourselves within mixed cultural and faith communities. The one theme that is mentioned more than any other is that of doing good while living a life that is peaceable. But we would be remiss to leave it there; the content of the letters also defines for us what the apostles meant by *good* and *peaceable*. Our greatest challenge in living that life is the values pollution of the world with its appearance of wisdom. And the apostles don't let us forget that the greatest source of that dangerous pollution of our minds may originate in the religious community itself.

We seek first to be an example in our personal life and work, regardless of what the social norm is. The kingdom of God is within us. We take action where we can. In the letter of Philemon, Paul uses his influence as an apostle to help a runaway slave. He then seeks out the owner, a convert of Paul's, to secure the safety of the man and, if the owner is willing, his freedom. Paul is even willing to pay the cost of the man's freedom, but he appeals to the brother's conscience, reminding him that he owes Paul everything already because of Christ. Paul may not be able to change the law of slavery in the Roman Empire *yet*, but at least this believer can stop owning this slave. And someday the church will be instrumental in changing the laws of slavery and the status quo.

Jesus told the tax collector not to collect more taxes than he was supposed to. Jesus told the converted soldier not to misuse his power in treating people abusively. The prophets tell us, "Don't use false weights and measures! Don't water the wine! Don't lie in court, or anywhere else for that matter!" "But that is the way we do it!" we cry. And Jesus says, "Exactly! You have absorbed the idolatry of the cultures around you."

God does not give us detailed professional instructions because we do not need them. We have the Holy Spirit and the values of God's eternal Word. We have access to the Father in every situation—personal or familial, professional or political—to give us instructions as individuals, 24/7.

We are to act in everything with faith! Faith . . . meaning that to the best of our ability we have consulted God for understanding of his next step for us and we are taking that step. We are not looking to other believers or leaders for our strategy but to God and his reliability to direct our course or correct our course. We listen to advice and then discern in God what to use and what to leave behind. Where is our authority? We are heirs of the kingdom, co-rulers with Christ. If he is not our source of authority, we do not have any. If he is, we need no other.

And now we come to John's revelation of the end . . . and the beginning.

CHAPTER 25

THE END AND THE BEGINNING

Revelation

G od takes time at the end of his chosen narrative to give us a glimpse of what is coming, a momentary release from the responsibilities of our life in the present. As apocalyptic literature the book of Revelation is by design cryptic and full of symbolic images. Applying the specifics of apocalyptic writings to time and space is difficult at best. However, the overarching themes and messages of Revelation are clear, and the emotional impact they convey is overwhelming.

Surely no single book of the Bible has more to do with political justice. As God reveals times to come and the closure of this age to John, he makes it clear that "proper order," or justice, will be restored to every part of creation.

THE TRIALS

In that time to come, God will judge the living and the dead of his human creation. He will judge the nations and their peoples, governments, and cultures. He will judge his church. He will judge the angels.

The King of Kings will sit in the Judge's seat, dispensing final justice. The final trials are comprehensive—they will cover everything—and are for all of God's created beings.

God alludes to the criteria he will use for the various trials. In judging the church, he will measure the values perpetuated and multiplied by the church against the revealed values of the Scriptures and the kingdom. We as members of the church, the body of Christ, do not have to wait for this judgment, of course; we can begin holding ourselves accountable to God's values now. Likewise, in the final judgment of individuals, dead and alive, God will hold us each accountable for what we knew and what we did. We set our own standard of judgment by what we ourselves condemn. Angels, fallen or not, will be judged by the same values, but we are given no details about their judgment except that some of us will participate in that judicial process.

In a similar way, the nations will be judged by the values on which they have built their cultures. Everything that is of "Babylon," the anti-kingdom—all principles and values that are the opposite of God's—will be destroyed. But those values that reveal the truth of God will be brought into the City of God and laid before the throne. They will be part of the glory of God, revealed through all nations in the new creation.

There will be no problem with evidence. The cosmos records all light and sound, and there will be an abundance of witnesses. Motive, culpability, and the timeline of evidence will be transparent. Whether churches or nations, humans or angels, we will all be held accountable for our choices. These final procedures are less about determining our guilt and more about revealing for all time the infallible innocence of God and his immutable justice.

Through these judicial procedures, we will see ourselves, as well as other individuals, whole peoples, and angelic beings, for what we are corporately and personally. The consequences of our actions have been foretold since the days of Adam. There is no appeal, as the process has been exhausted. We now have a finding from the King. This judgment is final! Proper order, justice, is dispensed.

THE CITY OF GOD

And proper order is established in a new community: a system of justice that is built on exactly the same values that God has been revealing from the very beginning of time.

God continues John's revelation by giving him a glimpse of the new heaven and the new earth. "One of the seven angels who had the seven bowls full of the seven last plagues came and said to me, 'Come, I will show you the bride, the wife of the Lamb.' And he carried me away in the Spirit to a mountain great and high, and showed me the Holy City, Jerusalem, coming down out of heaven from God. It shone with the glory of God, and its brilliance was like that of a very precious jewel, like a jasper, clear as crystal" (Rev. 21:9–11).

Until this point in Scripture, we have regarded the bride of Christ, the people of God, as a body. We have seen that body gathered together as the church, meeting together apart from the world in order to worship, praise, witness, give testimony, take the sacraments, and pray. As the bride of Christ, we gather to remember who we are in a world filled with lostness. But God sees that body dispersed, living out the kingdom all day in everything we do.

Now, in this future picture, the bride is the City of God. The part, a body, has become the whole, the community. In Christ, God has made it possible for us to fulfill the original mandate, laid out in Genesis 1 and 2, to become the community of God by applying God's nature, character, values, and ways to all of life, revealing God in every sphere of our lives and community. And Jesus is living with us!

Now we are the "chosen people," those called by God to reveal the kingdom of God. But there is one startling difference. Not only has God chosen us but *we have all chosen him*. Jesus will live among and through those who have willingly chosen him as their sovereign. God will not build his kingdom with slave labor.

We, the bride of Christ, the City of God, come from every tribe, tongue, nation, and people. We have refused the "traditions of men" our cultures clung to and have chosen to pattern our thinking and lives after the ways of God. We are from all tribes, but we have new passports—we are citizens of God's city. Now false ways of thinking are gone, and with freedom, unencumbered by sin, we build the kingdom of God in his presence, with his authority as heirs, realizing the dream of God from the mandate of creation.

What will the kingdom, this community of God, look like? We have no idea because it hasn't yet been realized. But we do know whose values it will embody. We could ask:

- Will it be beautiful?
- Will there be clean streets?
- Will there be enough housing?
- Will there be poverty?
- Will there be enough food and water?
- Will there be health?
- Will we continue learning?
- Will there be justice?
- Will we be able to communicate with each other?
- Will anyone be left out? forgotten? devalued?

But we already know the answer to all these questions. The key question is how and by whom will this all be accomplished? What will it look like? We don't know yet. Is it possible that we don't know because we will create it with God? Regardless, we can prepare here and now for our future by revealing as much of the kingdom of God as we can in our own lives, communities, and nations.

THE TEMPLATE OF THE KINGDOM

The threads of God's weaving that we first saw in Genesis 1 and 2 continue through this present age and into the coming kingdom. The new heaven and new earth are built on the same foundations and values as the first.

Three beings of authority and power still exist: God, humans, and angels. We humans, like God, live forever. If we begin at the end of the book of Revelation with the new heaven and new earth, we can follow the template of God's kingdom beyond the book of Revelation into eternity.

The material world is real, good, and essential for all of life and continues on into eternity. The City of God, we are told, has land, streets, homes, food, walls, gates, trees, fruit, horses, and a river. It is now the dwelling place of God as well as of his human creatures. It has boundaries, and those boundaries can be measured. Everyone in the City of God owns a home. Well, not just a home; Scripture says Jesus has prepared for us a "mansion." Apparently, this house is free.

The wealth and opulence of the city's infrastructure is hard to describe. John struggles for words rich enough to convey what he sees. The streets are made of transparent gold, the foundations of the buildings are precious gems, the twelve gates are each made of a single pearl, and the water, which abounds, runs through the city, clean and free to all. The city registry is perfectly maintained. There is neither material need nor poverty in this city.

Human beings are made in the image of God and are the purpose of creation. The whole point of creation and Christ's redemption is the creation of a community of heirs in fellowship with God and one other. God not only redeems us and gives us a new heaven and earth, but he comes to live with us in this community. Once again he walks and talks with us in the new garden, helping us to fill our community with quality, kingdom life. In this city, we have work to do and a purpose in God to fulfill as we create, manage, and govern a nation of kings under the King.

Words have power, and we are accountable for them. In the revelation to John, the books of heaven are opened and the facts they contain are used as evidence for final judgments. Satan, the deceiver and word twister, is dealt with, and his source of lies and half-truths is removed. Proclamations are still made in the new heaven and new earth, and God is still recording his words. There is no falsehood in this city.

Everything is affected by the fall, and everything needs redemption. Jesus declares from his throne, "I am making everything new!" (Rev. 21:5). In the City of God redemption is complete. The Lamb is on the throne. So what do we do now? We create and live life and live it more abundantly, all as acts of worship. We build the City of God with Christ, our King.

Life is sacred. The sacredness of life is the overriding value of the kingdom. Life is sacred because God created it and sustains it. Because life is sacred, the material world, essential to life, is also sacred. Because the material world is essential to life, we as God's co-rulers are to work it and develop it so that all of life is sustainable. Because life is sacred, work is sacred, time is sacred, and the provision they create is sacred. In the new city, everyone has a home, a job, and all that is needed to sustain life, because life is sacred.

The four institutions of authority and their domains go through radical transformation in the new heaven and new earth. God is king on his throne, but is there any government? There is no temple, but is there any ecclesial institution at all? In the City of God, we do not marry and are more like the angels, but is the concept of family still in use in any way? Of the four institutions of authority, the individual, as co-heir with Christ, is what obviously remains, in addition to God himself. What does that mean? The kingdom of God is within us, but now what does that look like as we live it out? What does the bride of Christ look like as the City of God? We don't know.

We are given few clues about this in Scripture. The values of the community are clear, but Scripture tells us almost nothing about the form and structure of the community.

The attributes of justice, provision, learning, discovery, beauty, love, worship, and communication will all be present, as they are all fundamental to the nature and character of God and therefore to his kingdom. But what do these corporate attributes of God look like when purged of evil and their need to deal with evil? How will they be administrated in eternity? Why such silence? Part of God's purpose in keeping silent must be that we are to devote ourselves to the task at hand—the here and now is our job. We do not yet live in paradise; we are currently God's ambassadors on earth!

Another reason for God's silence may be that he is waiting for us to create this community together. I love the way God allows Adam to work his way through naming all the animals, as recorded in Genesis 2. In that process Adam experiences great aloneness in his uniqueness. God allows him to experience desire for something before fulfilling the desire. The value God places on choice and collaboration is evident in this most basic decision of creation. Adam male and Adam female then choose each other, giving themselves willingly to one another in creating family. God created the first garden and entrusted his human creatures with the earth's cultivation. From the very beginning, a fundamental characteristic of God's kingdom is that we, God and human beings, work together. Because God needs us? No! Because he wants us.

Is it possible that we aren't given more information about the City of God because we are the co-creators of that community with God? Is our eternity to be filled with multiplying and creating communities that embody brilliant new interpretations of justice and provision? Will we make new scientific discoveries? Will our work evoke yet more of God's beauty? Will we fill the cosmos with the cities of God, communities that reveal who God is and how he works, but in infinite variety? Imagine! It is possible that the universe holds enough galaxies that each one of us could have our own to cultivate and fill with the glory of God.

In the kingdom of God, the future is the future and the present is now. We get ahead of ourselves. For now, we are still God's heirs on earth, surrounded by sin and lostness. How are we to abide in Christ and do the work of God here and now? As the angel said to John: "Let the one who does wrong continue to do wrong; let the vile person continue to be vile; let the one who does right continue to do right; and let the holy person continue to be holy" (Rev. 22:11). We, God's people, are here to reveal what can be, and what will be, when all are surrendered to Christ, beginning with our own life and work.

What are we to accomplish for God here and now, in this place where our days are numbered?

CHAPTER 26

HERE AND NOW

From Genesis to Revelation, the kingdom of God is, in part, a social contract. This revelation is there in microcosm in Genesis 1 and 2: God, the Creator of all things, gives human beings dominion on earth and the mandate to multiply, fill the earth, and create communities, tribes, and nations. The kingdom of God is revealed in its infinite diversity through the ways we, his co-rulers, choose to live together as neighbors; it is demonstrated in the values by which we agree to abide.

This kingdom community is there again in the last chapters of Revelation as we, the individually redeemed, gather to inhabit and create the City of God, the bride of Christ, with the groom in residence. The elements of the kingdom remain the same from the beginning of Scripture to the end: God, the individual, and the community. God is the origin, the individual with the Holy Spirit is the active agent, and community is the objective of the kingdom. The royal law remains our mandate. As Jesus said:

> "Love the Lord your God with all your heart and with all your soul and with all your mind." This is the first and greatest commandment. And the second is like it: "Love your neighbor as yourself." All the Law and the Prophets hang on these two commandments. (Matt. 22:37–40)

"The most important one," answered Jesus, "is this: 'Hear, O Israel: The Lord our God, the Lord is one. Love the Lord your God with all your heart and with all your soul and with all your mind and with all your strength.' The second is this: 'Love your neighbor as yourself.' There is no commandment greater than these." (Mark 12:29–31)

He answered, "'Love the Lord your God with all your heart and with all your soul and with all your strength and with all your mind'; and, 'Love your neighbor as yourself.'" (Luke 10:27)

Every book of the Bible holds in tension these three elements of the kingdom: God, the individual, and God revealed in the community. Think of Adam, the first man and first woman, and the effect of their actions on the future of the human race; or of Noah and his obedience to God in spite of his community's rebellion; or of Abraham and his influence on the future nation of Israel; or of Moses, called by God to take his people into freedom; or of Esther and her courageous act in securing the future of her people; or of Jesus and his commitment to live with us, in our human condition, incarnate, for thirty-three years, demonstrating for us what it means to actively love our neighbor and calling each of us to follow his example; or of the bride of Christ fulfilling its destiny as the City of God in Revelation. Wherever we turn in Scripture, as in life, the tension is there: God, the individual, and the community.

ACTS OF OBEDIENCE

Sometimes, throughout Scripture, the acts of obedience of these individuals are small and apparently insignificant: Ruth, faithfully following God and her mother-in-law, gleaning in the fields of Boaz; Esther, a slave in exile in a pagan country, competing in a beauty contest; Noah building the world's largest boat with no water in sight; the prophet Ezekiel cooking his food over dung; or Jesus going to weddings and making wine. These small acts of obedience had a big impact on the kingdom.

Sometimes individuals are asked to do something that has dramatic implications and obvious importance: the priest Jehoiada hiding little Joash in safety, protecting the last heir to Judah's throne and establishing him as king when he was seven; Queen Esther foiling Haman's plot, securing the lives and future of her people; Rahab hiding the spies of the invading Israelite army and lying to her government; Jesus refusing to do what would save his life; or Paul appealing to Rome for justice.

Whether the acts of obedience were large or small, God is telling us that these individuals made history and impacted the future of their nations. They were all building the kingdom of God.

WE ALL WANT JUSTICE

All human beings want to receive justice. The kingdom question is: Will we give justice? Will we act justly? Every individual has a role in achieving political justice, whether as a citizen or in a public vocation. All believers carry the mandate of God to be salt and light in every part of society, including the political life of their communities. As followers of Jesus, we are to pursue justice for our neighbor even if we are being treated unjustly.

Some of us are called to political justice as a vocation, in roles as police officers, civil servants, lawyers, members of the armed forces, or holders of political office, among many others. Paul said we are to consider those in government "servants of God." Whether we work within the justice system of a nation or are ordinary citizens, God has given us a clear set of values and priorities. We are to seek the mind of Christ in applying God's values to every part of our own life, and we are to seek the mind of Christ in applying God's values to the life of our community, as far as it will allow.

Violence is our gravest concern. What is killing people in our communities? Abortion, faulty construction, inadequate food or water supplies, suicide, jealousy, substance abuse, disease, religious fanaticism, poverty, political anarchy, political tyranny, greed? As Christians we don't focus myopically on designer issues or pet causes. We don't limit our scope to issues of personal consequence. Our focus is not on where I, the individual, am experiencing violence but on where we, the community, are allowing violence to flourish. How can we even begin to see God's perspective if we do not even know what is killing our neighbors?

In one community, the issue may be the absence of building codes or the lack of enforcement of those codes. Schools fall on top of children, or factory workers are burned alive because exits are locked. In another region, the vast majority of deaths occur because there is no clean water supply or sanitation. If our community's most prevalent cause of violent death is a high suicide rate among a particular group, we need ask ourselves what in our culture and values is driving these people toward taking their own lives. In another place, terrorism may be the most pressing concern, or the government itself may be committing the most violence against the people. Crime, organized or not, may be committing wholesale slaughter of people. It may be AIDS, it may be abortion, it may be drugs—we do not care. Whatever is violently taking lives is our concern. We do not have Christian issues. All of God's issues are our issues.

What do we do? What can you do? Think about who you are and where you are. Can you pick up a man beaten senseless on the side of the road and take him to get medical care? Can you help pay for his care and go back and check on him later? This is building the kingdom of God. Did you see something or hear something related to a violent crime? Can you give testimony? Are you in construction? Do you build safe buildings? Are you a counselor or psychiatrist? Can you help your neighbors understand why your community has the highest teenage suicide rate in the world? Do you hear a cry for help on your street? Are you willing to put your own life at risk to respond to the plea? Will you help the officials and your neighbors make your streets safe? Would you offer your home or your church as a sanctuary for people fleeing violence? Would your invitation stand no matter the race, religion, or economic status of the victims? Would you be a whistle-blower if you had knowledge of a government or military abusing its own power with violence? Would you demand that your government be more proactive in reducing violence of all kinds? The kingdom of God is built from small acts of obedience, "like yeast that a woman took and mixed into about sixty pounds of flour until it worked all through the dough" (Matt. 13:33). As Jesus did before responding to the Pharisees' accusation against the woman caught in adultery, we can all take time to scribble in the dust, seeking the thoughts of God, in order to know how God would have us respond now. You have the Holy Spirit and access to the mind of Christ!

If you are in government, are you constantly looking out for the needs of the most helpless, the forgotten, and the unrepresented?

Violence is most often the reality of society's fringes. What is the issue in front of you? Why look for a different way to be involved when there is an issue—or person—right in your face needing your action? Are you a lawyer? Could you make an adequate living representing those no one else represents? Are you a police officer? Do you use excessive force in your duties? Do you seek to treat all people with dignity, recognizing their value, even while enforcing the law? Are you a judge? Can you use this case in some way to curb violence by changing the interpretation of the law? Are you a legislator? Is there a way to make your community safer through legislation? Christ's ambassadors are constantly vigilant in looking for opportunities to apply God's life-sustaining values wherever we are. We are looking for revelational understanding from the Spirit of God to use in the circumstances that are in front of us, as Jesus did.

Consider the influence of one national leader, a doctor and Christian serving his country as chief medical officer. During this doctor's tenure, three critical issues confronted him: AIDS, abortion, and the dangers of smoking. As the nation's chief medical officer, this leader was able to influence the administration's views and to some extent the administration's policies on AIDS and abortion, but the results were disappointing. On the issue of smoking, however, he was able to turn the tide. His work changed public opinion and resulted in national legislation. It moved the government and the tobacco industry toward discouraging, restricting, and banning smoking in certain places and making the public aware of the dangers of smoking and secondhand smoke, as well as the public cost of smoking-related illnesses. The ideas and laws spurred on by this doctor have spread around the world, improving health in other nations and changing the way business does business. Did this public leader save lives? Was his work against smoking deaths any less important than outlawing abortion or stopping the AIDS epidemic? Those issues are also extremely important. We must continue to seek change. But the antismoking revolution was the change this one man could bring at that time.

IMAGES OF BIBLICAL POLITICAL JUSTICE

Biblical political justice requires a healthy tension of power between individual, government, family, and religious rights. Each of these institutions of authority serves God's purpose. We are to be vigilant to strengthen the one that is weak in our culture. One culture may suffer from the tyranny of anarchy by which every other right is made subservient to individual rights. In another culture, tyranny may take the form of one religious belief subjugating the rights of all other parties. When this happens—it does not matter what the religion is—tyranny, or the effort to control all of society from one religious value set, is not the kingdom of God, even when that control is put forth to support biblical values. In another culture, tyranny takes the face of family. The rights of family dominate. Are family structures seeking total control of family members? Of spouses, daughters, children? Do they defend their right to do whatever they like because they have the authority of family? Of course we are all familiar with political tyranny. Too many governments declare all else subservient to them, acting as though their power players are the only authority and the only party with rights. Each of these kinds of tyranny exists in our world and the societies we come from.

Daniel understood the limits of King Nebuchadnezzar's authority when the king built a golden idol and ordered all his subjects to bow down to it. Daniel drew a distinction. The king had the authority to build the idol. He did not have the authority to require Daniel to worship it. Daniel refused.

In the case of a woman left for more than a decade and a half in a coma and on life support, there was a confluence of family, religious, and legal rights. The husband, who was proved to be of sound character and motive, felt that his wife would not have wanted to spend decades more on machines and sought to have the support stopped. Her parents, who were Catholic, were sure that she was still communicating, and it was their desire to keep her on life support. The government had a clear legal position that the spouse had the authority to make the choice in the absence of a declaration of the patient's preference. The family, the church, the doctors, and the government were all weighing in on this case. But in the absence of other evidence, the issue was to whom to give legal authority over an incapacitated married adult: the parents, the religious authorities, the doctors, the government, or the spouse? This part of the case was a question of strengthening or weakening the legal boundaries of the institution of marriage. It was a question of where to place authority for this kind of decision. A decision had to be made.

What is weak in our community? What has too much power in our culture? Where are we blind to tyranny in the name of tradition and culture? Any believer pursuing biblical political justice must ask, "Where is the tyranny in my culture, and do I perpetuate it in my own life and action?" We must break with the godless traditions of our culture.

Biblical political justice is passionate about land laws, ownership, and boundaries. We believe that God has given the land to the people to provide for our material well-being. The broader the land ownership, the less corruptible the resources. The issue is not the necessity of every individual owning a plot of land, but rather a broad national objective to keep massive amounts of land from being controlled by the few. In some nations, land is almost entirely owned by the tribe or government, and in others it is monopolized by religious institutions or by corporations. No matter who holds the monopoly, no matter how good the intention of the monopoly, the fact is that resources are more corruptible in the absence of checks and balances. Broader ownership of land will lead to slower growth, but it will also lead toward empowerment of the many over the few and toward more interest in land development.

Remember King Ahab who wanted the vineyard, so his terrible wife, Jezebel, had the owner murdered and stole his property? You have to follow the story through to the end. The king comes to the terrible demise that God says he will. He dies where? On the land he stole from his neighbor. Serious stuff!

Land matters! Consider this one example among many. A group of Christians were negotiating with a government. They wanted to use outside investment to help a community of impoverished farmers in that country brand their product. There was no doubt that this product could be branded internationally, increasing the product's value multiple times. The money was there, and the government was amenable. But the key question was who owned the land on which the farmers grew their crop. In this case, as in most nations where producers suffer systemic poverty, the government owned the land. If the objective was to help the farmers, land reform would have to be part of the negotiation. Without it, the government would multiply its profits while the farmers remained impoverished. The global evidence for this is phenomenal.

We need dynamic revelations of God's values for strategies that will truly change nations. The issue is never just money.

Biblical political justice is passionate about the protection of the accused and due process. Vigilante law is natural, and revenge is human nature. If societies do not protect their people, violence will rage out of control. Just governments must have a means by which society is protected from the individual and the individual from society at large. In some societies, the system leans toward protecting the accused, in others toward protecting the victim, and in others toward protecting the community. In seeking political justice, we want to keep pulling the system back toward a healthy tension of the best possible protection for all parties. The actual system of due process is not as important as the fact that it allows for an impartial, objective conclusion to the conflict. To achieve this conclusion, due process has to depend on evidence, reliable testimony, an impartial judiciary, and a process of appeals that allows all of this to be tested. Due process requires time, and for time to be available, individuals must be protected.

Violence and vigilantism increase when the system of due process is so slow that cases may take years to get to court. God designed a system with practical representation at the grass roots; one would not have to wait long for a hearing. In God's design, whole communities were devoted to the protection of those awaiting trial. Life could continue for the accused with some level of normality while they awaited trial, but the victims and the community they came from were also protected. Measures were taken to protect the innocent who were still in danger of community retribution as well. Some liberties would be lost, but at least their lives would be saved.

What happens when the judicial system becomes as violent as, if not more violent than, the outside community? What happens if a person is more likely to experience violence or die in the judicial system than outside? If we, through our governments, cannot make people safe in our custody, how do we ever hope to decrease the violence in our communities at large? If human life is sacred, it is sacred everywhere, including in prison.

What can we do? Well, who are we? Where are we, and what do we do? What is Christ saying to us in this situation? Do you live in a neighborhood where the government is trying to place halfway houses and prisoner release programs? Do you live near a jail or prison that needs volunteers? Is your church in one of these neighborhoods? Are you a prison guard or a probation officer? Would you like to be one so that you can help protect human life? Are you a legislator looking at judicial or prison reform? Are you a lawyer responsible for protecting the rights of victims, the accused, the convicted, or the community? Are you one of these affected parties, or a family member of one? Are you a business-person who could help rehabilitate released prisoners? Do you watch shows that consistently use the threat of violence in custody in order to get a witness or suspect to talk, supposedly in the name of justice?

What is in front of you? What can you do? God holds our whole community responsible for the safety of our community.

Biblical political justice is constantly measuring the political system to make sure power is moving down and not up, moving toward individual responsibility and not toward responsibility by the few. The few cannot effectively take care of the many. It is not a sustainable system of justice. But the many, given opportunity and incentive, can take care of themselves. A political system that is based in massive popular support is stable, if sometimes chaotic. A political system that is based in the control of the many by the few may achieve some good, but it is not stable or sustainable. As God's ambassadors to the fallen world, we want to move our communities toward greater individual concern for each other and an increased sense of responsibility on the part of the individual for the community as a whole.

How do we do this? Again we must ask the essential questions: Who are we, where are we, and what do we do? God does not work in a vacuum. He works with us in our circumstances. What can you do? In some places, you are able to vote. You must at least begin there. If you live in a culture where voting is not possible, how could you work to change the thinking, to shift the tradition of the few being responsible for the many? What is Christ putting in your hand today? Do that! We can help take responsibility to protect our neighborhoods, being vigilant, being a witness, developing and participating in community watch. We can help our neighbors who may be in need by giving them a ride to the store, offering to pick up medicine for them, or helping them keep their house up. We can work for an environment where we all know our neighbors and are known by them. What if every Christian in the world prayed each morning, "Lord what can I do for my neighbors today?" and acted on whatever the Holy Spirit told us to do? We do not have to wait for governments to show concern for those around us. We can, in the authority that God has given us, take kingdom action. We can pick up that trash on the side of the road! All of us caring about each other creates a sustainable, loving community.

Biblical political justice is aware of the limits of law to control sin in our societies. It focuses on those things that are provably the most destructive to the community, and it changes what the political process allows it to change. We do not measure our success by fighting losing battles. God has given all human beings a measure of autonomy and freedom, and they will use it. Our job is not to control human nature but to offer a better way and seek to influence what we are allowed to influence. We do not win or lose. Our communities win or lose based on their choices, if they have a choice. We are salt and light, not power and control. If you are unable to affect the issue most important to you, what issue of justice can you affect? What is in front of you? What is Christ giving you now, great or small?

Biblical political justice is always looking for ways to move our judicial system away from punishment toward redemptive restitution and restorative justice. With the exception of loss of life, consequences can be restorative. The consequences of any other crime can be assigned a temporal material cost. As in the Old Testament's prescriptive law, the loss of an ear or of a month's work can be measured. The destruction or theft of property can be given a monetary value. A biblically just system will focus on reparations as a requirement and redemption as a possibility. A criminal's work can provide for those reparations. Punishment will not be the major objective, but it will be a by-product of loss of financial freedom.

Any human being's time and labor has value! If there are one million people in jail, that's a loss of forty million hours of work a week plus the cost of incarceration, with no one gaining anything! Everyone loses, and repetitive crime increases. There is something fundamentally wrong with this way of thinking. Something at a values level is missing, and all of society is suffering for it. This system produces vindictive thinking, loss of individual value, loss of recompense for the victim, and a huge cost directly and indirectly to the community at large. In Scripture, a criminal "paying his debt" meant *paying his debt*. The only exception was violent destruction of human life.

There is a better way! God has inspiration to share with us that no one has thought of yet.

Biblical political justice seeks ways to work with whatever political leadership we get, not accepting the myth that one leader will be all good and another all bad. As God's people, we acknowledge human fallenness. We accept that the best of leaders will let us down somehow and the worst of leaders may be used of God in some redemptive way. Our perspective at the end of the election is simply, "What can God accomplish for his kingdom through this leader and how shall I pray for him or her?"

God did not want Israel to have a king, but Israel wanted a king and it was their choice. So God did his best to bless and use the king he did not want. We do not win or lose our kingdom influence at the choice of a political leader. We have a job to do and advancements to make in discipling our nation regardless of who the political leader is. We do what God gives us to do in our circumstances.

Biblical political justice understands the signs and the times. As the prophets did, we seek to know when it is too late for the nation to turn around and move on or what we must do to stop the decline. In those times, God will show us how to use our captivity in our Babylon. Nations have risen and fallen throughout human history, and nations continue to rise and fall today. On the long line of time, God expresses his sovereignty in a nation's demise or blessing. We must align ourselves with God's judgments. If things are going terribly wrong in our nation, God is speaking to us through the circumstances. He is trying to tell us that our traditions—traditions and values that even Christians may uphold—are killing us. Can God's people be the first to acknowledge that the systems must go? Can we be the first to see the significance of God's sending our nation an enemy? Can we move beyond "good nation/bad nation" thinking and ask, "What is God trying to accomplish in us through this enemy?" Will we, God's people, be the first to judge our nation, tribe, or community as wanting, including ourselves? It is easy to see the enemy without. The enemy within is the greater foe.

It is easy to blame our nation's difficulties on the current designer sins. But why would God judge a nation for sexual sin among a minority of the population while leaving the majority, even Christians, committing sexual sins without responsibility? Can we accept that we do not deserve to be blessed and yet hold on to God for revelation of how to bless our nation?

Biblical justice is passionate about measuring political systems by the quality of justice the system secures for the poorest of the poor and weakest of the weak. It is not enough to say, "Well, we have a better system than such and such a country." That is not God's perspective. He does not measure us by the nations around us. He measures us by his standard. There is something to improve in every country and every judicial system, and God's priority for the *something* is whatever is destroying the *least* in our societies. It is impossible to say that we have God's heart for our community or nation without knowing who constitutes the disenfranchised in our community or nation and addressing the issues that leave them out. A biblical perspective begins with justice for the weakest of the weak.

Biblical political justice will be moved forward in our nations by those who are dependent on the Holy Spirit within them to seek and carry out "morally original" responses to the issues of our day. In his devotional *My Utmost for His Highest*, Oswald Chambers writes: "The one mark of a saint is the moral originality which springs from abandonment to Jesus Christ. In the life of a saint there is this amazing wellspring of original life all the time; the Spirit of God is a well of water springing up, perennially fresh. The saint realizes that it is God Who engineers circumstances, consequently there is no whine, but a reckless abandon to Jesus. Never make a principle out of your experience, let God be as original with other people as He is with you."[1]

Finally, biblical political justice accepts the imperfection of the world and our judicial systems. We accept that we will not perfect our nation. We seek to serve, preserve, and bless, making our society as just as possible. But we know we will have limited success.

As believers in Christ, we are looking to a future kingdom. It is not here yet in completion, but its coming is assured. It is here in you, though. It is not our job to worry about when it will come but rather to continue to do what God has called us to do here and now to bless our fallen world. We are the Red Cross, making the best out of humanity's disasters for the sake of the King. And what better place to reveal the light than in the darkness? What easier solution than to salt the tasteless pot? We should love our times. We should see the potential of our circumstances. Christ is ready to reveal the next step to each of us.

Ask! Seek! Knock!

NOTES

CHAPTER 2: THE ORIGINS OF POLITICAL JUSTICE

1. I intentionally do not use *Eve*, as that is not her name until after the fall, and it is Adam male, rather than God, who gives it to her. The name *Adam* is plural in Hebrew, as is *Elohim*, the word for "God."

CHAPTER 4: THE RED THREAD OF VIOLENCE CONTINUES

1. Adele Berlin and Marc Zvi Brettler, eds., *The Jewish Study Bible* (Oxford: Oxford University Press, 2004), 69.

CHAPTER 5: THE BUILDING BLOCKS OF THE KINGDOM

1. Leong Tien Fock, "Transform: Nation Agenda," in *The Great Commission and the Creation Mandate* (National Evangelical Christian Fellowship, Malaysia), 22.

CHAPTER 6: THE ESSENTIALS OF BIBLICAL THOUGHT

1. Os Guinness, *The Gravedigger File* (Downers Grove, IL: InterVarsity Press, 1983), 25.

CHAPTER 8: THE TEMPLATE OF LAWS

1. Historical law is law told in history form, exemplifying values.
2. Prescriptive law is law given in instruction form, i.e., "do this and do not do this."
3. It is very tempting to make this list number five as well by adding "God," from whom all authority and power come. The author is resisting the temptation to numerical perfection.

CHAPTER 9: CIVIL LAW

1. Readers may find it helpful to refer to chapter 6 in *An Introduction to the Old Testament Template: Rediscovering God's Principles for Discipling Nations*, 2nd ed. (Seattle: YWAM Publishing, 2011), for the overview of

347

governance in Scripture. A version of this is available online at http://templateinstitute.com/the-old-testament-template-book-chapter-6/.

CHAPTER 10: LAND

1. Berlin and Brettler, *Jewish Study Bible*, 12.
2. Berlin and Brettler, *Jewish Study Bible*, 347.

CHAPTER 11: CITIES OF REFUGE

1. Further study passages on cities of refuge: Num. 35; Deut. 4:41–43; 19:1–13.
2. Further study passages on witnesses: Exod. 23:1–2; Num. 35:30; Deut. 5:20; 17:5–7; 19:15–21.
3. Further study passages on law courts: Deut. 1:15–18; 17:8–13.

CHAPTER 12: CRIME AND CONSEQUENCES

1. Further study passages on false prophets: Num. 25:1–5; Deut. 13:1–5; 18:17–20.
2. Berlin and Brettler, *Jewish Study Bible*, 404.
3. Further study passages on idolatry: Lev. 20:1–5; Deut. 13:1–5, 6–11, 12–16; 17:2–7; 18:17–20.
4. Further study passages on murder: Exod. 21:12–14; Lev. 24:17; Num. 35:16.
5. Further study passages on manslaughter: Exod. 21:12–14; 21:20–25; 21:28–32; 22:2–3; Lev. 27:29; 24:17; Num. 35:16–21; 35:30–33; Deut. 19:11–13.
6. Further study passages on sexual sin: Lev. 15; 18; 20; Deut. 27.
7. Berlin and Brettler, *Jewish Study Bible*, 82.
8. Ibid., 268.
9. Ibid., 255.
10. Ibid., 154.
11. "Antisocial Personality Disorder: Definition," Mayo Clinic, April 12, 2013, http://www.mayoclinic.org/diseases-conditions/antisocial-personality -disorder/basics/definition/CON-20027920.

CHAPTER 13: CRIME AND CONSEQUENCES

1. Berlin and Brettler, *Jewish Study Bible*, 416–17.
2. Ibid., 416.
3. Ibid., 221.

CHAPTER 14: MEASURING POLITICAL JUSTICE

1. Berlin and Brettler, *Jewish Study Bible*, 157.
2. Further study passages on justice for the poor: Exod. 22:21–22; 23:2–3, 6–9; Lev. 19:15, 33–34; 24:22; Deut. 1:16–17; 10:17; 17:14–15; 24:17–19.

CHAPTER 16: JOSHUA AND THE JUDGES

1. Aram is in modern-day Syria.
2. Moab is in modern-day Jordan, east of the Dead Sea.
3. Ammon is in modern-day Jordan, east of the Jordan River.
4. The Amalekites lived in the Sinai Peninsula and modern-day Israel.
5. Midian is in modern-day Saudi Arabia, across from the Sinai Peninsula.
6. Sidon is in modern-day Lebanon.
7. The Philistines lived in modern-day Gaza and Israel.
8. Edom is in modern-day Israel and Jordan, south of the Dead Sea.

CHAPTER 17: SAMUEL AND THE WANDERING PRIESTS

1. Berlin and Brettler, *Jewish Study Bible*, 548.
2. Ibid., 549.

CHAPTER 18: THE KINGS IN ASCENT

1. Dates and length of rule for each king in this and the next chapter are taken from Edwin R. Thiele, *A Chronology of the Hebrew Kings* (Grand Rapids: Zondervan, 1977). Overlaps of coregencies have been ignored in the date line and only "official" reigns noted.
2. Both Ammon and Jabesh Gilead are east of the Jordan River.
3. Sheba is in modern-day Yemen and Ethiopia.

CHAPTER 19: THE KINGS IN DECLINE

1. Cush is in modern-day Sudan.
2. Ramoth Gilead is in modern-day Jordan.
3. The Assyrian Empire began in modern-day Iraq and covered much of the Near East.
4. Babylon is in modern-day Iraq, and the Babylonian Empire inherited most of the lands of the Assyrian Empire, covering much of the Near East; Kuthah is in modern-day northwestern Iraq; Avva is in modern-day northern Syria or southern Turkey; Hamath is in modern-day Syria; Sepharvaim is in modern-day Syria.

CHAPTER 24: THE APOSTOLIC MESSAGE

1. Further study passages on family and sexual immorality: Rom. 13; 1 Cor. 5, 6, 7, 11; 2 Cor. 12; Eph. 5, 6; Col. 3; 1 Thess. 4; 1 Tim. 5; Heb. 13; 1 Pet. 3; 2 Pet. 2; 1 John.

CHAPTER 26: HERE AND NOW

1. Oswald Chambers, *My Utmost for His Highest*, June 13, http://utmost.org/classic/getting-there-3-classic/.

ABOUT THE AUTHOR

Landa Cope is the founder and executive director of The Template Institute, a ministry of Youth With A Mission committed to providing seminars and materials for the development of biblical thinking in all professions. Since 1971 her work in missions has taken her to more than 120 nations. She is the founder of the University of the Nations' College of Communication and a pioneer of the international ministry of Mercy Ships. She published the first book of the Biblical Template series, *An Introduction to the Old Testament Template*, in 2006. The book has been translated into seventeen languages and counting, evidencing the global hunger for a biblical approach to discipling nations.

The TEMPLATE INSTITUTE
AT THE UNIVERSITY OF THE NATIONS

Founded in 2005 by Landa Cope, The Template Institute (TTI) is committed to a comprehensive biblical approach to issues in the public forum. The goal of TTI is to reveal Christ in all of life and enhance the effectiveness of professionals in all spheres to meet the needs of their communities through their vocations.

Working from the Books of Moses through to Revelation, TTI is dedicated to understand Scripture applied to daily life and work.

The structure of TTI is an independent institute seeking to create a training bridge between the professional community, Youth With A Mission (YWAM), and the University of the Nations (UofN). TTI is part of the family of ministries of YWAM.

The target audience of TTI is Christian professionals in the marketplace and professionals of all persuasions with an interest in the biblical foundations for nation building.

Strategies include:

- authoring the Biblical Template series
- publishing
- web resources
- virtual and real-time seminars and conferences
- book, video, and audio resources
- forums dealing with critical issues in the public domain
- biblical foundations for positions and values

For further information, events, and resources,
please visit: www.templateinstitute.com